BECOMING
MULTICULTURAL

CRITICAL EDUCATION PRACTICE
VOLUME 19
GARLAND REFERENCE LIBRARY OF SOCIAL SCIENCE
VOLUME 1079

CRITICAL EDUCATION PRACTICE

SHIRLEY R. STEINBERG AND JOE L. KINCHELOE, *SERIES EDITORS*

BECOMING A STUDENT OF TEACHING
*Methodologies for Exploring
Self and School Context*
by Robert V. Bullough, Jr.
and Andrew Gitlin

OCCUPIED READING
*Critical Foundations for
an Ecological Theory*
by Alan A. Block

DEMOCRACY, MULTICULTURALISM,
AND THE COMMUNITY COLLEGE
A Critical Perspective
by Robert A. Rhoads
and James R. Valadez

ANATOMY OF A COLLABORATION
*Study of a College of Education/
Public School Partnership*
by Judith J. Slater

TEACHING MATHEMATICS
Toward a Sound Alternative
by Brent Davis

INNER-CITY SCHOOLS,
MULTICULTURALISM,
AND TEACHER EDUCATION
A Professional Journey
by Frederick L. Yeo

RETHINKING LANGUAGE ARTS
Passion and Practice
by Nina Zaragoza

EDUCATIONAL REFORM
A Deweyan Perspective
by Douglas J. Simpson
and Michael J. B. Jackson

LIBERATION THEOLOGY
AND CRITICAL PEDAGOGY
IN TODAY'S CATHOLIC SCHOOLS
Social Justice in Action
by Thomas Oldenski

CURRICULUM
Toward New Identities
edited by William F. Pinar

WRITING EDUCATIONAL BIOGRAPHY
*Explorations in
Qualitative Research*
edited by Craig Kridel

EVERYBODY BELONGS
*Changing Negative Attitudes
Toward Classmates with Disabilities*
by Arthur Shapiro

TEACHING FROM UNDERSTANDING
Teacher As Interpretive Inquirer
edited by Julia L. Ellis

PEDAGOGY AND THE POLITICS
OF THE BODY
A Critical Praxis
by Sherry B. Shapiro

CRITICAL ART PEDAGOGY
*Foundations for
Postmodern Art Education*
by Richard Cary

THE POST-FORMAL READER
Cognition and Education
edited by Shirley R. Steinberg,
Joe L. Kincheloe,
and Patricia H. Hinchey

BECOMING MULTICULTURAL
*Personal and Social Construction
through Critical Teaching*
by Terry Ford

Becoming Multicultural

Personal and Social Construction through Critical Teaching

By
Terry Ford

Falmer Press
A member of the Taylor & Francis Group
New York and London
1999

Library of Congress Cataloging-in-Publication Data

Becoming multicultural : Personal and social construction through critical
teaching / by Terry Ford.
    p.   cm. — (Critical education practice ; vol. 6. Garland reference
Library of social science ; vol. 1865.)
    Includes bibliographical references (p. 217) and index.
    ISBN 0-8153-2199-6 (alk. paper)
    1. Sex—Reference books.   2. Reference books—Sex.   3. Sex—
Library resources.   I. Title.   II. Garland reference library of social
science ; v. 836.
    Z7164.S42L55   1999
    869'.3—dc20   93-37236
                                                                    CIP

Printed on acid-free, 250-year-life paper
Manufactured in the United States of America

Contents

List of Figures and Tables   vii
Preface   ix
Acknowledgements   xiii

CHAPTER 1
Defining Perspectives   3

CHAPTER 2
Being and *Becoming* Multicultural   21

CHAPTER 3
Constructing a Critical Context   41

CHAPTER 4
Constructing Self as Object:
Salient Autobiographical Experiences   57

CHAPTER 5
Deconstructing Self as Object   119

CHAPTER 6
(Re)Presenting Self as Subject   143

CHAPTER 7
Lived Truth and Distorted Honesty   157

CHAPTER 8
Implications for Critical Teaching   195

References   217
Index   225

Figures and Tables

FIGURES

Figure 2.1   A conceptual model of a grounded,
             multicultural self   24
Figure 2.2   A model of becoming multicultural   25

TABLES

Table 3.1   Opening Doors Schedule of Events   46
Table 6.1   Opening Doors Research Projects   145

Preface

I have identified with critical pedagogy since graduate school when I was introduced to the writings of Gloria Anzaldúa, Debra Britzman, Cleo Cherryholmes, Michelle Cliff, Paulo Freire, Henry Giroux, bell hooks, Joe Kincheloe, Patti Lather, Audrey Lorde, Peter McLaren, Ira Shor, Shirley Steinberg, and Michelle Wallace, to name but a few. Finally, for me, these were authors who validated my being in the world; a being that can best be described by the two favorite hats I have possessed since junior high. One reads QUESTION AUTHORITY and the other, WHY BE NORMAL?

Many of my graduate cohorts argued that the theoretical language of critical pedagogy was too much of an obstacle to overcome. I remember extensive discussions about the intimidation of terms such as *social transformation, critical or radical education, social construction of reality,* and *critical reflection.* Today these phrases are supplanted by others, such as *border pedagogy, crossing borders, marginalized other, politics of difference, politics of location, situated knowing, postmodern,* and *post structuralist,* among a myriad of others.

One of the often cited criticisms of critical theorists is that they are long-winded about identifying everything that is wrong with our classist, sexist, racist, and homophobic education system, and describing in infinite detail the sociohistoric events that have led to unequal treatment of the "other." However, they are short-winded about making practical suggestions for change. Thus, my primary intent, through the autobiographical stories I retell in the following pages, is to provide the reader with a concrete example of the often unreachable theory critical educators espouse.

When I was invited to assist in implementing a new program for undergraduate minority students, titled "Opening Doors: The World of

Graduate Study for Minority Students in Education." several events helped shape my decision to participate. The most influential reason for my decision was the birth of my niece. Her father is African American, and her mother's family is European American.

The nine months of my youngest sister's pregnancy were a trial that divided my family in two. Being the oldest, and the only one to have gone to college, I have always been the one the others looked to for answers. This situation was no different. I was bombarded by complicated issues of what was right for the baby, for my sister, and for various family members. Somehow all the academic talk about multicultural education and the language of critical theory was of little to no help in this real-life instance. The trials of our family feud over the birth of this biracial child heightened my awareness of how much I did not know. I realized my lack of personal experience, as well as the knowledge that this was only the beginning of never-ending challenges to which I would need to respond. I viewed the invitation to participate in Opening Doors as a way to find some practical, experiential answers.

My hope is that reading this account of the Opening Doors experience will provide raders with insight on the practical application of critical theory into practice. To that end, I have tried to avoid the use of intimidating language in order to make these theoretical concepts more accessible for classroom practice. However, some use is unavoidable. I have labored from various angles not to trivialize or romanticize the Opening Doors experience. I avoided reporting the results in a simplistic compare-contrast of what African Americans, Native Americans, Asian Americans and Latinos bring to the learning situation. To do this I had to go beyond superficial recognition of the contributions from individual ethnic groupings (use of *grouping* denotes the particular individuals assembled in this context), to the core selves brought together in this particular context. In doing so, I found that it was not ethnicity itself that drove the interpretations of meaning, but that ethnicity was a salient feature of the core *self* of the individuals.

At times it is difficult for me to separate critical education from education that is multicultural. To me, critical teaching is the obvious avenue through which multicultural understandings can be generated and supported through classroom experiences. Therefore, it appears I use the terms *critical* and *multicultural* as synonyms. For me they are, although I also acknowledge that for others they are not synonymous.

I hope the detailed description of critical teaching strategies and decision making as well as the outcomes of these practices will provide a model for classroom teachers who are seeking ways to generate multicultural understandings in their classrooms. I also hope that the detailed outcomes of these practices will assist teachers in being prepared for the messy, sometimes unpredictable, conflictive, confrontive, and always, to me, rewarding experience of critical pedagogy for becoming multicultural.

Acknowledgements

No matter how independent and self-determined one is in life, independence and determination are not developed in isolation. Therefore, there are several individuals whom I wish to thank for their encouragement, support, love, and friendship. First, I must thank the Opening Doors participants for allowing me to experience, for a brief moment, the lives they endure daily. They taught me much in eight short weeks. I would also like to thank Sherry C. Vaughan and Cynthia B. Dillard both of whom were instrumental in my original conceptualization of this piece. Marie Churney and Jan Lewis provided helpful feedback, suggestions, and comments for which I am deeply grateful. Mona Roach was a ruthless editor, cutting and splicing her way through the text when I needed it the most. Thanks also to Shirley Steinberg and Joe Kincheloe for taking a risk on this newcomer. And finally, to my niece, Mariah, whose presence in the world was the influence and my inspiration throughout the project: this one is for you. May this be an effort to make the world a better place for you to grow up strong, healthy, and proud of who you are.

BECOMING
MULTICULTURAL

CHAPTER 1

Defining Perspectives

*When a subject is highly controversial . . . one cannot
hope to tell the truth. One can only show how one came
to hold whatever opinion one does hold. One can only
give one's audience the chance of drawing their own
conclusions as they observe the limitations, the
prejudices, the idiosyncrasies of the speaker.*

—Woolf (1929, p. 4)

This book details the interactions of twenty-one ethnically diverse
undergraduates through one eight week classroom experience titled
"Opening Doors: The World of Graduate Study for Minority Students
in Education" (referred to as Opening Doors or OD throughout the
book). Through the analysis of classroom experiences, dialogue journals, and interviews, I attempt to answer the question, What does it
mean to become multicultural?

Proponents of multicultural education focus on the process
whereby a person becomes multicultural or develops competencies of
perceiving, evaluating, believing, and doing in multiple ways.
However, when practically applied, the dynamic, fluid, and changing
qualities central to the process are often translated into mastery of a
product, focusing on static features of generalized groups rather than on
the individuals who make up those groups. Therefore, to clarify the
actual process of developing a multicultural perspective, this book is an
interpretive ethnography of the Opening Doors program.

The book has two primary purposes. First, it identifies crucial
elements, influences, and interactions that enable students to develop

the complex multi faceted understanding of diverse cultures that is necessary for true multicultural education. Second, the book develops an explanatory model of the process of becoming multicultural to be applied across educational settings. As the interactions of the Opening Doors participants will illustrate, *being* multicultural is a much more complex process than simply being born a person of color. Being African American, Asian American, Latino, or Native American guarantees the individual has *a* perspective, but it does not guarantee a multicultural perspective.

MULTICULTURAL EDUCATION RHETORIC

In order to truly recognize, accept, and affirm cultural diversity and individual differences, it is essential that we adopt an overriding educational philosophy that respects the cultural and individual differences of all people, regardless of their racial, ethnic, cultural or religious backgrounds, or physical differences. The belief that all people must be accorded respect is undergirded by a fundamental acceptance of the premise that all people have intrinsic worth. It should thus be the goal of society's socializing institutions—especially our schools—to recognize the worth of all people and to instill and maintain the importance of equal respect for all.

—Grant (1977, p. 65)

Definitions of multicultural education have focused on the dynamic, fluid and changing individual, a process whereby a person *becomes* multicultural or develops competencies of perceiving, evaluating, believing, and doing in multiple ways (Banks, 1981; Bennett, 1990; Klasen & Gollnick, 1977; Nieto, 1992). Defined as a process of "becoming," multiculturalism is then a perspective or a shared frame of reference from which reality is perceived (Shibutani, 1955). Being multicultural is a way of being, perceiving, thinking, and acting in the world in ways that symbolize the equal respect of all humanity regardless of the racial, ethnic, or cultural differences. Multiculturalism is a way of viewing the world in general.

Contrary to the rhetoric that calls for an inclusive, process-oriented perspective that supports every child's learning and development, the practical application of multiculturalism in the classroom has been product-oriented packaged sets of isolated skills. For instance, in her text *Comprehensive Multicultural Education,* Christine Bennett (1990) provides model lesson plans for implementing the multicultural curriculum model discussed throughout that text. In one lesson, historical facts about the contributions of Dr. Daniel Hale Williams (an African American male) in performing the first open-heart surgery are added to a lesson identifying the causes, care and treatment, and components of a heart attack. The evaluation strategy, written by the contributing teacher, reveals the additive nature of the multicultural component: "A short multiple-choice test will be given to test the student's achievement on each of the four segments in the strategy section. In addition, a brief report on the contributions of Dr. Daniel Hale Williams will be required" (pp. 326–327). This strategy is more an afterthought than an integration of the physician and his brilliantly conceived treatment. Other lessons include having students listen to Black blues music and write their own blues compositions; perform German and Israeli folk dances and then write reports about folk dancing; read and perform the play *Indians* written by Arthur Kopit; and compare the phonetics of Spanish and English (pp. 328–346). These "model" lesson plans illustrate how the *process* of becoming multicultural has been implemented as mastery of a *product.* This product focuses on static features of generalized groups of people rather than on the people themselves.

Democratic education assumes that all individuals are diverse and learn best when topics, issues, material, and methods grow out of student concerns, and that in order for education to serve society's needs, it must first meet the needs of the individual. However, educators have responded with product-oriented, object-centered curricula that fail to meet the needs of diverse learners. These objectifications of differences do not begin with understanding the qualities and/or traits of real human beings but with stereotyped and static descriptions of the generalized other. What does it mean to develop a perspective that respects and values the needs of individuals rather than identifying objects? What teaching strategies facilitate a process-oriented view of the individual?

Not understanding what it means to *become* multicultural causes attempted solutions to become part of the problem. First, there has been a misunderstanding of the relationship between the individual and the curriculum in the creation of product-oriented curricula. Second, there has been a misunderstanding about the nature of learning, or meaning making. Learning has been conceived as a matter of transmitting knowledge to students rather than constructing knowledge with students.

Product-Oriented Curricula

Global Approach

One example of a product-oriented application of multiculturalism is the global approach to social studies curricula. Kniep's (1989) work in social studies curricula stresses the interdependence and global connectedness of society as a whole. The global approach to social studies curricula intends to provide an avenue for a process of understanding, in valuing and appreciating human differences, including those from other nations, ethnicities, races, and cultures (Kronowitz, 1987; Metzger, 1988). However, the outcome of this curricular approach is to identify and label artifacts from specific cultures rather than explore the lived experiences of the individuals for whom these same artifacts hold meaning.

The global approach to social studies curricula seeks an appreciation of individual differences and cultural diversity by having students identify and label the objective content of various cultures (food, dance, dress, and other commodities) across curriculum areas. Simply identifying the objects of differing cultures ignores the historical, social, and political ways in which the cultural meaning of these objects is constructed by its people. By centering curriculum content on the objects of the culture rather than on the actions, intentions, and achievements of individuals from the culture, the individual human beings who construct the culture also become objects.

For instance, identifying Mexican culture with tacos, rice and beans, piñatas, Spanish language, Cinco de Mayo, sombreros, and siestas, allows no possibility for interpersonal understanding. There is no "person" in the picture with which to interact. The person is just another object on the list of cultural artifacts. There is no room for individual differences to be recognized. What of the U.S. born Mexican who has never been to Mexico or may not even speak Spanish? What of the Mexican who has never been out of his or her country? What of the Mexican immigrant farm worker who crosses the border into the United States to seek economic employment to support his family left behind in Mexico? What of the Latina from El Salvador who is mistakenly categorized as a Mexican because she speaks Spanish? Would the cultural artifacts have the same meaning for each of these individuals? Would one even think to ask the question of individual interpretation if individuality is not considered when lists of cultural features are constructed?

Focusing on objective artifacts of the culture rather than relating to the actual human beings who create culture makes the subject an object. Critics stress that objectifying the subject in this way leads to further marginalization and alienation of those people the dominant culture intends to understand (Brown, 1988; hooks, 1990). By focusing on the artifacts of a culture rather than encountering and understanding individual people, stereotypes are strengthened rather than lessened. Students objectify the content knowledge, keeping cultural diversity at arm's length so it remains something out there, different, and therefore strange and unfamiliar. No interpersonal connection between human beings is established. No sense of bonding or shared emotions that comes with human relations can be realized. Because there is no human connection, there is no human understanding. Cultural differences remain distant, pertaining to people who live "over there" whom we will never meet, not to the individual sitting in the seat next to us.

Learning Styles

A second product-oriented application of multiculturalism capitalizes on the notion of individual differences and diversity by neatly packaging these ideals into learning styles inventories and strategies (Dunn & Dunn, 1978; Myers & Briggs, 1976). Teachers across the nation are encouraged to buy ready-made materials and attend in-service workshops to assess and match their teaching styles with the individual learning styles of students in their classrooms. Longstreet (1978) has developed a scheme specifically for identifying ethnicity in the classroom. He identifies five aspects of ethnicity that serve as guidelines for pinpointing potential sources of misunderstanding in the classroom: (1) *verbal communication* (grammar, semantics, phonology, discourse modes); (2) *nonverbal communication* (kinesthetics, proxemics, haptics, signs and symbols); (3) *orientation modes* (body positions, spatial architectural patterns, attention modes, time modes); (4) *social value patterns* (ideal models of conduct such as cleanliness, hardwork, promptness); and (5) *intellectual modes* (preferred ways of learning, knowledge valued most, skills emphasized). The assumption underlying a learning styles approach is that if teachers have the knowledge to identify the ways in which individual learners respond in the classroom (e.g., Longstreet's guidelines) then that knowledge can be applied to adjust teaching styles to accommodate learner differences.

Objectifying Learning Styles

Though potentially an avenue for developing human understanding of complex cultural issues, application of cultural diversity knowledge may further objectify the differences people intend to understand. With this approach, the curriculum promotes an objectified, product-oriented view of differences in four ways.

First, teachers may overgeneralize cultural characteristics, which leads to further stereotyping of students and their cultures. The perceived images "Native Americans won't look you in the eye," or "male Hispanic students will have problems with female teachers because women aren't valued as authority in their culture," or "Asians are quiet and good at math and science" are examples of these over-generalizations. The conceptualization of stereotyping alone marginalizes individuals. The individual becomes one of "those"—a nameless, faceless, objectified entity. Rather than be José, a boy with a particular name, a particular family, with hopes, dreams, and goals in life, the boy in the front row becomes the "Hispanic" in the class.

Second, stereotyped overgeneralizations can also lead to a self-fulfilling prophecy in which teachers perceive differences where there may in fact be none. For instance, assuming a student is Hispanic, and therefore an immigrant with language difficulties, may keep a teacher from finding out that in fact the student has lived in the United States all his or her life and English is the first language. Prejudging, pre-sorting, and precategorizing students based on assumed social and cultural characteristics furthers stereotypical images and minimizes the personal understanding process between individuals.

Third, such prescriptive interpretation of cultural differences can hinder rather than facilitate communication. If the teacher believes he or she already *knows* why a student behaves in a particular manner, there is no need to speak with or question the individual. Both teacher and student continue to make assumptions about what the other *thinks* and no attempt is made to verify these interpretations. Interpersonal connection is again avoided rather than encouraged.

Fourth, ethnographic studies illustrate how differences are often interpreted as deficiencies. When students exhibit behaviors different from the European mainstream behaviors valued and practiced in the school system, these differences are targeted for change. For instance, Gilmore (1985) focused on how definitions of attitude and what constitutes *good* and *bad* behavior determine access to academically tracked classes. Steps and stylized sulking, both cultural aspects of Black communicative behavior and reflective of a particular ethnic style and socioeconomic class, were isolated events of the study. Because these behaviors did not match the expectations of the European middle-class values supported in the schools, Black students who practiced steps or engaged in stylized sulking were interpreted as having a bad attitude toward school and were tracked into remedial classes. Similarly, Gee (1985) describes how an African American second grader who engaged in exaggerated storytelling, an ethno-linguistic feature of her African American culture, was sent to the school psychologist because the teacher judged the student's story to be rambling and disconnected. It did not fit the European American teacher's narrative style. Finally, Delgado-Gaitan (1988), in her study of Hispanic achievement in schools, reveals through ethnographic interviewing how the Lationo students who succeed are the ones who change their cultural practices to conform to the mainstream. In this way, differences are identified in order to annihilate them.

Cultural Difference as Product Knowledge

Product knowledge concerning cultural differences is clearly not a sufficient condition for developing a multicultural perspective in which students learn appreciation and acceptance of others. Teacher knowledge of cultural differences transmitted to students without opportunity for interpersonal interaction can lead to overgeneralized stereotyping, misinterpretation of individual intent, less interaction between teacher and students, and pressures for students to conform to mainstream society. Much depends on how individual teachers interpret the knowledge and apply it to contextual situations.

Though teachers have created and implemented identification strategies in an effort to provide and affirm cultural diversity, the focus on product rather than process causes these efforts to consistently fall short of the intended goal. Both attempts, global social studies curricula and learning styles inventories, have been knowledge-based approaches. In other words, schools have responded to the need of multiculturalism by providing information—to students through objectified curriculum content about cultural artifacts, and to teachers through objectified stereotypes of cultural and behavioral styles. Implicit in these reforms is the belief that by providing the product of information, the process of human understanding will naturally follow. Perhaps because these curriculum strategies objectify differences at a social or generalized group level, they have failed to develop human understanding at a personal level.

Recruitment Strategies

The latest strategy to implement multicultural perspectives in the schools has moved from curriculum packaging and planning to more intensified recruitment of ethnically diverse undergraduate students into the education field. Ethnically diverse teachers, by virtue of having experienced ways to cope and succeed in the European American dominant school system, may or may not have developed a multicultural perspective. A potential flaw in recruitment logic lies in assuming that an individual naturally transfers personal experience to a social understanding of others. To assume multiculturalism is a static product, addressed by merely adding more teachers of color into the classroom, is to assume that every teacher of one race or ethnicity will think, act, believe, and respond in a manner similar to others of that same race. This rationale raises two questions. First, does being ethnically diverse from the European American mainstream necessarily assume that the teacher will bring a multicultural understanding to the classroom? Second, what qualities, factors, or influences might ethnicity bring to the learning situation, and how does that in turn affect learning?

Learning as Transaction

These efforts to achieve multiculturalism in the classroom oversimplify the personal meaning construction process of learning and knowledge as the outcome of learning. Knowledge is not objective, static, or additive as the traditional, transmission model implies. Rather, knowledge is constructed or results from a transaction between the knower and the to be known. In contrast, constructivism, grounded in the ideas of Dewey (1909), Piaget (1959), and Vygotsky (1978) views learners as "active participants in the creation of their own knowledge. Because learners interact with and interpret the world, knowledge is a function of the learner's background and purposes" (Hiebert, 1991, p.2, emphasis added). Learning, as a meaning construction process, does not transfer; it is transactional. A transactional perspective implies that the sociocultural background individuals bring to a learning situation influences the perceptions and actions of those individuals in a given situation. There are multiple social factors within an individual's personal history which influence personal ethnic identity construction.

Minority Types

Ogbu (1992) illustrates how multiple factors influence meaning construction of ethnicity. He identifies three categories of minority people. First, autonomous minorities are those who are minority in a numerical sense in relation to the dominant culture. Examples in the United States include Jews, Mormons, and Amish. These groups share religious perspectives and beliefs that govern the way in which they lead their lives. Second, immigrant or voluntary minorities are those who choose to come to the United States mainly for economic enhancement or political freedom. Hispanic agricultural workers are an example. Third, castelike or involuntary minorities, such as African Americans, were brought to the United States against their will through slavery, conquest, or colonization.

The particular historical relationship between the dominant culture and ethnically diverse cultural groups influences the way individuals interpret the meaning of education. Ogbu (1992) asserts that "the meaning and value that students from different cultural groups associate with the process of formal education vary and are socially transmitted by their ethnic communities" (p. 7). All ethnically diverse groups, even if they have similar cultures and languages, may have different histories. Different histories shape different social contexts, which shape different meaning interpretations and perspectives brought to the learning context.

Situationally Constructed Ethnicity

Teachers bring to the learning context their own meanings and values constructed through individual histories in their particular cultural communities. Culture, including ethnicity, is situationally constructed (Banks, 1981). Factors such as geographic location, family ties, peer groups, and socioeconomic status influence the ways in which individuals perceive the meaning of their ethnicity, whether positive or negative. John Ogbu describes the situational construction in this way: "If you are in Kenya, you say you are an American. If in New York, you are a Californian. In L.A., you are from Frisco. So how you identify yourself will vary, depending on the situation" (Semons, 1991, p. 141).

Individuals differ in their constructed meanings of ethnicity. For some, ethnicity symbolizes a sense of cultural pride and group affiliation. For others, ethnicity represents marginalization, alienation, or a source of internalized oppression. Further, much of the interpreted meaning of ethnicity is influenced by the history of the ethnic relationship with the mainstream culture (Ogbu, 1992). Research studies in the field of social psychology (Becker & Geer, 1960; Bordieu, 1977; Hargreaves, 1967; Lacey, 1970; Woods, 1980) illustrate how cultural views, values, and belief systems are dynamically constructed rather than static entities as suggested by a product-oriented model of multiculturalism. Race, ethnicity, gender, age, social class, peer groups, sexual orientation, and family relationships (such as mother, wife, father, uncle) are among the cultural aspects that can simultaneously influence how an individual perceives or interprets a context-specific event. Which cultural aspect is most influential at any given time is dependent on situation-specific contextual factors and is therefore a dynamic interaction between the individual and the contextual factors, rather than a static feature that can be affixed. Reducing this complex *process* of multiculturalism and perspective development into *product-oriented* curricular units, scope and sequence, and even recruitment of ethnically diverse teachers suggests an anemic view of what is required for one to *become* multicultural. It is no wonder that Grant's (1977) goal of true multiculturalism is unfulfilled. It is likely that we have not even understood what it means.

To complicate matters even further, teachers, whether people of the dominant European American culture or of color (African American, Asian American, Latino, Native American), bring their histories and personal meaning constructions of ethnicity to the learning context just as students do. It is naive to asume that because an individual is ethnically diverse from the dominant European American culture, he or she is multicultural.

Ethnicity, as personally and socially constructed, is one aspect of culture for any individual, but it is not the only cultural aspect. Nor is it as static and socially objectified as arguments of recruitment numbers imply. Multiculturalism is not a product that can be neatly reproduced and distributed to students as suggested by curricular attempts in social studies. Neither can teachers become multicultural by acquiring a body of knowledge about cultural differences as learning styles programs suggest. It is also impossible for students to absorb transmitted multicultural understandings by virtue of being in the classroom with an ethnically diverse teacher. The dependence on a transmission model of learning continues to oversimplify the role of social factors and ignores the personal nature of learning as a meaning-making construction.

Perspective Building

Balance between the personal and the social is needed to develop a multicultural perspective. Multiculturalism is a perspective that develops through the process of human interaction. It is a way of being, perceiving, thinking, and acting in the world. It cannot be a specific teaching strategy. It is a perspective through which to view and implement appropriate teaching strategies. It is a way of viewing the world in general and a way of perceiving the teaching-learning context within that worldview.

To become multicultural implies undergoing a personal developmental process influenced by social factors. Multiculturalism is defined as a process. But what does this mean? What does the process look like? How can teachers facilitate the process with students in the classroom? How can teachers engage in the process themselves? What role does ethnicity play in the construction of cultural meaning? What characteristics describe one who is truly multicultural? What kinds of social constructions within classroom contexts facilitate the process of developing a multicultural perspective?

MULTICULTURALISM AS A PERSPECTIVE

The intent of this introductory discussion is to highlight the dichotomy between current theory and the reality of its implementation into practice. The recent prescriptive writing on the topic of multicultural education for teacher educators does little more than portray culture as an object. List after list of suggestions detail for teachers the ways to change classroom methods to accommodate the "stylistic" differences (learning styles, thinking styles, interaction styles) of diverse learners. These teaching methods or strategies are merely superficial and cosmetic. Changing a teacher's lesson plan or rearranging rows of furniture into cooperative learning groups rather than rows of individual students does not necessarily indicate an intent to address issues of diversity.

Instead, a multicultural perspective indicates a transformational change from the dominant Eurocentric perspective shaped through socialization in the United States to an inclusive view of multiple perspectives and multiple realities. Having a multicultural perspective inherently means accepting the reality of many truths or many versions of truth. Multiculturalism also requires acknowledgment that any insistence on a singular version of truth implicitly excludes all others.

Applied to classrooms, multiculturalism is neither prescriptive, nor diagnostic, nor a foolproof method strategy applied *to* students or even *with* students. Multiculturalism is a way of being, perceiving, thinking, and acting in the world. As stated earlier, multiculturalism is a way of viewing the world in general and a way of perceiving the teaching-learning context within that worldview.

DEFINING LABELS

Language chosen to define and describe experiences is simultaneously inclusive and exclusive. Each term or word itself defines and portrays much for the individual user. Most words used to describe groups of people are inadequate for just that fact: the words describe groups, not individuals. Avoidance of overgeneralizing the ethnic groups represented acknowledges and affirms differences. Therefore, the word *grouping* symbolizes and characterizes the particular experiences and perspectives of the twenty-one individuals of African American, Asian American, Native American, and Latino descent in the Opening Doors program.

The terms *White, Anglo, European,* and *mainstream* are each inadequate to describe the variations in the European American experiences of individuals across the United States. However, individuals in Opening Doors often used these terms interchangeably to represent the dominant cultural view of schools and curricula. *European American* represents a concept that parallels labeling of other ethnic groups: African American, Asian American, and Native American.

Similarly, the generalized term *Hispanic* to describe all Spanish-speaking individuals is also inaccurate. As one program participant explained in her autobiography, the term *Hispanic* symbolizes Spain and ignores the Latin roots of her culture as she experienced it in El Salvador. And as Maria Lugones (1990) explains, Hispanic is an Anglo construction of convenience. "To be Hispanic in this country is, in a dominant Anglo construction purposefully incomplete . . . . Who counts as a Hispanic? Are Latinos, Chicanos, Hispanos, black dominicans, white cubans, korean-columbians, italian-argentineans Hispanic? What it means to be a 'Hispanic' in the varied so-called Hispanic communities in the US is also up in the air. We have not yet decided whether there are any 'Hispanics' in our varied 'worlds'" (p. 395). The category *Hispanic* can represent any race. However, European Americans most commonly use the term to describe the Mexican population in the United States, whether the person is a Mexican immigrant or U.S. born. Though accurate description of the particular experiences of individuals is important, the continued string of Hispanic/Mexican/Chicano/Latino is cumbersome for the reader. Thus, as a matter of reading ease, this text uses the generalized term *Latino* rather than the Anglo term *Hispanic*. Hispanic is only used when directly quoting from the participants.

Minority as a term referring to the ethnically diverse experiences of those other than European American in the United States is not used in this text except in direct quotations from another source. Politically speaking, the label *minority* symbolizes an ethnocentric relationship of power and has little to do with demographics. *Minority* is a label assigned from the Eurocentric view of the world that presumes only those different from European Americans have ethnicity. All individuals have ethnicity. As Guillermo Gomez-Pena (1988) rightly questions, "That Anglos themselves aren't also an 'ethnic group,' one of the most violent and antisocial tribes on this planet? . . . That the five hundred million mestizos that inhabit the Americas are a 'minority'?" (p. 132). Finally, the phrase *people of color,* though an overgeneralization, represents the underlying common bond of struggle and solidarity shared by those ethnically diverse from the dominant culture in the United States.

RACE, CULTURE, ETHNICITY, AND IDENTITY

> *There isn't a shred of evidence for any of this . . . . It's a*
> *reconstruction out of the whole cloth . . . . Yet it has a*
> *certain air of verisimilitude . . . . It's both appropriate to*
> *the facts and creative. Perhaps that's the best that can*
> *be said for any biography when all is said and done . . . .*
> *After all, the Greeks turned Crete from a matriarchal to*
> *patriarchal culture, not only in fact but in memory . . . .*
> *I believe it was John Maynard Keynes who said, "Both*
> *when they are right and when they are wrong, [ideas]*
> *are more powerful than is commonly understood.*
> *Indeed the world is ruled by little else.*
> —Cross (1990, pp. 191–192)

Interpretive research is "both appropriate to the facts and creative." In striving to reconstruct a story having verisimilitude, interpretive research is necessarily uninhibited by preconceived notions of what to find or what to prove. Therefore, it is imperative for this type of research that the investigator's mind be unclouded by specific frames in which to make the data fit. However, this does not mean abandonment of conceptual frames of reference or strategic analysis. On the contrary, as Strauss and Corbin (1990) note, the research question itself sets some boundaries. It is toward the setting of boundaries that a discussion of ethnicity in relation to race, culture, and identity is necessary.

Race

Though race can be a symbolic identifier of ethnicity, race and ethnicity are not one and the same. Race is biological and therefore a fixed, static set of physical characteristics (Benedict, 1934). Ethnicity, on the other hand, is socially constructed and therefore dynamic, fluid, and changing from one situational context to another.

Culture

Ethnicity and culture are not synonymous. Ethnicity is assumed to be only one aspect of culture. Culture is a fluid, dynamic, socially constructed system of shared knowledge and beliefs that shape human perceptions and generate social behavior (Banks, 1981; Bennett, 1990;

Carr & Kemmis, 1986). Therefore, as one part of an individual's culture, ethnicity is symbolically constructed and can only be interpreted by discerning the individual's intentions of the symbolism. In defining *cultural theory,* Geertz (1973) suggests, "Culture is most effectively treated, the argument goes, purely as a symbolic system (the catch phrase is, "in its own terms"), by isolating its elements, specifying the internal relationships among those elements and then characterizing the whole system in some general way" (p. 17). In Geertz's terms, ethnicity is *one* of the "isolating elements" within the whole cultural system of an individual.

Ethnicity

Ethnicity identifies a particular group within a larger society. It is a means of social distinction by others or self primarily based on race and cultural characteristics (religion, tradition, language). Its interpretation can vary greatly within an individual at different times in life as well as across varied settings and situations (Banks, 1981; Bennett, 1990). Nash (1989) asserts that "*ethnicity* and *ethnic group* are among the most complicated, volatile and emotionally charged words and ideas in the lexicon of social science" (p. 1). He further explains that ethnicity has "all sorts of unwanted ideological and evolutionary accretions" (p. vii) that contribute to the complexity and mythology of its usage. As an anthropologist, Nash's study of ethnicity theory defines an ethnic group as "people not politically dominant in the nation-state and who had significant cultural markers of difference" (p. 2). Thus, from an anthropological perspective, individuals construct symbolic meanings of ethnicity personally, socially, historically, and politically.

Identity

Some confusion results from the two different meanings of *identity.* One meaning indicates sameness and the other distinctiveness. "On a superficial level, distinctiveness seems to refer to individual identity, while sameness is rather connected with a sense of commonness between several persons who constitute a group" (Jacobson-Widding, 1983, p. 13). However, the matter is further compounded in that both meanings of *sameness* and *distinctiveness* can be applied to (1) personal identity and (2) social identity. Erik Erikson (1959/1980) defines personal identity in terms of continuity, which refers to the persistent sameness within a person. Tajfel (1981) defines *social identity* as "that part of an individual's self concept that derives from his knowledge of his membership of a social group (or groups) together with the value and emotional significance attached to that membership" (p. 255). both the personal and social dimensions as well as the sameness and distinctive dimensions of identity imply a complex interdependence of multiplicity of which ethnicity is only one element. Saharso (1989) states that "Both the content of ethnic identity and its significance in relation to the aspects of identity (such as gender, class and generation) are to a large extent dependent upon the reaction of the environment" (p. 98).

Applying situational and contextual dimensions of social identity to personal constructions of ethnicity suggests that (1) ethnicity is not necessarily a central factor in an individual's experience of identity, (2) there are multiple variations concerning the way in which individuals (eventually) give meaning to their ethnicity, and (3) ethnic identity cannot be studied in isolation from the social context in which it is constructed. Ethnicity, then, is one contributing meaning in what Goffman (1959) calls the collaborative manufacturing of self.

Self

Study of the self as object has been the focus of social psychologists, in particular the symbolic interactionists within social psychology. There are three characteristics of the self. The self is *reflexive, social,* and *symbolic.* The reflexive nature of the self is the ability to be both subject and object. This is what Mead (1934) referred to as the "I and Me" of the self. The "I" is the individual as subject, the personal self. The "Me" is the individual as object, the social self (Charon, 1992, p. 90). The social self emerges out of interaction and actively assigns meaning to symbols that constitute the concept of self. The nature of the self is an active process of emergence within a given situation. Goffman describes how the socially situated self "must be produced anew each and every occasion of social interaction" (Charon, 1992, p. 81).

This book focuses on analysis of the situated self. The identities that emerged out of specific social situations during the Opening Doors program, the effect of ethnicity in those identities, and the actions that individuals used to maintain a positive self will be described and analyzed.

CRITICAL POLITICAL AND SOCIAL REALITIES

> *All I can do is to offer you an opinion upon one minor point . . . . Lies will flow from my lips, but there may perhaps be some truth mixed up with them; it is for you to seek this truth and decide whether any part of it is worth keeping.*
>
> —Woolf (1929, p. 4)

This book portrays the process of becoming multicultural through the reality of myself as a European American woman. I would be naive to assume my own European American ethnicity had no influence on my interactions and ability to establish relationships of trust among the participants in the Opening Doors program. My European American self might well have proceeded in substance and in a manner different from those of an African American, Asian American, Latino, or Native American.

Not only am I European American, but my roles in the program and thus my interactions with the participants varied. I am cognizant of my precarious position. I was the numerical minority (being the sole European American actively participating on a daily basis), but in regard to power I was still a symbol of cultural dominance. Therefore, I have struggled with the question, Whose story can I legitimately tell? I am convinced that it is not their story that I can tell, only my own version of their story. I can legitimately tell of my interactions, observations, and the ways in which I interpreted meanings from the eight-week Opening Doors program. I do not assert that this is the definitive analysis or the *one* or *true* interpretation of events. hooks (1990) warns that many cultural studies "highlight notions of difference, marginality and otherness in such a way that it further marginalizes actual people of difference and otherness. When this happens, cultural studies re-inscribe patterns of colonial domination, where the 'Other' is always made object, appropriated, interpreted, taken over by those in power, by those who dominate" (p. 125).

It is not and never has been my intent to objectify, appropriate, or dominate interpretations of the events or the people in the Opening Doors program. In fact, it is the exact opposite that I wish ultimately to achieve. I do not wish to talk *about* ethnic perspectives—to compare or contrast learning, teaching, and communication styles—all of which are superficialities of the people they represent. I have chosen not to dwell on the differences in communication and learning styles of ethnic groups. Further articulation of differences already researched and described by others (see Au. 1981; Cook-Gumperz, 1986; Erikson & Shultz, 1981; Markus & Kitayama, 1991; McDermott & Gospodinoff, 1981; Peyton, 1990 ; Phillips, 1976) is contradictory to my purpose which is to develop an interpretation and understanding of multiculturalism that does not objectify the subject.

With these social, political, and personal realities in mind, the analysis and portrayal of the individuals in this book were driven by my personal motive to construct an account "with no single voice being identified as more or less authentic . . . but rather to construct social realities that celebrate, acknowledge and affirm differences" (hooks, 1989, pp. 11–12). My primary goal is to represent the multiplicity of meaning construction, to the best of my acknowledged Eurocentric ability. However, hooks and West (1992) assert that White scholars bring "certain baggage with them when they look at Black culture, no matter how subtle and sophisticated the formulations. Therefore we must always be on guard to bring critique to bear on the baggage that they bring, even when that baggage provides certain insights" (p. 36). Thus, I invite the reader to heed hook's and West's caution and keep in mind that the detailed descriptions I have written are interpreted and constructed from the perspective of one European American who participated daily with the eight African Americans, three Asian Americans, seven Latinos, and three Native American undergraduate students learning about the intricacies of graduate school.

CHAPTER 2

Being and *Becoming* Multicultural

If we analyze those people and actions by linear models,
we will create dichotomies, ambiguities, cognitive
dissonances, disorientation, and confusion in places
where none exist.

—Brown (1988, p. 17)

Elsa Brown (1988) suggests that strict adherence to one particular theoretical perspective may exclude relevant explanatory information to the lives it portrays. bell hooks (1990) criticizes cultural studies, arguing that such studies actually perpetuate the domination and objectification of the people and cultures studied. Extending the discussion of objectification to ethnicity theory, Nash (1989) warns: "One of the chief hindrances in the understanding of ethnicity has been the premature drive to forge a general, all-encompassing theory" (p. 3). Nash further argues that a "polythetic" view which combines a "more general theory of social, cultural and psychological systems . . . into a general all-inclusive social science" is the framework needed to enable different instances to enrich mutual understanding (p. 3).

With these warnings and criticisms in mind, one of my goals, as hooks (1990) advocates, is to "attempt to rethink cultural practice, to re-examine and remake ethnography, to create ways to look at and talk about or study diverse cultures and peoples in ways that do not perpetuate exploitation and domination" (p. 128). I discuss the diversity of individuals in the Opening Doors program through detailed accounts of personal construction of self as object (Chapter 4), the necessity of critical reflection on self-knowledge to deconstruct perceptions of self

21

as object (Chapter 5), the (re)presenting of self as subject enabling subject-to-subject interactions with others (Chapter 6), and finally, the interpersonal conflicts that arise when individuals, acting politically from their varying perspectives of self, come together in social interaction (Chapter 7).

It is imperative to be informed by diverse theories in order to maintain the intentions, multiplicity, and integrity of the twenty-one OD participants. Postmodernism challenges the duality of Cartesian logic. Because my purpose is to represent the multiplicity of reality construction, my analysis and conceptualization could be termed postmodern. Critics of postmodern analysis claim that "a post-formal mode of thinking with its emphasis on multiple perspectives leads to uncertainty, fragmentation, chaos, and an ethical relativism that paralyzes social action" (Kincheloe & Steinberg, 1993, p. 298). I argue that identifying, deconstructing, and representing multiple realities is the necessary process through which new social realities and common understandings are constructed.

I draw from anthropological, feminist, critical, psychological, and social psychological theoretical perspectives as analytical levers to explain and inform the interactions that took place during the Opening Doors program. This polythetic framework can be likened to Kanpol's (1992) description of the "new sociology of education . . . where a Marxian, neo-Marxian and combination of phenomenological/ hermeneutic approaches (employing either ethnomethodological or symbolic interactionist techniques) gives new meanings and multiple interpretations to the functions of schools and its protagonists" (p. 5).

Methodologically, my collection and analysis of the autobiographies of the OD participants is influenced by the educational biography work of William Pinar (1978, 1981, 1989) and Madeleine Grumet (1987, 1991) where "*currere* entailed a triple tell as reflection was sorted into past experience, present situation, and future images" (Grumet, 1987, p. 324). As already described in Chapter 1, I draw from symbolic interactionists to explain formulations of the self, and in particular the contextual situatedness of self. In addition, I have particularly focused on the anthropological perspective of Nash (1989) for his theory of ethnicity.

My analysis and proposed process for becoming multicultural also draw from the areas of overlap between postmodern, feminist, critical, and postcolonial thinking. Each of these perspectives places an emphasis on (1) merging rather than fragmenting the social from the personal self connecting politics and epistemology i n conversation that i s power sensitive (Giroux, 1991); (2) correcting the invisibility and distortions of experience be they race, class, gender, o r sexuality (Britzman, 1995; Giroux, 1991; Lather, 1986); (3) the "situatedness and plurality o f possible meanings"(Greene, 1994), including the partiality of all knowledge claims and the indeterminacy of history; (4) interpretation as always "contingent and the specific" (Giroux, 1992; Greene, 1994); (5) "a conscious struggle to transform a social reality which in turn will transform consciousness" (O'Brien, 1 9 8 1), "to renegotiate t h e boundaries of knowledge that claim the status of master narratives, fixed identities, and an objective representation of reality" (Giroux, 1992).

Finally, Britzman (1995) states that "anti-racist and postcolonial scholars have rethought the concept of cultural capital to account for multiple and conflictive radicalized dynamics: culture is analyzed as a significant site for producing codes of whiteness and discourses of Eurocentricity." Throughout, I have relied heavily on the critical perspectives from colonial, antiracist academics of color (Anzaldúa, hooks, Lorde, Lugones, Wallace, and West, among others) to analyze both the autobiographies, and the interpersonal interactions of the participants in Opening Doors.

BEING MULTICULTURAL

Drawing from these anthropological, feminist, critical, psychological and social psychological theoretical perspectives, I have constructed two conceptual models. Figure 2.1 depicts what it means to *be* multicultural, while Figure 2.2 represents the process of *becoming* multicultural. Both models rely on basic concepts of critical theory. Kincheloe (1993) describes critical theory as being "concerned with extending a human's consciousness of himself or herself as a social being" (p. 109). Thus, Figures 2.1 and 2.2 illustrate that to be and become multicultural means that an individual must be and become more conscious of his or her own positionality and how life experiences influence that location. Critical theory is driven by self-reflection. It is an introspective process where individuals "undoubtedly come to know themselves better by bringing to consciousness the process by which their consciousness was constructed" (Kincheloe, 1993, p. 109). As shown in Figure 2.2, critical self-reflection is the action through which individuals become more conscious of themselves, and more under-standing of how others also operate in the world.

Figure 2.1. A conceptual model of a grounded, multicultural self

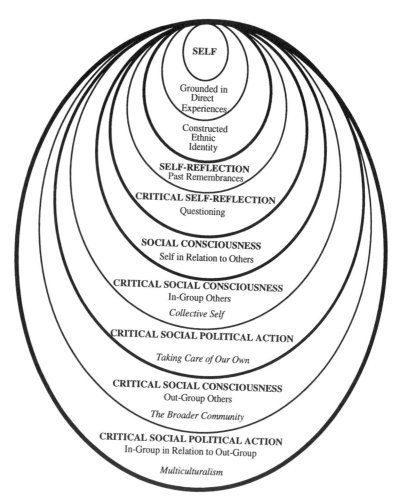

Figure 2.2. A model of being multicultural

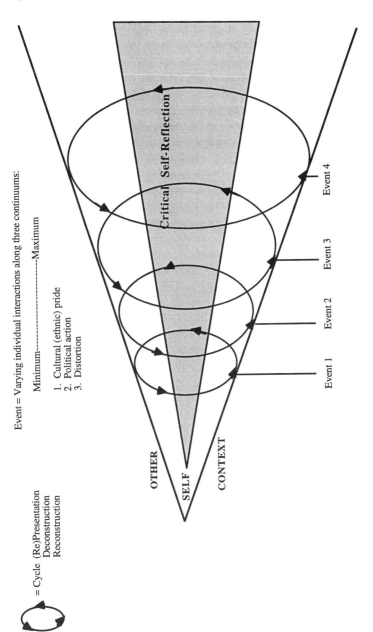

Multicultural Self

Beginning with the self, grounded in direct experiences, each expanding and recursive circle in Figure 2.1 illustrates how the four interactive phases of self represent the developmental phases of *being* a multicultural self. In subsequent chapters, I argue that any group of individuals who come together in social interaction will vary in these phases of self-development, and that the present nature of self-development influences the immediate actions of the individual in the present, as well as shapes his or her interpretation of the past. A major criticism of applied curricula in multicultural education is that current attempts objectify the self by beginning with the social self and ignoring the personal self. The emphasis of the grounded self in the model in Figure 2.1 is the process of achieving a multicultural perspective beginning with the personal self—or self as subject.

The multicultural self is similar to the concept of self as subject (Brown, 1988; hooks, 1990; hooks & West, 1992; Cliff, 1990). In particular, Cliff (1990) explains how understanding the history of the United States as a racist nation includes understanding that in order to oppress Blacks and people from Third World nations: "The person who is oppressed is turned into an object in the mind of the oppressor" (p. 271). Furthermore, the one who is oppressed also begins to view himself or herself as an object. Conceptualizing people as objects represses the emotions of fear, pain, guilt and shame that come from interpersonal interaction with a fellow human being. Objectifying artifacts of culture or grounding beliefs in stereotypes rather than interacting with actual individuals keeps us as human beings from relating to one another on a personal level. It keeps us from knowing, and more important it keeps us from understanding one another. However, one must first understand oneself as subject before one can understand, relate to and appreciate another also as subject.

Self-Construction

Understanding self as subject begins with the past experiences that shaped or constructed the individual in a particular context in the present. Chapter 4 addresses the self-construction process of the Opening Doors participants. In "Voices of Past Experiences," the direct experiences and influences shaping OD participants' sense of self are discussed. As symbolic interactionists assert, it is not the act itself but the symbolic meaning individuals construct from the act that influences the self-identity of the individual. Therefore in "Ethnic Idenity from Past Experiences," I delineate the particular ethnic identity constructions shaped by these direct experiences. Because self-identities are situationally constructed, "Effects of Ethnic Identity on Learning Experiences" follows these ethnic identity constructions into the particular context of the Opening Doors experience. Referring to Figure 2.1, Chapter 4 addresses the first three circles: the self that is grounded in (or shaped by) direct experiences. In turn, individuals construct personal ethnic identities from those direct experiences, and those identities are reconstructed in particular situational contexts.

Self-Knowledge

Chapter 5 explores self-knowledge. Self-knowledge is crucial for understanding self as subject and involves self-reflection on past remembrances as well as critical questioning of those experiences in the present. Having experiences and being consciously aware of the meaning those experiences hold for future interactions are two different aspects. Self-knowledge "has to do with critical recovery and a critical revision of one's past, of one's traditions, of one's history" (hooks & West, 1992, p. 6). However, not all individuals have been allowed or afforded the opportunity to explore the traditions of their historical past to enable them to understand themselves in the present.

Social Consciousness

Referring again to Figure 2.1, Chapter 6 portrays the two foci of the social consciousness of self: self in relation to in-group others and self in relation to out-group others. The notion of the collective self, or perceiving oneself as part of a larger, broader community, is similar to Mead's (in Charon, 1992) concept of the generalized other. Mead used the term *generalized other* to describe the culture of the group: "A generalized other is a set of rules that develops in interaction and which individuals use to control themselves in that interaction . . . . It is the conscience of the group that individuals are expected to follow in interaction" (p. 172). Two foci of social consciousness are in-group others and out-group others. The social consciousness of the in-group is the first phase of the social self in acting toward self as subject rather than self as object. Social consciousness of the out-group refers to the individual's ability not only to interact, but also to have a sense of responsibility and belonging to all humanity, going beyond one's own ethnic identity and culture, to view oneself as a collective part of a broader world community. Expanding the conceptualization of the social self to include others outside one's own ethnic grouping occurs when a multicultural perspective is achieved.

Political Action

Whether the reference group for the individual is the in-group or the out-group, the individual acts toward his or her conceptualization of the generalized other. Those actions, or political actions, and the symbolic meanings of those actions are the focus of Chapter 7. When some individuals act from an in-group consciousness and others act from an out-group consciousness, conflict is inevitable.

BECOMING MULTICULTURAL

Figure 2.1 provides a conceptual model of *being* a grounded, multicultural self, while Figure 2.2 depicts the process of *becoming* a grounded, multicultural self. The process can be described as recursive cycles of (1) deconstructing self as object, (2) reconstructing self as subject, and (3) engaging in subject-to-subject relations with others. An overview and description of the model serves as a guide for the following chapters, which describe, through personal accounts, the model in action.

Role Internalization

Society involves individuals engaging in cooperative action with others (Charon, 1992). In order to maintain collective cooperation within a society, roles (sets of rules) are negotiated by the individuals who interact within the society. Most individuals internalize several roles. Mother, daughter, teacher, businessperson, student, brother, and sister are just a few of the roles we internalize. These roles operate as a "set of shoulds" or rules governing action. For instance, one of the role expectations of the oldest child is that he or she should help care for and look after younger siblings. Likewise teachers should be respected for their knowledge and authority. Students should respect and not question the authority of teachers. Children should be seen and not heard. Most often, these sets of shoulds have been internalized and operate without question. However, when perceived as the role rather than as the individual, the self becomes objectified. Individuals become an object of domination; the set of shoulds controls the individual's actions.

For most, the shoulds are subtle and pose only minor conflicts when the roles and rules governing behavior instilled in the smaller society of the family match the rules of the larger societies) of the community, city, state, nation, and world. However, when the cultural values, beliefs, and rules of interaction (set of shoulds) in the smaller society differ from those imposed by the larger society, a major conflict arises. Ethnicity is one of the factors in the United States that creates tension.

Core Self

Individuals enter any new situation-specific context with a personal reality constructed through their transactions in past experiences. From a social psychological perspective, the individual comes into the context having developed a core self including basic motivations, values, beliefs, and identities (Bush & Simmons, 1990). Ethnic identity is one aspect of that core self. Nash (1989) describes how ethnic identity is one aspect of the core self, or what he terms "primordial ties":

> Ethnic ties have been bundled together with other kinds of deep, core, and primary bonds . . . into a category of "primordial" ties. Primordial ties lie at the core of the person. They form the basic identity, and . . . are thus the social expression of the psychological basis of identity, selfhood, and of others who are like the self, and yet others who are different from the self. (p. 4)

For a person of color interacting with the dominant European culture of the United States, ethnicity becomes a particularly salient identity of the core self because of the experiences of objectification. However, individual experiences vary in degree and effect on self-identity of the individual. Transactions with community, family, religion, gender expectations, and schooling experiences contribute to the construction of personal histories. Ethnic identities resulting from these transactions are socially constructed and in turn socially transformed. Nash (1989) describes the fluid reality of ethnic identity as being a "historical product . . . subject to change, redefinition, and varied salience in the lives of members of the group" (p. 5).

The direct experiences of the self result in the individual's self-concept, the individual's own thoughts and feelings about self (Rosenberg, 1979). For people of color, the concept of self as object develops through the daily transaction of struggle to overcome images of a dominant culture and the invisibility of images similar to their own. Mead asserts that the self develops in two stages. In the first stage, the self develops "through the particular attitudes of other people toward the developing individual" (Bush & Simmons, 1990, p. 140). This first stage of self-development, or primary socialization, is the self construction process. For individuals in the United States who are ethnically diverse from the European American mainstream, the attitudes developed toward them are attitudes of objective invisibility.

SELF AS OBJECT

Issues of invisibility and internalized perceptions of self as object are the focus of theoretical writings from critical feminist women of color such as Gloria Anzaldúa, Michelle Cliff, bell hooks, Audre Lorde, Maria Lugones, Michelle Wallace, and others. In particular, Wallace (1988) explains how cultural invisibility functions to foster self-hate in persons of color:

> It is not just a matter of white people at the top and people of color at the bottom (although that's often the way it turns out), it's about the notion of order as an arrangement in which some people are always better off than others because it helps foster the exorable self-loathing that keeps everybody in their place. (p. 166)

When self is perceived as object, often the self becomes an object of hate. Hate from others is internalized into self-hate, or internalized racism. When one internalizes the external hate-filled actions of others and perceives oneself as an object of hate, self-worth decreases. Wallace (1988) explains the effect invisibility has had on her perception of herself as a person of color in the dominant European American school system:

> I kept to myself and read voraciously but came to loathe the superbly well-educated, articulate whites who shared my classes. I feared I would never catch up. When the fear became too much for me—I was no brave person either—I dropped out. But the project of catching up will always be my existential plight. (p. 169)

The existential plight of catching up that Wallace describes is one of the effects of construction of self as object that students of color bring to the school setting.

In the self-construction process, the view of self that the person of color develops is often one of self-hate as the individual internalizes the anger and hostility of others. Individuals begin to view themselves as others view them: language "deficient," a set of generalized cultural assumptions, a basketball player, an agricultural worker, and above all else, an object of ridicule. And as one of the OD participants poignantly questions, "Who the hell wants to be part of a group people laugh at?"

Critical Reflection to Deconstruct

Meanings constructed from past experiences, and particularly the constructed meanings of ethnic identity, directly influence social interactions in the present. Critical reflection on one's individual experiences and the symbolic meanings constructed from those experiences is the place where becoming multicultural begins. Symbolic interactionism asserts that "the meaning of the symbol is not found in nature, but only through arbitrary designation by people" (Charon, 1992, p. 44). Thus, the multicultural process begins with individuals reflecting on their own symbolic meaning making to understand the arbitrary or idiosyncratic nature of the symbol. Only by identifying one's own personal and arbitrary assignment of meaning (such as invisible, hatred, deficient) are individuals enabled to recognize the same arbitrary designation in others.

Critical self-reflection is the process through which individuals begin to deconstruct themselves in order to bring to consciousness the symbolic meanings of past events. However, to enable the critical self-reflection process, time and place for reflection as well as others' responses are necessary. When individuals share their personal histories with one another, interpersonal similarities are recognized. By sharing the pain and struggles of personal and individual experiences with others, a common bond of interpersonal understanding develops. Or as Nancy Bereano states in her introduction to *Sister Outsider,* the critical reflection process enables individuals to "confront the worst so that . . . [they] may be freed to experience the best" (Lorde, 1984, p. 11). For people of color, the worst is the deconstruction of past internalization of self as object in order to experience the best, a reconstruction of self as subject in the present.

Reconstructing Self as Subject

As individuals act, reflecting on the intended meanings of their actions and the perceived meanings others place on their actions, a dialogic process of self-reconstruction in the immediate context emerges. Reconstruction begins when the individual acts from his or her own personal perspective, receives feedback from others, and changes consequent interactions based on the feedback. Charon (1992) states that "interaction creates perspectives . . . . Our approach to reality is social; it changes as our interaction changes, and it is stable when our interaction is stable" (p. 160). Through cycles of external interactions with others followed by internal reflection on those interactions, cycles of instability and changing perspectives are experienced.

The dialogic process occurs on two levels. First is the external dialogue between self and others, or social interaction. Second is the internal dialogue between the acting self and the reflective self. Or as Mead (1934) explains, the essence of the self lies in the internalized conversations that constitute thinking. It is through the constant reflective process that the constructed self as object can be dismantled and reconstructed as subject. The longer one views the self as object, the more time it will take to concentrate on the deconstruction process. For people of color who have been marginalized and made invisible through a Eurocentric curriculum, the reconstruction process may take intensified time and effort. Explicit efforts to reconstruct a positive ethnic identity are vital to the multicultural process. When individuals can know themselves as subjects, they are enabled to know others as subjects as well. They are enabled to have a consciousness of self in relation to others.

In the learning context, this same external-to-internal dialogic process is the essence of Vygotsky's (1954) internalization process. It is through language that we make sense of our world, language used in concert with others, and language in dialogue with ourselves. As Vygotsky notes, "A word is a microcosm of human consciousness" (p. 153). Language of the environment (others) shapes a child's (or learner's) generalizations about the world. Only through dialogue with others who perceive the world differently from ourselves can our inner dialogue reshape those generalizations.

Conflict

However, the process is not a smooth or painless one. When individuals act from personal perspectives that do not match the perspectives of others, conflicts are inevitable. Symbolic interaction suggests that individuals act toward a generalized other or referent group with which the individual shares a common perspective. This shared perspective then acts as a set of rules which guide social interactions (Charon, 1992). The task of communication is eased when all refer to the same generalized other. However, the difference of in-group and out-group referents as the generalized other is a potential source of conflict. Charon (1992) suggests: "Sometimes the smaller societies cause us to challenge and try to change the larger society because the emerging perspective and generalized other regard the larger society to be immoral or incorrect" (p. 179). The more negative the interactions people of color have with the European American dominant out-group, the more immoral the out-group is viewed and the more focused individual action is toward the in-group in order to reconstruct self as subject.

For example, negative experiences such as rape, drug addiction, divorce, ostracism, alienation, no positive role models, and denied access to schooling can become vehicles for a passion to replace the present dominant European American school system. On the other hand, the experiences of positive role models and successful schooling experiences can offer a construction that seeks to change the present system rather than reject or completely redesign it.

Though views of how to implement change in the present system differ, there are people of color who perceive change as necessary to enable future students of color to know themselves as subject and not be alienated from their ethnic identity. Actions are focused toward making those changes for future generations. Nash (1989) describes how this sense of giving back in the future is strongly tied to the individual's sense of tradition, or past. Tradition lends group cohesion and continuity to the individual. This notion of preserving the historical past in order to merge the lives of individuals in the group toward the future is particularly strong for some African Americans who have had their historical roots intentionally extinguished. Insistence that African Americans need to learn more about themselves and find out more about their own history is indicative of efforts to strengthen African Americans as a group by placing "authority, legitimacy, and rightness to cultural beliefs and practices" in past tradition (Nash, 1989, p. 14).

Audre Lorde (1984) asserts that efforts of people of color to reclaim the past are essential to reconstructing self as subject in the present to act toward the future. She writes:

> As we come more into touch with our own ancient, non-european consciousness of living as a situation to be experienced and interacted with, we learn more and more to cherish our feelings, and to respect those hidden sources of our power from where true knowledge and, therefore, lasting action comes. (p. 32)

Critical Social Consciousness

To survive in the European American dominant culture of the United States, people of color have had to become adept at role taking or following the governing rules (or perspective) of the larger society. In doing so, their own personal perspectives have been marginalized and silenced. When individuals acquire the self-knowledge to perceive themselves as subjects, questioning of present situations follows, creating a critical social consciousness. Critical, in this sense, implies questioning—questioning in order to reconstruct. Hooks (1989) defines critical social consciousness as the "process by which we move from seeing ourselves as object to acting as subjects" (p. 27). Social rules and situations are not taken for granted as impenetrable structures. They are questioned through the perception of self as an acting subject that can contribute to changing those structures through political action. Personal perspectives are not sacrificed in order for the social perspective to prevail. Instead, personal perspectives are viewed as having an equal responsibility to share in negotiating and constructing changed social structures.

When the individual acts on the personal reality previously alienated by the larger society, that action designates political and socially conflictive action. Personal action is political action. When those traditionally silenced by the larger society choose to act from self as subject, they act in order to engage others in the same role-taking behavior they have been practicing themselves for their lifetimes. When the other, who has been perceived as object, begins to act as subject, conflict is likely. However, the farther removed the action is from the mythical norm (to borrow from Audre Lorde's, 1984, terminology), the greater the conflict.

Minimum-Maximum Action

Out-Group Conflicts

Nash (1989) explains how the action aspect of ethnicity involves symbolic claims to social parity to other groups. Action to claim status of equity can be placed on a continuum of minimum-maximum action. A minimum action is one that allows a group to practice their group's way without hindrance from the larger society group. The right to celebrate cultural holidays and festivals is an example of minimum action. A maximum action, however, insists on the "domination of social and cultural life by ethnic considerations" (p. 15). The current civil wars in Eastern Europe are an example of maximum action.

Actions toward the minimum end of the continuum obviously cause lesser conflict with the larger societal expectations, while actions toward the maximum end cause much greater conflict. Applying the minimum-maximum action line to the classroom, students who choose to act toward their ethnic self as subject by researching and reporting on the historical contributions of their cultural heritage are less likely to create much disturbance for others. The action toward the personal self is within the boundaries of acceptable behaviors as deemed by the rules governing the larger society. However, when students of color refuse to participate in classroom activities led by European Americans, the action is perceived as being in direct opposition to the governing rules of the larger society. The more toward the maximum end of the action line the actions of individuals are, the more those actions are labeled and distorted by larger society in an effort to control and extinguish such behaviors. *Militant, isolationist,* and *separatist* are among the labels assigned to those who, in an effort to enact change, choose actions that oppose the larger societal expectations.

In-Group Conflicts

Minimum-maximum actions not only cause conflict between in-group and out-group, but can also cause conflict between in-group members who do not agree on the degree of personal action taken by others within the in-group. This conflict arises in the area of trust. Individuals who act from either end of the continuum tend to perceive the other as going about making change in the wrong way. Those at the maximum end perceive those toward the minimum end as not committed enough to the cause. Those at the minimum end, however, perceive those at the maximum end as being too violent, angry, or hate-filled, determined to get their way no matter how many others are injured in the process.

Confrontation for Change

Whether acting from the minimum or maximum end of the action line, choosing to act personally is choosing to disrupt the status quo. In acting politically the individual purposefully and deliberately breaks the walls of invisibility and silence of their personal self, which creates discomfort for others. As Lorde (1984) states: "The transformation of silence into language and action is an act of self-revelation, and that always seems fraught with danger" (p. 42). The result of broken silences is that others must now engage in the same critical reflection and role-taking process that people of color have done daily in this nation. Only when the personal is no longer silent can social perspectives change to include rather than exclude the personal. Only when the personal is respected within the larger social perspective will individual needs be valued in order to change individual self-destruction into societal production. Audre Lorde's daughter explains the self-destructive nature of silence when she advises her mother:

> Tell them about how you're never really a whole person if you remain silent, because there's always that one little piece inside you that wants to be spoken out, and if you keep ignoring it, it gets madder and madder and hotter and hotter, and if you don't speak it out one day it will just up and punch you in the mouth from the inside. (Lorde, 1984, p. 42)

Personal action involves dialogue with others, sharing personal perspectives in order to create new socially shared perspectives. The longer one has been silenced as an object, the more apt the first utterings of personal perspectives will be laced with tones of anger. However, anger must be made conscious in order to deconstruct its objectified roots. In this way, a voice of anger should be positively acknowledged as the first initiating step forward from silence, the first step toward reconstructing self as subject.

Conflictive experiences may be outwardly viewed as negative. Often negative encounters with others engage the critical self-reflection process. For those not able or willing to self-reflect, being in situations that cause them to do so becomes threatening and therefore incites defensive behavior from them. The more an individual views self as object, the more defensive the behavior is likely to become. However, the process is initiated. As Audre Lorde (1984) describes, "the learning process is something you can incite, literally incite, like a riot. And then, just possibly, hopefully, it goes home, or on" (p. 98).

BEING AND BECOMING

Learning is the construction of new patterns of behavior or information through transactions with the environment. Socialization is a special kind of learning through which we internalize values and symbols of culture. The self is constantly being socialized with each new context, and therefore has no end state. So, too, there is no end state in becoming multicultural. Each time the self is (re)presented in a new context, a new cycle of development begins. Multiculturalism is more than just a learning process. It is a socialization process that involves qualitative degrees of self-development. One does not discontinue to know oneself at a certain age or stage in life. Self-knowledge cannot be measured by an objective measurement or assessment tool. It is an individual and personal process that includes the necessity of acknowledging the role of personal experiences in constructing the view of the personal self.

Linguistically, the prefix *re* means to do again. The process of *becoming* multicultural is characterized as recursive because the process recurs again and again from one situational context to another. One cannot become multicultural and transfer multicultural ability from one situation to another. Multiculturalism, like any other objectified learning skill does not necessarily transfer. Knowledge of others in one situation cannot be automatically transferred from one contextual situation to the next. However, generalized knowledge concerning the underlying nature of human interaction *can* facilitate understanding in new situations.

For example, a European American student may learn how to cooperate with the Asian American student who sits next to him in his fourth-grade classroom. In fact, the two may even develop a life long friendship of caring and sharing. This does not mean that the same European American boy can transfer the multicultural knowledge of understanding his friend to knowing how to cooperate with all Asian Americans, or even to understanding and appreciating the new Asian American classmate who enters the class part way through the year, for that matter. However, if our hypothetical student were to reflect on his own interactions with his Asian American friend, bringing to consciousness the ways in which their friendship developed (Did they fight at first? Who initiated the interaction in the beginning? How did they resolve conflicts? How did they find out about their differing lifestyles? How did they react to that knowledge of differences? What enabled their understanding to develop? What hindered their understanding?), then that social consciousness of relating to others, resulting from self-reconstruction, will facilitate understanding in the new contextual situation.

This is what is meant by cultural sensitivity. Sensitivity is bringing one's own personal construction into consciousness in order to be more sensitive toward the other's personal construction. In other words, the more sensitive we are to our own sense-making processes or constructions, the more apt we are to take the role of the other and recognize the same idiosyncratic constructions in them. Hence, through recognizing ourselves in others, we respond with more cultural sensitivity.

In sum, Figure 2.1 represents the development of the grounded self. Any group of individuals who come together in social interaction will vary in the phases of self-development. Kincheloe and Steinberg (1993) suggest that "we have missed the rather obvious point that individuals operate simultaneously at divergent cognitive stages" (p. 299). So, too, in developing a multicultural self, individuals may operate at several layers of the grounded self depending on the context, situation, and individuals involved. It is not a static development such as age, where once you are twelve you can never go back to being eleven again. Instead, the development varies with each new contextual situation encountered. The present nature of self-development influences the immediate actions of the individual in the present, as well as shapes his or her interpretation of the past. The beginning of a grounded self, or perceiving self as subject, is reflection on the direct experiences that shaped the present self.

Figure 2.2 illustrates the process of *becoming* multicultural. The recursive cycle begins with the individual who, upon encountering others in the present social situation, reflects on his or her own self-construction of the past in order to reconstruct the self in the present situational context. The reconstruction process then enables the self to socially interact in subject-to-subject relations. The more often the process is repeated, the more able the individual is to view the other as subject, or to take the perspective of the other. Just as with any other kind of learning, the more the process is repeated, the more habitual and facile it becomes. The more facile one is in processing new situations, the more readily one is able to engage in subject-to-subject relations. In other words, the more role taking in the perspective of the other is experienced, the more multicultural understanding is developed.

CHAPTER 3

Constructing a Critical Context

> *The overall goal of the program is to encourage ethnic
> minority students to participate in and pursue graduate
> study in teacher education. Central to this goal is the
> establishment of close personal relationships between
> undergraduate student participants and the faculty and
> graduate students who serve as mentors and role models
> in this process . . . . In addition to providing an excellent
> educational research experience, the Opening Doors
> program will also seek to provide for the social and
> cultural needs and education of the talented minority
> student participants.*
>
> —Dillard and Parkay (1991, p. 9)

The Opening Doors program, was implemented for the first time at a
state university in the Northwest during the summer session of 1992.
This federally funded program was "an intensive eight-week summer
research and study experience" in which twenty-one talented minority
college juniors and seniors participated in an effort to increase minority
participation in graduate education (Dillard & Parkay, 1991, p. 1). The
program focused on the following elements: "1) understanding self
including self-identity, personal perspectives, and values; 2) knowledge
of graduate study; 3) the role of research and scholarship; 4) involvement with current graduate students and faculty in one major research
activity; 5) academic and career counseling; 6) selection and application processes for graduate school in their chosen area of study: and 7)
on-going communication and mentoring by university faculty" (p. 1).

41

The overall goal of the program was to encourage students from traditionally underrepresented groups to participate in and pursue graduate study in teacher education. The program planners were of the opinion that ethnically diverse groups are underrepresented because college campus efforts do not adequately attend to socioemotional and sociocultural needs of minority students. Therefore, central to the goal of Opening Doors was the provision of an interactive, supportive environment designed to meet the social and cultural needs of the OD participants. Social activities were planned to enable the establishment of close personal relationships between the undergraduate OD participants and other graduate students on campus who serve as mentors and role models in this process. In addition, several of the activities provided academic and career counseling necessary for the students to pursue graduate study effectively in education. Faculty mentoring and sponsorship, fellowship with other ethnically diverse graduate and undergraduate students, and a regular forum to express feelings, frustrations, and uncertainties were structured into the program to provide the foundation for academic success "to assist the traditionally underrepresented student in being able to compete more effectively with their European-American counterparts" (Dillard & Parkay, 1991, p. 15). Opportunities for ethnically diverse participants to do academic research in a context that also provided personal counseling, mentoring, guidance, and support gave this program an interactive nature, one that is ideal for exploring what it takes to become truly multicultural.

OPENING DOORS PARTICIPANTS

The Opening Doors committee (consisting of the program director, the administrative director, a representative from the graduate school, a representative from the Division of Minority Affairs, and a representative from the Career Development Office) selected twenty-one undergraduate juniors and seniors on the basis of (1) academic performance (2.75 GPA and above); (2) two letters of recommendation from college professors; (3) a statement of purpose written by the student; and (4) a telephone interview. To search for students meeting these criteria, preliminary contacts were made with college presidents and/or directors of minority affairs at all regional institutions of higher education. Subsequently, flyers were distributed throughout the state and the western region of the United States (Alaska, California, Hawaii,

Idaho, Montana, Oregon, and Washington). For those students who met the four minimum criteria, a fifth criteria—financial need—was also considered in the final selection process to identify those students who would benefit most from the program (Dillard & Parkay, 1991, p. 17).

The OD participants selected included eight African Americans (six females and two males), seven Latinos (four females and three males), three Native Americans (two females and one male), and three female Asians and/or Asian Americans. Eleven of the participants were undergraduates at the university sponsoring the Opening Doors program. Their ages ranged from twenty-one to forty-six years old. Twelve participants can be described as *traditional* juniors and seniors, in that they were single and in their mid twenties. The remaining nine were *nontraditional:* older students in their mid thirties to mid forties, with children and married, divorced, or separated. Twelve named education as their academic area of study, while the other nine listed the areas of communication, liberal arts, life sciences, psychology, protective sciences, cultural history, and urban studies.

OPENING DOORS STAFF

Celeste, the program director, is an African American female, and Assistant Professor of Multicultural and Bilingual Education in the College of Education. As director of the program, her role included organizing and facilitating all Opening Doors activities, acting as a liaison between the participants and other university personnel (financial services, bookstore, residence housing, registrar), and teaching the academic coursework in the program. Her individual research interests include the study of sociocultural contexts of schooling, language, and literacy.

My primary role in the program was research and data documentation of all activities. However, as an experienced teacher, including two years with undergraduate education majors, I also assisted Celeste in planning and implementing the instructional activities of the program. My research interests (sociocultural contexts of schooling, language, and literacy) arose from observing the evolution of gang activity in the middle school where I previously taught for seven years. The location of the school district in an agricultural region of the state included over 60 percent of the student population as Latino, largely Mexican American. My experience interacting with parents, students, school staff and administration, and the business community served as a driving force behind my interest in the Opening Doors program. In my sometimes failed efforts to facilitate cooperative discussions across the interest groups in my local community, I realized that I needed to know more to foster an understanding of diversity in others.

Kristy, a staff assistant, is a Chinese American female in her first year of doctoral study in cross-cultural counseling. Kristy had minimal teaching experience before the program: an instructional assistantship for one year, where she ran study sessions for the professor of the course. Her primary role in Opening Doors was to be a participant-observer, documenting field notes during class sessions.

Wes, the other staff assistant, is an African American male who was just completing his first year as a master's student in counseling psychology. Wes had no prior teaching experience before the program. Rather than a formal teaching role, Wes's primary contribution to Opening Doors came through his active, personal involvement with group members. His personable, casual style enabled others to talk freely and easily when he was around. His primary role in the program was the same as Kristy's, to document field notes during class sessions.

As staff members, the four of us divided roles implicitly among ourselves, but not necessarily explicitly for OD participants. Since this was Celeste's first year after receiving her degree, and I was only one year away from receiving mine, she and I were the most experienced and most familiar with the roles and demands of graduate school. Thus, we assumed the teaching roles in the class, while Kristy and Wes assumed research assistant roles. I was the only European American who participated on a daily basis with the Opening Doors group. Celeste invited me to be part of the program because of our previous work together in which we collaborated on two projects: a multimedia presentation on critical pedagogy for a national conference and a Multicultural Education in a Global Society graduate course where I served as her assistant. This experience provided Celeste with a familiarity with my academic work, research interests, and perspectives on issues of diversity. In turn, our experiences together provided me with insights about diversity from other than my own European American vantage point.

The contributions and expertise of each staff member varied in nature. Whereas Celeste invited me to participate due to my strong academic record as a graduate student, she invited Kristy and Wes as role models for graduate students of color. The contributions of each staff member were purposefully designed to be complementary. Though I could provide guidance and support about the academic work of graduate life, my obviously nonexistent experience offered no insights into the specific social and cultural needs of being a student of color on a predominantly White campus. Therefore, the role modeling and personal perspectives as graduate students of color that Kristy and Wes could provide were vital and essential contributions to the goals of this program.

EVENTS OVERVIEW

Celeste described to OD participants on the first day that the overall purpose of the program was to demystify the notion of graduate school. She explained her view that those with "alphabets behind their names" are not any smarter than anyone else they just have more tenacity than others. "I'm convinced," she elaborated, "that the ones who succeed are bold, brave, and stubborn enough to get in there and get it. It's not about who is smarter or brighter, but who wants to stay in there longer." Table 3.1 illustrates the intense and rigorous academic schedule in which OD participants engaged to develop this tenacity. This overview schedule is useful to illustrate two points. First, OD participants engaged in an integrated program of academic coursework to meet personal research interests and non academic events to facilitate social interaction among the OD participants with university professors, staff, and personnel on campus. Second, the schedule provides a context for viewing the important timing of events. The timing of social and academic events became a crucial factor because interpretations of social encounters often affected the interactions among individuals in the academic setting and vice versa.

The program consisted of three types of events: (1) academic, (2) social, and (3) special events. Following Table 3.1 is a brief description of each of these event types.

Academic Events

The academic agenda for the first week set the stage for the OD experience, putting into motion a full range of types of activities encountered in a graduate school experience. Events of the first week focused on the first stated objective of "understanding self including self-identity, personal perspectives and values." Celeste told OD participants:

Table 3.1. Opening Doors Schedule of Events

	Monday	Tuesday	Wednesday	Thursday	Friday
Week 1	Class 9-12 Orientation	Class 9-12 Autobiography Dean's barbecue	Class 9-12 Autobiography	Class 9-12 Autobiography Video: The Rise of College Campus Racism	Class 1-4 Journals due "Hows and Whys of Grad School"
Week 2	Class 9-12 Journal sharing Speaker: Associate Dean, "Issues in Education Research."	Class 9-12	Small group planning BCD 1[b]	Class 1-4 Speaker: Dr. Can, Dissertation Research. Small groups research method presentations	Class 9-12 Journals due Small groups research method presentations Sunday: Minority Affairs Picnic
Week 3	Class 9-12 Journal sharing Proposal discuss Speaker: Gang Research and Qualitative Methods	Class 9-12 Library present CD-ROM	Independent study Journals due	Independent study	Day off
Week 4	Class 1-4 Journal sharing Lit review/research prop Mentor names given out	Independent study	Independent study BCD 2	Cleveland Conference 8:30-11:30	Class 9-12 Journals due Proposal present

Week 5 [a]	Class 9-12 Journal Sharing Scenarios	Work with mentors	Work with mentors	Work with mentors	Class 9-12 Journals due Mentor impressions
Week 6	Class 9-12 Journal sharing Scenario debrief Associate Dean's Pool Party	Work with mentors	Work with mentors	Work with mentors BCD 3	Class 9-12 Journals due At-risk planning
Week 7	At-risk planning	Class 8-9 Journal sharing At-risk Conference 9-11:30	Work with mentorss	Work with mentors	Class 9-12 Journals due Presentation practice
Week 8	Class 9-12 Presentation practice	Colloquiam 9am-4pm Reception Night out at Local Restaurant	Class 1-2 Final evaluations Final paper due		

[a] Celeste was gone this week
[b] BCD = Behind Closed Doors, a social event

This week we'll spend a lot of time talking about issues of identity, what it means to be a graduate student, a faculty member, a TA, on a campus. Also what does it mean to be a student of color? You'll hear a little about, and we'll talk about, issues of race and racism because I think it's important to talk about those things up front before we get into the business of what we're going to be doing . . . . It may be a little different reality sometimes on a campus, being a student of color, than it is for other students. So we'll be talking about those issues this week as sort of an orientation for what you're about to do.

Autobiographies

The first assignment designed to focus on issues of self and identity invited students to create an autobiography presentation to share with the group. At the end of the first day, Celeste explained that participants would present their autobiographies to the group beginning the following day. She asked that in preparing the autobiographies OD participants consider, "What is it I bring and understand? And, what is it that will enable others to know the world the way I do?" She further explained: "We come to an event all that we are. It matters what I bring, what background, what history I bring to an event. We'd like to know more about who you are. What has made you up to this point? The autobiography should answer two questions: (1) Who am I? (2) What are the important people, places, and experiences that have influenced me?" She concluded by explaining that the form was to be any genre other than expository writing. Song, dance, poetry, art, anything but expository writing may be used.

The Rise of College Campus Racism Video

Whereas the autobiography assignment provided a means for individuals to look inward and focus on issues of personal identity, the second activity focused on looking outward, dealing with issues of social identity. We watched the video *The Rise of College Campus Racism,* developed by Black Issues in Higher Education as a teleconference presentation. Panelists included two African American scholars, Naim Akbar and Jawanza Kunjufu, who were familiar faces to several of the African Americans in the group. The video addressed and discussed current issues and incidents of racism on college campuses. After viewing the first half of the panel discussion, OD participants formed four small groups to conduct their own discussions. Celeste framed the viewing of the video by saying,

> All of you have mentioned ethnicity and race sometime throughout your autobiography . . . . And many of you talked about both intra . . . as well as inter, or cross-cultural conflict, discrimination . . . . These issues are still alive and well. Regardless of whether we choose to embrace them, they are issues. Taking into account who we are individually, and then collectively, these are the two questions I'd like you to keep in mind as you watch. First, what is my responsibility as the person I have described to this group, in relationship to some of the issues that will be presented? Secondly, what could be some of my possible responses? Those will be the questions we'll ask that you talk about in small group discussions after the viewing.

Text Readings

Vital to program objectives but not included in Table 3.1 are the assigned readings from the two required texts: Jaeger's (1988) *Complementary Methods for Research in Education,* Washington, D.C.: American Education Research Association, and Becker's (1986) *Writing for Social Scientists: How to Start and Finish Your Thesis, Book, or Article,* Chicago: University of Chicago Press. OD participants read assigned chapters weekly from each book. In addition, OD participants also consulted the *Publication Manual of the American Psychological Association Manual* (3rd ed.) during the research process to format their written projects.

Dialogue Journals

Each week, OD participants wrote a response journal. The course syllabus stated that the purpose of the journal was "to generate a dialogue between class members that will assist in extending and broadening our individual and collective understanding of educational issues." OD participants typed one to two pages on whatever topic of interest they chose each week, whether that interest was personal, social, or academic. Two copies were brought each Friday: one to share with a peer, and the other for Celeste. Then, on Mondays journals from the previous week were returned to their owners with a written response from the trading partner. OD participants traded with whomever they chose each week.

Along with the journal from their peers, OD participants also responded to journals from Celeste and me each week. The original plan was that Celeste, as the group leader, would write each week. However, after the first week, the staff met and decided I would also write each week. The purpose of my writing was to enable OD participants to get to know me better, and also to keep them informed about the data collection and to invite their feedback in my on going analysis of the program. Implementing this strategy assisted the development of trust between the OD participants and myself as the participant-observer and also as the only European American in the group. After the first week of listening to several negative generalized comments about the atrocities caused by European Americans, I felt it vital to establish communication to alleviate skepticism about what I must be thinking. Therefore, responding to the events and learning activities of the week was the purpose of Celeste's journal. The purpose of my journal was to keep OD participants informed about the on going ethnographic research data being collected. Even though Celeste and I tried to keep the purposes of our journals separate in theory, reality proved that human interactions are not that easily separated. Thus, our journal themes overlapped on several occasions.

Weekly Journal Sharing

On Mondays, after trading journals and reading the responses, the first fifteen minutes or so of class time was spent discussing journal themes. After the reading of peers' journals, these discussions became a vehicle for communicating and sharing ideas and for the development of a professional as well as personal support system. Individuals found trading journals an invaluable experience. The written journals enabled individuals to express thoughts and feelings on paper they might not have spoken out loud in large group settings. Therefore, OD participants gained further insight into the perspectives of their fellow OD participants through this process.

Research Process

In an effort to demystify the research process, the program was designed for students to conduct their own piece of original research during the eight-week program. Each OD participant came to the program with a research topic of interest. Unlike most introductory research courses in which students start only with a review of literature, the entire research process was explored: literature reviews, annotated bibliography, proposal for study, a final report, and a formal colloquium presentation of findings to a public audience. To facilitate the process, each OD participant was assigned an individual faculty mentor (either within the College of Education or across the university) to assist with the research project. Meeting times with mentors and the level of mentor involvement were negotiated by the individual pairs. Mentor involvement ranged from those who met two to three times a week to those who met their mentor once and chose not to engage with him or her anymore.

Small Group Presentations

After reading and discussing the introductory chapters of the methods book, OD participants signed up for one of the research traditions in their text: philosophical, historical, case study, experimental, quasi-experimental, ethnographic, and survey. OD participants studied their chosen research tradition in groups of three, and presented to the class their understandings of the methodology and underlying assumptions using participatory examples for illustration. OD participants were given two half days and one whole day for preparation. Celeste explained their responsibility:

> You all will get together in small groups and . . . . study one particular area, one type of research. Then we'll come back together and you will teach the rest of us about historical research, or ethnographic research, or case study, [or] experimental. So each group is going to have the responsibility to teach us. Don't think you're going to have to go find it all out yourself. There's a chapter in your text for each one of those. You will have to figure out how you will present that research to us so that we understand that information. So we all will be teachers. We'll look at the different types of research that are done so that you can see where your particular questions may lie, within which tradition.

Guest Speakers

Five guest speakers shared with OD participants their knowledge and perspectives on varying topics relevant to graduate study. A

representative from the graduate school spoke on issues regarding
entrance requirements such as GRE testing, types of programs and
degrees, funding possibilities, and the like. One week after his defense,
an Asian American Ph.D. candidate came to talk about his experiences
with the dissertation process. Next, to provide an example of what
qualitative data might look like, I presented a research project I had
conducted on the topic of Latino gangs. The associate dean of the
College of Education came and spoke on current topics in education
research. Last, the Opening Doors group visited the main library on
campus where a Native American librarian demonstrated the procedure
for conducting CD-ROM searches and helpful strategies for finding
information in the library system on campus.

Scenarios

Each of the five small groups was given a different scenario which
described a situation of an ethnically diverse student in an educational
setting. The scenarios, adapted from Sue and Sue's (1990) book on
cross-cultural counseling, included (1) a European American male
English teacher correcting the Black dialect of two African American
boys having a personal conversation outside of class, (2) a White
female high school teacher designing role-playing activities to force
Asian American students' participation, (3) a Latino male who is failing
schoolwork because of attending to his family's needs first, (4) a
European American female history teacher changing lesson methods to
try to force two "sullen and withdrawn" Native American boys into
class participation, and (5) a Latina student asking to receive a C or D
for a course because she felt she knew the material even though she
flunked the exams. In an effort to broaden understanding of the other's
perspective in learning events, the scenarios were purposefully
distributed to match as closely as possible the ethnic make up of the
groups where OD participants were sitting. The group with the most
Latinos was given a Latino scenario, the group with Asians and Asian
Americans was given the Asian American scenario, and so on. After
recording individual responses to the scenario questions provided each
small group compared answers through discussion. Then the small
groups reported their findings to the whole group, and group views
were recorded on the chalkboard.

Social Events

Time for social interaction outside the classroom setting was consciously built into the schedule. Though all but three OD participants resided in the same dorm on campus, it was necessary to provide scheduled times for OD participants to talk among themselves, as well as opportunities to meet and interact with other university people.

Behind Closed Doors

Celeste described the event Behind Closed Doors on the first day:

> It's sort of a play on words. This is called Opening Doors and that's exactly what we're trying to do. But we all know that in the work that we do, oftentimes there are those conversations that need to be had behind closed doors. What those sessions are, are [a time] for us to get together . . . to say there are some other issues of graduate students and students of color that don't often have a place to be talked about in a university setting. What we want to do is to provide a place where people could come and have refreshments and that kind of thing, and just talk without having to worry about who's going to say what about what, or who's going to be there, or who's going to see it. It's just this group . . . . It's just that kind of chat. Behind Closed Doors. Whatever you want to talk about . . . . It's a place we get to learn more about each other . . . . Again, to strengthen our own understanding about what it means to be a graduate student, or faculty member, or teacher, in this country in this context.

Social Gatherings

Along with Behind Closed Doors (soon shortened to the acronym BCD), other social events were scheduled for OD participants to meet and interact with faculty and personnel on campus. Both the dean and the associate dean from the College of Education volunteered to sponsor informal gatherings at their homes. The dean had an informal barbecue at his home the second day of the program. Having not yet gotten into the academic demands, participants spent time in informal, getting-to-know-you conversations. Then, during the sixth week, the associate dean sponsored a pool party at her home. At this time, several

OD participants were sitting pool side engaged in collecting data from one another for their research projects. Tape recorders, interview questions, and surveys were at hand as individuals mixed their social time with accomplishing academic tasks. The last social event was sponsored by the Minority Affairs group on campus. This was the only weekend activity on the schedule. On this Sunday afternoon OD participants were invited to attend a potluck picnic to meet and interact with other ethnically diverse students and other ethnically diverse faculty affiliated with the research university.

Special Events

As the professor with the expertise on multicultural issues on campus, Celeste was often called on by other professors to present, respond to, or coordinate activities concerning multicultural issues for their courses. During this summer session, two occasions arose in which Celeste was asked to participate. She used both these situations to actively involve the Opening Doors participants in the varied roles and responsibilities of being a graduate student or faculty member of color.

C. Conference

Each summer, the university sponsors a three-day conference for the state's school administrators called the C. Conference. The focus of this year's conference was on restructuring education. Celeste was asked to be one of three respondents to the keynote speaker. She explained to the Opening Doors participants that one role they may encounter as graduate students is that of respondent. Therefore, this would be a good opportunity for them to see what it's like to have to respond, impromptu, to someone else's ideas. She also added that it would be a good opportunity to meet and get to know some of the names and faces from around the state and begin making connections (especially for those nine OD participants who were education majors) for teaching positions in the near future. All OD participants attended and actively asked questions of the panel and keynote speaker in the session in which Celeste responded. They were also invited to attend any of the other sessions.

At-Risk Session

The second opportunity OD participants had was an invitation to participate in a seminar on at-risk K-12 students that was taking place on campus during the summer session. Originally, the professor who ran the seminar asked Celeste to be a guest speaker about the views of ethnic minorities on issues of at-risk students, to which she responded, "Why not let the *minorities* speak for themselves?" The result was that at the end of week six, for the first time since they had been there, OD participants were purposefully divided into groups based on their ethnicity. The four groups were given one and a half hours of class time on Friday to discuss and plan an eight-to-ten minute presentation on what they perceived as relevant issues related to members of their ethnic grouping who may be at risk of school failure. Groups were left to decide who was going to speak for their group, what issues they considered vital, and what they wanted to say about these issues in relation to at-risk students in education.

On the day of the presentations, all Opening Doors participants joined the graduate students enrolled in the at-risk seminar for the summer. Since the seminar was a satellite course being taped for future national broadcast, the room was complete with cameras, microphones and monitors. The four elected presenters gave their talks, while others were members of the interactive audience. In order to prepare the Opening Doors participants for the new experience of classroom technology, Celeste discussed and planned with them the types of questions she might pose to the audience as she moderated a discussion following the presentations. Preparation also included discussing the types of experiences from their own lives that OD participants might share in response to the questions. The situation of going to a new classroom, complete with graduate students who were enrolled in the class and had been in the environment for six weeks, was awkward enough. Adding television monitors, cameras, and microphones, and then asking OD participants to spontaneously respond to questions posed created a situation of unknowns that would cause even the most assured graduate student to be stressed. Therefore, the preparation work was designed to reduce the number of unknowns and ease nervousness.

The chronology as well as the type of events in the Opening Doors program affected the interactions that took place. In addition to the scheduled activities, all four staff members maintained regular office hours for OD participants. Even on days when they were left to work on their own or with their assigned mentors, a staff member was always available to assist or answer questions. Table 3.1 shows the sequence of learning and social events and illustrates the balance of social and academic assignments. It will serve as a helpful reference guide as events and interactions that emerged from this constructed context are described in more detail.

CHAPTER 4

Constructing Self as Object
Salient Autobiographical Experiences

*Each of us looks upon the common world from a
particular standpoint, a particular location in space and
time. Each of us has a distinctive biography, a singular
life history.*

—Greene (1978, p. 24)

The stories each individual initially shared in the formal autobiography
presentations surfaced time and again through various activities during
the eight-week program. The same stories of the past, as well as
additional ones, were spoken or written as illustrations of a particular
perspective. Personal histories were also expressed to interpret activities and issues examined in the present and to justify reasons for future
goals. Tellings and retellings of personal narratives appeared in the bio
sheets filled out the night before the first class meeting, in small and
large group discussions, in weekly journal writing, and in formal and
informal interviews. As Pinar (1981) describes the autobiographical
method, recounting the autobiographies of the OD participants allows
us to "excavate layers of intention and experience which antedate and
live below the text which is daily life" (p. 177). In other words, the
personal narratives expressed through classroom interactions in the
Opening Doors context provide an understanding of the personal and
individual constructions of ethnicity individuals brought into the
program.

From social psychology, we learn that two processes forming the
self-concept or self-judgment are reflective appraisal and social

comparison (Gecas, 1982). In the case of individuals ethnically diverse from the European American mainstream, reflective appraisal and social comparison often results in construction of self as object. Audre Lorde (1984) describes growing up as a Black woman in the United States as "absorbing hatred" (p. 146). Being laughed at, ridiculed, ignored, silenced in a racist society meant "growing up metabolizing hatred like daily bread" (p. 152). For some participants, personal histories revealed metabolizing hatred in much the same way as Lorde describes. Internalizing the perceptions of the dominant European American perspective constructed a sense of self as object: An object of hatred because ethnicity kept them from being "like everyone else." For others, especially those coming to the United States later in life, their stories reveal less of a negative construction of ethnic identity.

Though common themes developed among the stories, no two individuals' interpretations of ethnicity were the same. Lived past experiences, and the meanings constructed from those experiences, influenced the interpretation of the learning events that occurred in the context of the eight-week session. Pinar (1981) states that "the autobiographical method can be employed to cultivate such attentions to situation as element of the self, to self as situation, and reconstitution of both" (p. 184). Here, the gathering and analysis of the personal narratives illustrate how personal lived experiences in the past shaped individuals' views of themselves and their interpretation of ethnicity as an integrated part of self in the present situation.

Birthplaces, geographic locations, demographic makeup of childhood communities, and family ties each play different and significant roles in shaping "singular life histories" (Greene, 1978). To better understand who the OD participants are, their past experiences are categorized here by five major themes: community, family, religion, gender socialization, and schooling. The first significant theme discussed is the role of community. Four types of community influence include (1) the effects of the all-White community, (2) immigrating to the United States, (3) bridging reservation and mainstream lives, and (4) the all-Black community.

The second theme is the contributing role of family in constructing self-identity. Within this theme, strong family ties, both positive and negative effects of strong ties, and explicit parent teachings are explored. A related theme is religion. Some participants experienced religious affiliation from an early age, while others came into religious influences later in life. Even the one participant for whom religion and a god are non existent explicitly referred to religion as she described herself.

The fourth theme is gender socialization. The discussion in this chapter includes the explicit accounts of four women who have endured breaking cultural and family traditions, negative self-esteem, and denied access to schooling because of being born female. Male gender socialization is not addressed. However, rather than deny the relevance of male gender socialization, it is evident that none of the males in this particular group chose to explicitly state how gender roles affected their experiences.

The fifth and final theme is schooling. The discussion illustrates how the education system treated, sometimes mistreated, and oftentimes ignored the cultural differences and needs of the OD individuals. Being left out of the curriculum elicits serious issues of unavailable role modeling and consequent negative self-identity. The few images presented are negative and stereotypical. One participant offers an explanation of why she believes only the European American perspective is presented in schools and another questions the responsibility of the media in providing the images that schools have neglected to provide.

Together, these five themes: community, family, religion, gender socialization, and schooling create autobiographical portraits of the twenty-one individuals comprising the Opening Doors group. As Maxine Greene (1978) says, "What we understand to be *reality* is interpreted or reflected on experience. We live in continuing transactions with the natural and human world around us" (p. 24). The autobiographical retellings reveal the experiences through which participants reflected to interpret the learning events and activities of the Opening Doors context.

VOICES OF PAST EXPERIENCE

Community

All-White Communities

Paul, an African American male, and Rochelle, an African American female, each grew up in all-White communities. For his autobiography, Paul wrote a poem to express his feelings of marginalization, of not knowing whether he was Black or White:

My family.
The most important part of my life.
They are there for me in the good times and bad times.
Then Boy's State.
Two seconds left in the game. Score is tied.
Am I a basketball player?
Or am I a person?
Am I Black or am I White?
I stood on the line thinking about my life.
When I look in the mirror who or what do I see?
Is it a member of the human race?
Or is it a human of some race-type?
As long as my cultural identity is in doubt there can be no true identity.
I'm left in the limbo of social marginality.
Alienated, and directionless on the landscape of White America.
Who am I? What will I be after the game?
My mother told me, "The game is over. You're still my son. And I
     will always love you."

When issues of interracial dating were discussed, Paul explained that one reason why he dated outside his race was the community where he grew up. Being on a college campus with only eight Black men and four Black women didn't provide many options for him. Because of sheer numbers, either he dated White women or he didn't date.

Rochelle was born in Atlanta, but spent her high school years in Washington State, where she was the only African American in her high school. Though very strong, confident and proud of her African American heritage, Rochelle writes that her own ethnicity "makes me more aware of insensitivity toward people of color." After reading *The Invisible Man* by Ralph Ellison, Rochelle explains how her own experiences in her community are similar to those of the characters in the book:

> This story mirrored how I have often felt as an African American on
> a predominantly White campus. As long as I am not making waves,
> or contradicting the majority, I can be placed on a pedestal and fit in
> with everyone else. But when I speak out for myself and my people, I
> am often regarded as overly sensitive or prejudiced against Whites. In
> actuality, I am merely trying to take an equal step with the majority,
> and ensure that others have that chance, too.

Miguel, a Mexican-born American, experienced language and color issues which caused him to marginalize his Mexican culture until recently. He relates:

> The other thing about me is that I've learned over the last three years about my culture. I was born and raised here in Washington. My high school was predominantly White. Through the educational systems I was the only Mexican in the upper classes [tracked]. All my friends were White. The only time I spoke Spanish was to my parents. The only time I was Mexican was at home. The last two years I've found myself here at college. A song that I really like that reminded me of that is a Quincy Jones song called *Back on the Block.* . . . And that's the way I feel . . . I'm back on the block. I share my culture, and I'm proud of my culture.

Immigrating to the United States

Jesus, like Miguel, is also Mexican and grew up in an all-White community. However, unlike Miguel, he is one of the eight OD participants who was not born in the United States. In his auto-biography, Jesus poignantly portrays his family crossing the border as gaining shoes at the price of acquiring the handicap of a second language. He stood barefoot in front of the group and placed shoes and an ankle brace on the floor in front of him. "We had a really rough time in Mexico," he began. "We were very poor in Mexico. So I am bare-foot, which was most [of] the time. Coming into the U.S. as agricultural workers, we did get shoes," he continued as he put on one of the shoes in front of him. "But we also got a handicap," he explained as he reached to the floor and placed the ankle brace on his other foot. "This handicap is the color that we wear." Jesus explains:

> As I grew up in an all-White community, it was very difficult in the beginning for me to understand why these people resented me so much. I tried very hard to be like them, to speak their language, to wear the same clothes as them, to be accepted. As I became more accepted by them, I became more alienated from my family and my culture, and I could sense some resentment from them because I identified with my White peers more than I did with them. It was very hard to listen to my "friends" yell names like "wetback" and "spick"

to the other Mexican farm workers and turn to me and say, "Don't worry, Jesus. You're not a Mexican, you're one of us." I remember thinking to myself, "No, I'm not one of you, because I would never bad-mouth anyone like you just did!" But I could never bring myself to say that because I knew that I would be outcast. Now I wish I had.

Fabian also migrated from Mexico to the United States. However, he describes that even though he arrived in Texas, where the Latino population was the majority, he still faced problems similar to Jesus. He explains:

I came to the US in 1969. . . . Even though I grew up in a community that was about 99% Mexican or Latino, I was still discriminated against because I was the new one. The same thing that happened to you [Jesus] happened to me, except for me, all us new ones stuck together. It was the new arrivals against the so-called Chicanos.

Fabian also shares how his need to fit in led to destructive behavior:

I wanted to fit in when I was growing up. I grew up in the 60's, in kind of the end of the hippie era, so I had long hair. I also tried drugs because I wanted to fit in. Peer pressure and all of that. After a real traumatic experience with drugs I realized that wasn't the way. So in high school I became involved in athletics.

Tonya, like Fabian, also wanted to fit in, but she chose a different route. She describes the effects immigrating to the United States had on her:

I was born in Mexico. I'm the oldest of nine. My father came to the United States when I was eight, and then again when I was eleven. He was a migrant worker and followed the crops and he took us with him. We lived in all types of housing. They were not always very good houses, but it was the private side that made the house. . . . My dad saw dollar signs in the United States, and change in life. . . . I grew up and I loved school. School was my escape from home. I tried to be White. But when I had to speak they knew I was Mexican. So I made it my goal to speak with as little an accent as possible. I tried so hard to fit in.

Though Celia was born in the United States, she moved to El Salvador as an infant. This created a second-language barrier for her when she returned to the United States, similar to the experiences of Jesus, Fabian, and Tonya. She relates:

> I was born in East LA. Then when I was seven we moved to El Salvador and I was in El Salvador from first to ninth grade. I've been here since 1986. I came here speaking no English so I was put in ESL for two years. I was discriminated against by my own people, and marginalized in school because there are mainly Mexicans at my school. I struggled that I could go to school, and I finally got into UCSB [University of California-Santa Barbara]. I was determined that the language wouldn't stop me. My boyfriend has helped me in my struggle, and taught me a lot about the Mayas, Aztecs, Incas, and the major civilizations important to my culture.

Refuge, adoption, marriage, divorce, and fathers in the military are reasons why these next five individuals came to the United States. Debra's transition from Laos to the United States at age six was further complicated by having to leave her natural parents behind. Her adoptive parents traveled to Thailand to adopt her and her brother. Though her few remembrances of Laos are painful ones, being Laotian with Anglo-American parents in a White community has its painful side also. In her second journal, Debra raises several questions of identity she wants to explore. She writes:

> With me, I had my brother and sister who were adopted with me and who were also Asian. I felt support among them at home when we three played together. I didn't feel that safety at school. Even with the three of us the other kids made fun of us on the bus. What's so funny about slanted eyes? I don't see the humor.
> I was living with my adopted White parents from age six on. We did not go to Chinese parties or celebrations. Our family did not have Chinese friends that we socialized with. My parents had eleven Chinese refugees that they sponsored into USA, but they were not our socializing group. They were a group my parents were helping.
> Another thing I was thinking of is that I was brought into an American family. I was the one that had to change. (Don't get me wrong, I'm not bitter at having been adopted. I'm learning and questioning about my self-esteem and my feelings towards my Asian-

ness). I was the one that had to change. Maybe to a six year old's eyes having to change means that there is something wrong with me. If I was the one that was doing right, why would I need to do different? So maybe the process of moving to a different country itself was hurtful to my self-regard.

Charles, who is African American, was born in Bitburg, Germany, and experienced an array of communities through traveling with his military father. By the time he came to the United States he was in high school. He explains:

> I grew up overseas. I wasn't used to just Black and White like here. It was always German, English, Filipino, Japanese, Turkish, Israeli, Okinawan, Chinese, Korean, and everything else. That was my background. Until I got here and this was the first time I'd been called a nigger. And I almost killed somebody!

Charles goes on to relate how shocking this was for him because his mother and his aunts were raised in California and were part of the Black Panthers, who taught him to not let anyone call him that. "I didn't understand how different, how racist it was, how narrow-minded these people are in the States till I came here in high school."

Whereas the others came to the United States while still in their childhood years, Carol and Michelle were in their twenties and came for different but related reasons. Michelle came from Jamaica at twenty because of a divorce, and Carol came from China at twenty-six to get married. Both Carol and Michelle have very strong and vocal views about the effects of their moves. Carol talks fast and animated as she describes her childhood in China:

> I'm from China. I'm Chinese. [Shrugs her shoulders]. I may have some genes, IQ., from my parents; but I don't know. I am female, you know, nothing you can do about it. You from different areas, you speak Chinese, you speak English. But the issue is, who dominant culture is. Here, the dominant culture is White. . . . You want to go back to Africa [points to the African Americans in the group] and find out about your ancestors and so on. I no want to go back to China. It's miserable! China is terrible! They are so competitive. They drive you nuts! Here in America you say, you're not together. [Indicates African Amercians]. You feel lonely, but at least you have

that peace. In Chinese we don't have that. It's so competitive, you have no friends.

Carol didn't feel comfortable in China because she didn't feel she fit in. She goes on to say:

> In China I was bigger than my friends. They were so small, and I was huge! With my friends, I had big feet, big everything, and they were so small. It's not funny because I always wear mini skirt because I never had the right size. So even though we don't have that race problem that's classification, I don't fit in. And there's nothing I can do about it. I'm always big, huge, compared to them. So when I met Americans they would say I was beautiful, so I liked Americans. All my life I grew up not having confidence. People would always say, "You're not smart enough." So right away I feel I'm not smart, I'm tall, I'm not delicate, I'm not woman, so I come here and I think I could be tall, and America would be just great.

Carol viewed America as a positive escape from the negative shame and lack of self-esteem she experienced in China. However, once she got here, she found she wasn't happy here either. She explains:

> Then I met Americans, and I feel very comfortable with Americans. But when I get here, I think everything will be just great, but I sit down and cry. Because there were other problems. I wasn't happy from the age of twenty-five to thirty-five. One reason is because America is so individual. And unless I know you for you to talk to me, I could sit there for the rest of my life. And that's what happened. I wasn't invited to anyone's home. I invited a couple to my home, but I have no common background to talk with you about. So I cannot have decent conversation. So that part is hard.

Carol faced isolation from European Americans, while Michelle describes facing isolation and alienation from other Blacks upon her arrival in the United States. Michelle explains some of the cultural differences between Jamaica and America she has experienced:

> Everyone here is trying to find their cultural identity. Reggae says Africa when you hear it. Jamaicans are into African culture, in a sense. But in Jamaica it's different from here in the United States. The

only time Jamaicans say Black or White is in reference to Americans. There are Whites, Blacks, Indians, Jews, Portuguese, Red Indians, Black Indians, Maroons (who live separate in the hills), but we never refer to each other by color. I grew up in Montego Bay, a tourist town. I'm in search of myself. I didn't know anything about Africa or anything about racism until I came to America. I'd never heard anything about Martin Luther King or Malcolm X until I came to America ten years ago. My relatives are not into the culture thing. . . . I motivated myself a long time ago that in order for me to know more about me I'm going to have to know about my culture. . . . In Jamaica, color wasn't part of our vocabulary. But after coming here I can see how I was discriminated against by my own people. I can see how the ones with the lighter complexion were favored.

She also describes the differences she has observed among Black people in Florida and those in Washington, where she has recently moved. In Washington, "everyone is concerned with finding themselves," she explains, "but in Florida people are too busy trying to find jobs to be able to find themselves."

Karen, born in Okinawa, Japan, of a Japanese mother and a European American military father, is the only one of the twenty-one participants who mentions nothing about her ethnicity in the opening weeks of the program. Describing her family she writes:

I am the oldest daughter in my family consisting of father, mother, and two younger sisters. My home has been made up of a variety of places because of my father's occupation—Army (now retired). I think we are a very close-knit, a private family. My father now works for the Post Office while my mother continues as a homemaker which I think has contributed very much to our family values and bonds/ strong ties. Although we are all different, our sense of family is very strong.

Reservation Life

Walter, Diane, and Kelly, the three Native American participants, had different kinds of experiences as they attempted to bridge the worlds of reservations with the European American mainstream. Walter tells of how his early years were influenced equally by the Christian world and the Indian reservation:

> I'm from Standing Rock Indian Reservation South Dakota, from Hunkpapa Band, which you might know is Sitting Bull's Band. My father was a college educated minister for the congregational church, so we moved . . . all around the state. On the other hand, my father's brother never went to school. He learned the old ways. So I have a history from both the Christian, and the Indian Reservation.

Diane is Nez Perce on her mother's side and Cherokee on her father's. Of growing up, she explains:

> First of all, I was born in Yakima WA. When I was ten months old we moved to Salinas, CA which is lovingly and affectionately called the salad bowl of America. We were only supposed to stay a couple of years while my dad was going to school, but it ended up I grew up there. My brother and sister were born there, and they're still there now. My dad being Cherokee, I don't know too much about my Cherokee side. I just know that he spoke the language until he started school. Then he learned English. Unfortunately he never taught us. He speaks it now still, to his parents on the phone, but he never taught us.

Kelly shares a more traumatic and transitory childhood:

> I tried to come up with something cohesive about my life. There is nothing cohesive about my life . . . . All these places on the map are places that I actually lived, except for Mexico, I went there for five weeks, and Alaska. The rest are different places we moved around, different Indian reservations . . . . I think it's the number of places. I've never been in one place very long.

After picturing her nomadic life growing up, Kelly reads a poem she wrote the night before which reveals to the group a violent and turbulent childhood of growing up on Indian reservations with a Native American father and an Anglo-American mother:

> Life began living next to Squaw Hill under a Big Sky
> Where at night you can hear a woman screaming, howling for her lost child...
> If you listen closely
>
> White girl. Where did you come from? White girl. Why are you Here?

It was an unheated swimming pool, it was a horse with hard mouth, it was White corn
Pow-wow. how much is that necklace?
Oh, no, no. I can only pay 3.
Look, White Girl. You had 5, you had 5 right There.

And a baby died at our house. And a man tried to shoot our house but my dad sat up with a shot gun, himself. He would wait. . . .
What's going on!! Go back to bed.

Then three tribes together? A White world figuring we would all destroy ourselves.
Run, run away with a knife, school girl.
Worse than an apple.
My sister came back with a baby.
Run, run to catch the school bus, Alison,
run with me, here, let me take your books.
We travel into a White world only 14 miles away through mint fields.
hate came back and the wheels of the truck spin away at 55 miles an hour.
Hate came back and our horse got away.
The seven drums will chase it, make it leave.

Oglala, Cheyenne, Crow, Makah, Wasco, Warm Springs, Piaute, Blackfeet, Eskimo
The smell of dry dust devils swirling, man-made under buck-skin, colors swirling everywhere. A distant wail begins.
The thump, thumping of drums.
The ching, chinging of a jingle dress.
The hollow rustle of quills.
The click, clicking of shells.
Yarn string, ribbons, beads patterned together that bring a butterfly to life, and feathers.
Hot, cold, round, round in unison,
pounding, thumping,
All eyes fixed, feet mimicking the dancers beat, forks pulling at an Indian taco.

Here we go again around the circle of life.

Having a very light complexion, Kelly was deemed the "White girl" on the reservation. But when she attended public schools she was labeled "that girl from the res."

All-Black Communities

Deirdre and Adrianne are the only two who specifically stated that they grew up in all-Black communities. Both remember having positive, nurturing family environments growing up. Though Deirdre was adopted like Debra, she doesn't appear to suffer the same negative consequences. She writes: "I grew up in a two-parent household. I was adopted at the age of six months. I was the traditional only child. Although my father was the one who mostly let me *have my way*, I took piano lessons, dance lessons, violin lessons, swim lessons, etc. at my mother's insistence."

Adrianne describes her father as "authoritarian" and her mother as "submissive and benevolent." She also explains that her childhood was "fairly stable growing up, except for a period of two and a half years when my dad was placed in a sanitarium for people who contracted tuberculosis. My father's expectations for his girls were to avoid pregnancy, graduate from high school, marry a fine young man or find a good job."

The positive, nurturing experiences of these two African American women can be contrasted with the negative experiences and hardships endured in the childhoods of two other African American women, Karma and Lisa. Karma writes: "I was brought up in a very abusive family with the focus on a patriarchal perspective." She describes growing up in Brooklyn as being surrounded by "abusive people." She started using drugs at age eleven. She lists reefer, crack, cocaine, and speedball as the substances she used to counteract the abuse she endured. In describing the effects of her childhood, she says, "I'm like a black widow spider. I had my children. Then I killed and ate up my mate."

Lisa, the fifth of eleven children, was born in North Carolina, and grew up in New York City. Standing with her Bible clutched tightly in her hand for support, she describes her life as periods of "light and darkness." As a toddler (age two or three) she was raped. This event began what she called her "season of darkness." She explains: " I became an introvert as a child and withdrew from the world in music and books, I was always the darkest sister. I got it from the White world and I got it from the Black world. So I withdrew." By her adolescent years, around the age of thirteen, she became a heroin and cocaine addict, which continued for twelve years. Feeling a sense of remorse and heartfelt depression fill the room, Lisa quickly reassured us, "There is light in here. God didn't totally abandon me, or I wouldn't be here today." Then, to qualify she said: "There are a lot of people I grew up with who aren't here today."

"I was a para-pro at New York Hospital. My back has always been straight," she offers as an explanation for why she had a hard time "copping" drugs on the street. "They wouldn't believe me," she said, laughing. "Everybody always thought I was a cop." She continues: "I did that for twelve years. Until God let me see my five-year-old son seeing me as a drug addict. Then I knew I had to change. I've been married twice. The first time was for two years. I thought that's what I was supposed to do."

Family Role Modeling and Support

Demographic makeup of the communities in which they grew up influenced the shaping of ethnic identity. So, too, did the various degrees of role modeling and family support.

Laura's family support provides her with a sense of positive self-esteem, as well as cultural pride in who she is. She writes:

> I am from Mexican descent, but I have been trained to teach European history and culture. My parents are very proud of their heritage and instilled me with that pride. I have values and customs that are different from my American (European influenced) environment. But just because I do not have a "European Experience" and my skin is not White does not mean I could not do a job as well as someone who has White skin.

Lilia has also developed a strong sense of pride and ethnic identity from her family. "You carry your life with you," she explains, spreading a blanket on the floor. "This is my foundation." Then, kneeling down with a picnic basket, she says: "I feed off my family and this is my picnic I'm going to share with you." As she pulls items out one by one, she tells us about the things most important to her. "The next thing I brought was a picture of my family. My culture. I went to Mexico. It's real important for me to know who I am and where I come from. It's important to me to serve my culture."

In her interview, Rochelle explains: "I had a good support system. Both my parents were always there pushing me, 'Rochelle, go get this.' They gave me a good basis. I feel I have good components to be successful." In sharing her high school photo album with us for her autobiography, she explains: "I chose high school because it reflects for me my family and parents' teachings that shaped what I am today." The adjectives she uses to describe herself and her pictures emanate a sense of pride and positive self-esteem. Flipping through the photos, she proclaims, "I come from kings and queens, and I'm a beautiful Nubian princess," showing a picture of her homecoming where she was crowned the first African American queen in her high school's history.

For Debra, even though memories of her biological mother are very painful for her, she appreciates the love, support, and nurturing from her adoptive parents. She relates:

> My adoptive mom loves flowers, beauty, homemaking. I think so much of her. She tries to help others have a better life. My adoptive dad is a veterinarian at the university. He's so intent and committed to teaching me about riding horses, geometry, health, courses I need to take. He's always so committed to everything in my life. That shows a lot of love to me that someone would care so much about my life. He tries to be silly, to make my mom laugh. I admire their love relationship. It's a good model for me.

Charles's autobiography graffiti mural consisted of a world of which he said, "The world is my backyard." His world or "backyard" consisted of symbols for his mother, father, and younger brother, who was in attendance at the same university with him.

Diane's separation from her family has brought her to a realization of their importance to her. She explains:

> I got the chance to talk with my mom this past weekend. I enjoyed our visit immensely. Although it was only two weeks since the last time I talked with her, it was a long two weeks and she let me know it! It's kind of hard being so far away from my parents because they give me so much emotional support. Their hard work and sacrifices have had such a difference in my life that if it wasn't for them, I probably would not be where I am today. Thank you creator for blessing me with a strong sense of family.

Kelly expresses a closeness in her family similar to Diane's. However, where Diane's absence from home has elicited a strong sense of security in knowing that her parents are there and support her, Kelly's separation from her parents creates conflict. In her first journal entry she writes:

> I feel like my greatest accomplishment and failure was seeking a BA. I left home, my mother. I scare them now. They don't understand me. We grew up so close and communications have become very strained over the last 5-6 years. There are a lot of misunderstandings. My parents are VERY proud, but frightened. They say, "You've been in school since you were 4 years old—don't you think this is enough?" It's hard. I worry about them. I feel like they've been upset all this time—it's hard to respect them and do what I would like to do.

Though Deirdre didn't endure the types of hardships like those of Karma and Lisa, she had her rough periods to survive. She attributes to her father the coping skills she learned in order to endure the daily routine of prejudice. She explains: "In terms of what is deepest within me,it goes back to what my father said: Treat people as individuals. Don't be mad at someone because someone else is mad at them. That's the way I was raised. I grew up in an all-Black city. I wasn't taught prejudice, at home or school. I learned it by experience. . . . It wasn't consciously or formally instructed."

Charles's mother also instructed him on how to get along. He reports: "One lesson that my mother taught me was to always accept others for who they are and take them in with love and respect."

Deirdre and Charles were explicitly taught how to get along with others, while Karen was told how to achieve. Karen explains: "Since I was little I remember Mom saying, 'We live in the United States. You're half Japanese and you have to be better than everyone else.' And that's something from really little I remember. She still says it occasionally, you have to be better because you're half and half. You're not all-White."

Lilia's mother taught her to be in control of her experiences. Lilia relates: "My mom always told me, just fix it."

Diane's competitiveness, as well as her willingness to accept others for what they are, was instilled through her parents' teachings. She explains:

My father was always playing basketball. I like to be competitive. Sure, I like to have fun, but my parents taught me to always do my best, so that's why I always try my hardest. They also always said to remember that other people are always trying their hardest too. They might not be as good, but they're trying too. So that's one thing I learned is to take people as they are. I look for the best in everybody. I do that a lot.

Religion

In describing the picture of a flower she drew to represent her life, Laura explains, "And at the center is a cross, because I want Jesus Christ at the center of my life at all times." Lilia also talks of her religious beliefs as being an integral part of her life saying: "One of the first things I feed off of is the Lord and the Holy Spirit."

Still recovering from a recent emergency surgery while in Colombia, Miguel shares his faith. He explains:

The first thing was the physical pain. This was my fourth surgery that I had. And I thought, Why me, God? Why Me? Why do you allow this to happen to me? And right before I went under the knife the poem, *Footprints* came to me. It's about a man who has a dream. And he's walking on the sands of the beach with Jesus Christ, and he's seeing all these wonderful scenes of his life. And every time life got hard for him he only saw one set of footprints. He asked Jesus why that was, and Jesus asked him, why do you always doubt me? Those times when there's only one set is that I was carrying you. And that's what he was doing for me.

Adrianne tells how she "came to know" her grandmother's God at the age of seventeen:

My grandmother was another figure in my life. She didn't have an education. She couldn't read or write. But I saw her struggle with that and she was able to read the Bible. So from her I was able to learn about God. I remember going to church with her and she was sanctified and filled with the Holy Ghost! I didn't understand that. But at seventeen I was able to identify with her God until today I have a personal relationship. So this has been a guiding force in my life. Two scriptures I have grabbed onto and passed on to my children

are, *You can do all things through Jesus Christ who strengthens you,*
and *Everything works out for the good of those who love the Lord and
live according to his will.*

Lisa, Karma and Deirdre each speak of "finding God" as a source
of strength later in life. Lisa credits her God throughout her
autobiography. "The Spirit has moved me," she exclaims as she jumps
up to stand before us with a Bible in hand. "I was afraid I wouldn't have
what I needed to do this. But then I remembered Exodus 15:2, 'The
Lord is my strength and my song.' He reminded me I have everything I
need right here."

Karma gives similar thanks to God for giving her the strength and
her current positive outlook on life. After recounting her escapades with
drug addiction since the age of twelve, Karma shares the events of just
two years ago:

> Then I decided to clean out my life. I checked myself into a drug
> rehab. I not only got rid of drugs by myself, I stopped using alcohol
> and cigarettes all in the same transition. And then I got this spiritual
> sense. I started thanking God for everything. For the rug, the grass,
> the sun, I mean things I would never thank God for before. I started
> smelling things again. I started seeing things again and I started
> appreciating who it was that made me. [God] made me the mighty
> woman I am today. Because right now through my own strength I am
> able to give my energy away. You'll never ever see me in a bad mood
> because I no longer have them. My mood is always lifted by God in
> the sense that I'm not going to allow myself to dwell on negativity.
> My negativity is over, and I'm not going to dwell on it.

That Deirdre draws her strength from God is evident as she writes:

> I will talk to Him as I am on my way back and ask Him for the
> strength to be all that He wants me to be: loving and dedicated to Him
> and His way of life. I will dwell on Him as much as I can and bring to
> mind all of the Scriptures that have fallen into the far corners of my
> memory. I will ask Him for more of His wisdom and character and
> for more faith that I will believe that I will receive it. In other words,
> I will use the time to re-establish the most important relationship that
> I have: the one with my Creator.

Walter and Diane express a sense of spirituality that is different than the others. For these two Native Americans, religion is not something outside, or an added part of their experience. Rather, it is one of the self-grounding, integrated parts of their circle of life. To begin her autobiography, Diane sits on the table in the middle of the semi-circle and starts talking about the symbolism of the circle for her. "There are many aspects of it, that I try to live my life by," she says. "That's the caring, sharing, loving, understanding equally myself and everybody else. So this circle means a lot to me." When it's time for his presentation, Walter takes out his leather pouch, and says:

> This always goes with me wherever I go. There's a circle here. If you notice the colors, we believe that this represents the four races of the earth. We believe we were all put here at the same time, and we worship the same God that you do. [pulls out a rod from the pouch] This is a step. It represents the biblical teachings of the straight and narrow. That's the Red Road. Everything we see in the world comes from Mother Earth. We remember that. In everything you see, no matter what you do, it all comes from Mother Earth. So this represents our people. This opening here represents the center of my universe. Everything you get isn't free. So we offer it something. We offer tobacco. This represents the people. [Holds the end of the pipe in one hand]. And this represents the way your life should be. [raises the stem of the pipe in the other hand]

Later, Walter describes how all of life works in harmony or in balance:

> I came to a conclusion we're all related whether we like it or not. Everything in this universe is related one way or another. The plants are here for a reason, the sun is shining for a reason. So the sooner we accept that and live by that, the sooner we can get along. . . . Indians believe everything goes in a circle. In this I found there's four areas you have to grow in: spiritually, mentally, physically, and emotionally. So when we're talking about being in balance, or walking a Red Road, these are some of the things we're talking about. For example, if you leave spirituality out, you're going to have to fill that void with something, like drugs or alcohol.

Several participants didn't explicitly mention religion as a significant factor in their lives. However, Carol was the only one who explicitly expressed having no belief in God. "I don't think a human being can be happy, no matter what you're looking for, if you're looking for unity, or God. I don't know, Chinese don't believe in God. I don't believe in God," she says quietly, with her head bent down to her chest, "which makes me unpopular."

Gender Socialization

In choosing to pursue educational goals, both Tonya and Celia chose to go against their socialized gender roles in their Mexican and Latino cultures. Tonya explains that the way she was raised was an example of negative role modeling. She says, "I learned from the way I was brought up how not to be." Being a woman meant her first and foremost obligation was to be submissive and subservient to the men in her family. She first tried to fulfill both the obligation of her traditional arranged marriage and her personal educational desires. But she found she couldn't make them both work. She explains:

> I knew that I was going to have to marry a certain man, and at the age of thirteen I knew that I had a marriage all set up. . . . We were supposed to be the perfect match. And for a long time I thought so, too. He made promises not kept. He didn't want me to go to school. So I left. I have two children and they are my inspiration, and I would not change anything because of them. They are in school here, and they support me.

Like Tonya, Celia also talks of having to fight against the male-favored tradition in her family. Her brothers were the ones who were given the opportunities and support for the aspirations. As a female, Celia's role expectation was similar to Tonya's. Her only concern was to be of service to the dominant male. Therefore, when Celia had career and educational goals of her own, she was not given the same encouragement and support her brothers received. Her struggle to gain entrance into college and to achieve academically meant also struggling against her father and his image of what she could do. She explains: "No matter how much I did I was never good enough. But inside me I know I'm capable of doing it."

Debra's Asian culture also favored males over females. Debra doesn't remember much of her birth mother, but what little she does remember includes feelings of shame for being female. She relates:

"Being a female has really influenced me in good ways and not so good ways. The first six years of my life my birth mom was ashamed of me because I wasn't a boy. And so I grew up with that shame of being female. I think it's really affected my self-esteem, because it hurts to have your mom not love you because you're a certain way."

Lisa describes how being an African American woman was an added strike against her, denying her access to the schooling she sought:

> I went back to school late. I went to enroll in a community college and I was told I couldn't do it. I was interested in math and science, and the counselor told me no, I wasn't. I was great in mathematics and they destroyed it. They told me I couldn't. One, because I was Black and two, because I was a woman. So even back to when I started college I told him [guidance counselor] I wanted to go into education. He said, "No, you don't want to do that, you want to go into vocational training." Luckily I knew who I was enough to say, "No, this is not what I asked you. This is not what I said I wanted to do. You don't know me. How can you tell me that's not what I want to do or I can't do that? You've never seen me before, how can you know?"

Schooling

One of the most disturbing and poignant issues of the OD participants' schooling experiences was how much of themselves they did not find in the school curriculum when they were growing up. Pinar (1991) describes how this process of being left out creates a fractured, repressed self: "'We are what we know. We are, however, also what we do not know. If what we know about ourselves—our history, our culture, our national identity—is deformed by absences, denials, and incompleteness, then our identity—both as individuals and Americans—is fractured. The fractured self is a repressed self" (p. 9). The OD participants described several ways in which by omission, schooling experiences created a repressed sense of self.

Laura writes of how she was taught to appreciate European contributions in art, literature, and music, and wishes that she could have learned the same appreciation for all views:

In High School I took a humanities course which taught music appreciation, art appreciation, and literature appreciation. Of course this class only covered European and American music, art, and literature. It sure would have been wonderful to learn about other types of literature, art, and music from other parts of the world. I would have also liked to learn about famous works in Spanish and about writers like Pablo Neruda.

I learned to appreciate the European contributions. Maybe that's why I feel multicultural education is so important. Students need to be aware of the contributions from many different groups of people. It is very difficult to appreciate something one knows nothing about.

Lilia draws from her recent student teaching experience to explain not only that much is left out, but what is in the curriculum is often irrelevant to the students in the classroom. She describes her experience at the elementary school where she did her student teaching:

The Mexican population is forty six percent so we're almost the majority there. So I did my student teaching there and I could count the White kids on one hand. The minorities are all these little Mexican kids. Yet when we were talking, it was still Thanksgiving and the pilgrims. Now how the hell does that relate to us? We didn't cross no ocean. We've BEEN here! How does that feel to the child when we're still making pilgrim hats?

From her experience in history class, Diane recalls an eager anticipation, followed by disappointment:

I remember looking at history books when I was younger and I'd see this little section on Native Americans just little, only a page or two, and I'd be all excited. We were going to learn about my Indian ancestors. I'd know just from my mom and dad that it would be just a small part, but there was so much more. It bothered me in a sense. But then I thought well I know it already. And then learning about Columbus, I mean, that's one of the first things I remember learning about.

Diane's recollections of Columbus are not positive ones. Nor are some of the sporadic images that Karma remembers of African Americans she encountered in her textbooks. She avoided taking social studies courses because "there weren't any images of me. Nobody looked like me. I mean, they got these ugly pictures of Harriet Tubman and they got her so raggedy, and you don't want to identify with that! I would rather not have had her in a potato sack!"

Paul places his finger on the problem in a practical sense. He tells his group, "Each one of us has our own place in history, but the fact that it's a quarter inch-thick in a twelve inch book! That right there says something's wrong." He goes on to tell of his discovery about some of the missing knowledge: "I read this book about the Civil War, and it showed about this Black regiment that was one of the most successful throughout the Civil War. And I've never heard anything about it. It's just things like that make me wonder why, and how much more is out there that I haven't heard?"

Wes echoes Paul's questions of how much more is left out:

> You know what? It's been there all the time that there was something that wasn't right about these stories. . . . As a child you see that. There had to be something. I mean, where did they come from? One day they're in Africa, then they were on the slave ships and they were slaves. There had to be something before that. But you never, I mean, I guess as a kid I would kind of think about it but never, like she said, question authority. That's just the way it was. And my parents and all that, they never really taught or had time.

Karma shares her theory on why nonexistent or stereotypical images have been allowed to persist in the curriculum. "You're not supposed to question authority," she says. "That's what we're taught." She furthers her argument by adding that it's not just a matter of the textbook materials at fault, it is also part of the pedagogical practices. She explains:

> I think the traditional way of learning had a lot to do with how we forgot about to question that. Because the traditional way of learning is you take this piece of paper and you memorize it. So when you get the test, see, that's all you know is what's on that test. And so when the test is over . . . that's it and you forget about it.

Paul, who majors in sociology and participates in sports, writes about the dangers of the way school athletic programs stereotype young Black athletes:

The blind pursuit of attainment in sports is having a devastating effect on our people. It starts with a belief that our principal avenue to fame and fortune is through sport, and seduced by a win-at-all-cost system that corrupts even elementary school students. Too many Black kids treat basketball courts and football fields as if they were classrooms in an alternative school system. A young Black athlete may say, "OK, I flunked English, but I got an A+ in slam-dunking." In the words of Dr. Harry Edwards, *We must put textbooks in front of play books.*

The failure of our public schools to educate athletes is also part of the school's failure to educate everyone. Of course, society as a whole bears the responsibility as well. Until training a young Black's mind becomes as important as training his or her body, we as a society will continue to perpetuate a system like that of the Roman gladiators—sacrificing a class of people for the entertainment of the mob.

Lisa views the lack of multiple perspectives in the curriculum as nothing short of sacrificing the lives of children. She tells her group, "These are not common known facts, that's all I'm saying. They're not in the history books yet." Then she asks, "How long do we have to wait? How many kids have to be sacrificed?"

Wes fuels Lisa's despair, saying:

And like you were saying in the elementary schools, they're not sensitive to us and therefore why should I respect them? My people know the people who have done all this. And a lot of people feel this way. We've given them so much and why do they still want more and all this kind of crap, you know what I mean? And I hear this and say, well man if there was just something in the history books that would show them where they got it from in the first place.

In voicing their concerns, Lisa and Wes describe how the drop-out cycle is set in motion by the present school system:

WES: Each one teach one, back in the days, are you familiar with that?. . . My stepbrothers took part in that. . . . They have a thing like with the African American men. They have doctors and lawyers, they'll come in for a day or two and teach the young Black boys about their culture, you know, and just so they can see them and see what type of people they are.

LISA: Role-modeling kind of thing. If you can't see it then you can't dream it. See what I'm saying? For so many years I didn't see African Americans going to college I thought—

WES: It must not be happening.

LISA:—I can't do it. I really believed I could not do it.

WES: That was one of the things that hindered my progress.

LISA: I didn't think I could do it because I didn't see it in my neighborhood. In my family, it didn't happen so . . .

WES: So people who see everybody in their family going to college, that's just another step in life.

LISA: Right. No big thing. But for people who aren't exposed to that kind of thing, people who have suffered under these, the present oppressive school system, we lose geniuses daily. We just lose them to gangs and drugs.

From Lisa's personal experience, she views a no-win situation for African Americans in the present system. If there are no role models, self-esteem is affected. In turn, having a low self-esteem leads to dropping out. Then the ones who drop out become the role models in the community for the next generation. Dropping out becomes the norm. The cycle continues. However, both are quick to qualify that lack of achievement is not due to lack of ability:

WES: I was checking out when they were having those riots. A lot of these gang leaders are intelligent. They were on *Donahue* and all this. I mean these brothers were dropping knowledge of the Black history.

LISA: Oh yeah, we don't have stupid kids. They just, they don't find anything, they don't find themselves in the classroom.

WES: And they're leaders, too. That's why they're picked to be the leaders of these gangs. That's somebody that can lead me, you know.

These brief biographical sketches of the eight African Americans, seven Latinos (including one Chicana, one Latina, four Mexican Americans, and one Mexican permanent resident alien), three Native Americans, and three Asians that comprised the Opening Doors participants the summer of 1992 illustrate how the life of any one individual cannot be the prototype for the generalization of an ethnic category. Being African American has a different meaning for Paul, who grew up in an all-White community in the Pacific Northwest, than it does for Adrianne, who was raised among Blacks in the South. Debra, Carol, and Karen might all check the Asian box on governmental forms, but other than that they share more differences than similarities. Debra comes wanting to find out more about her Asian self, while Carol would rather forget such a miserable experience. Karen, who is biracial, doesn't acknowledge an ethnic influence of any sort on her life. So also the Latino participants have varying degrees of knowledge and symbolic representation of their ethnicity. Celia is very firm about her political conviction that she is Latina, not Hispanic. Of the others born in the United States, Lilia prefers to be called Chicana, Miguel calls himself a United States-born Mexican, and Laura sees herself as Mexican American. Of those that migrated to the United States, Fabian and Jesus both call themselves Mexican Americans, while Tonya is not a citizen of the United States, but a Mexican who is a permanent resident alien. The three Native Americans have their differences, too. Walter has spent the forty-six years of his life in the Lakota tribe, and the last several years studying the "old ways" to be able to teach future generations. Kelly describes a violent, turbulent childhood marked by marginality from two worlds (reservation and mainstream society), and Diane portrays a solid grounding of her Nez Perce traditions while living and being educated in the mainstream.

Even though each individual had his or her own personal construction of ethnic identity, the demographic makeup, and racial attitudes in the communities where they were raised significantly influenced the events each individual experienced, as well as the meaning they constructed from those events. Frankenburg (1993) terms this phenomenon the social geography of race. In her words, "Geography refers to the physical landscape. . . . The notion of social geography suggests that the physical landscape is peopled and that it is constituted and perceived by means of social rather than natural processes" (p. 44). Who lived there, rather than where they lived and the specific interpersonal interactions encountered in the past, formed perceptions of ethnic identity.

Ethnic identity is only one of the perceptions influenced by social geography. Perceptions of schooling are influenced as well. Ogbu (1992) suggests that "the meaning and value that students from different cultural groups associate with the process of formal education vary and are socially transmitted by their ethnic communities" (p. 7).

ETHNIC IDENTITY CONSTRUCTION FROM PAST EXPERIENCES

I received the message of anglocentrism, of white supremacy, and I internalized it.
—Cliff (1988, p. 58)

All OD participants describe a continuing struggle in an attempt to find out who they are as people of color. The struggle, the degree, and the intensity of experiences create varying attitudes of ethnic pride, historical continuity, self-worth and self-esteem, and perceptions of self as a potential scholar. However, these hardships vary in degree, intensity, and longevity. Jesus, Fabian, Tonya, and Walter struggled with ESL battles from an early age, while Carol is still battling English at age forty. Lisa, Karma, and Fabian all share experiences of drug addiction, but her being raped at an early age makes Lisa's experience unique. Choices of divorce, separation, and failed relationships plague Michelle, Karma, Lisa, and Tonya, all of whom have children who command their attention at the same time these women are trying to figure out what is best for themselves. Ethnic identity eludes Debra, who searches for her "Asian self" lost in adoption by Anglo-American parents, while Donna's adoption, by African American parents, appears not to affect her sense of positive self-esteem.

All endured incidents of racism, prejudice, and discrimination. However, each individual's ethnic identity was shaped in different ways by these experiences.

Past experiences shaped the ethnic identity of individual OD participants. Three aspects of ethnic identity construction include (1) ethnic pride and cultural history, (2) ethnic identity conflicts, and (3) internalized racism. Schooling was a major influential force.

Three Aspects of Ethnic Identity Construction

OD participants' perceptions of cultural pride and embodiment of ethnic history varied in degree. At one end of the continuum are those like Walter and Charles who actively sponsor their cultural heritage for others to learn, while clearly articulating their pride in who they are and their manner of being in the world. Next are those for whom ethnic identity causes conflict. Being biracial, Karen and Kelly both endure conflicts from having adopted more of their European identity than Asian and Native American identities, respectively. Michelle, on the other hand, faces a different conflict altogether. Not having to contend with racial dualities,she struggles instead with the meanings, values, and rules of being a Black Jamaican, which differ greatly from those of being an African American. Last are those who are in the greatest conflict because they have turned racism inward to hate themselves. Debra and Carol both illustrate this phenomenon of internalized racism, though from very different viewpoints and resulting from very different past experiences. These three points on the continuum of ethnic pride are illustrative only of the beginning, middle, and end points. Others fit in varying degrees in between.

Ethnic Pride and Cultural History

Talk of ancestors, legacies, forefathers and elders was particularly prominent from the African Americans. Lisa talks of serving the diaspora, and "bringing her people together" in order to fight the injustice. Her belief is that the answers for African Americans today lie in first finding out about their own cultural heritage and the contributions of historical African Americans that have been kept silent in the Eurocentric curriculum. She explains:

> It's been one of my biggest challenges to get other African Americans to come together. When they planted that seed of divide and conquer that really took root, and we're still dealing with that. All my life I hated light-skinned Blacks because they hated me. I didn't know why. We need to deal with these issues. We need to talk about and learn about what our forefathers did for us.

Rochelle reflects a sense of historical pride when she introduces herself as coming from kings and queens as a "beautiful Nubian princess." Charles asserts his pride in being African American in all he says and writes. But it is not just enough for him to be proud of his heritage, he wants all people to be proud of their own culture, no matter what race or ethnicity. He explains: "This world really needs to change. It's amazing how much White America has taken away our identity. But as we've grown up and shared our experiences here, some of us are younger, some are older. We bring back ourselves and give pride back to those who need it and deserve it. And we give pride to ourselves."

Heritage is also a salient factor for the Latino participants. Celia considers herself a politically active as well as ethnically proud individual. She explicitly states, "I am not Hispanic. Spanish is not of the indigenous side of my culture. I'm not Chicana. I am Latina." She is active in her conviction that political action, revolutionary action, is needed for change. She asserts: "I believe that things have to change, and to do this you must be out of the norm, always fighting. I actively participated in La Raza. I have pride in saying who I am and my culture, which is Latin American. I am not Mexican. But I do things for my culture."

Lilia also mentions La Raza and the importance of her culture. "I went to Mexico. It's real important for me to know who I am and where I come from. It's important to me to serve my culture. We had a Somos—which means We *Are*—conference, which I attended."

Jesus has become actively involved in his Mexican culture through a folklore dance group on campus while Laura claims that "feeling proud and active in my Mexican community has helped me learn more about myself and teach others." Laura also illustrates the importance of her deep "roots" through a song she wrote for her autobiography. As an introduction to the song she explains:

> I also think of people as flowers. . . . The reason why I say that is because there are things in our lives constantly. But it goes farther back than my life here. It goes deeper into our past interior, and I think of that as my past history. And all those things impact me. I don't know all those things. But some I've been told about, and I can see the way my great-grandmother interacts with me, I hear the stories of my great-great-aunt, and it's all impacted me.

Diane also shares a song to represent her cultural roots. As the song played, she shared a history lesson about White Flag Day from her Nez Perce history:

> Today is a significant day in Nez Perce history. Today is the first day of the Nez Perce slaughter in 1877. It's the battle of White Flag. I have a great-great-uncle who was the one who carried in the white flag surrendering to the troops. As he was carrying the flag with other warriors, they were fired upon, and the battle started. Fortunately on

that day, no Nez Perce were killed. That was a good day for the Nez Perce. But that was not the only day. The Nez Perce lost many men, women, and children of their nation. That's the thing America is trying to celebrate with the arrival of Columbus. There's an organization called Indian Nation and they're celebrating five hundred years of survival. The Indian people are still here.

Different from others, Diane and Walter perceive their ethnic identity as an integral part of self. Diane demonstrates just how much her culture is an integral part of herself when she writes:

Yes, I have a proud culture. However, the culture is a part of me, I am not the culture. I am an individual who just so happens to be Native American.

It's a good feeling to know about one's culture and it should not be diminished.

Like Diane's, Walter's integrated sense of Native American history and culture exudes from his total being. He spent ten years studying the old ways. He relates:

I was going to be a minister like my father. For a year and a half I went to a community college in Mesa, Arizona. But it didn't fit me, so I dropped out. I went to my uncle and told him I needed some of the old ways because something was missing. So I went on what they call a vision quest. You go up way out in the middle of nowhere with no food and no water for four days. I came back with the vision that I had to teach children. That was my job. So I went back to school, got my associates' degree in 1981. In 1982 I was supposed to start my student teaching. So I went back to the council of elders and said I'm ready. They said no you're not ready. I didn't understand. They said I had to go back. Because I was chosen to teach the old ways. So even though I only had thirteen weeks of school left, there's a ten year gap because I had to learn the old ways. And it's all oral. Nothing's written down.

Ethnic Identity Conflicts

As stated earlier, Karen was the only participant who did not talk about her culture and ethnicity when she presented her autobiography. She also did not answer the questions on the bio sheets asking about the influences of ethnicity. When asked why these questions were left blank, she responds, "I left it blank because I don't know how it does or if it does. I never really thought it was an issue. I just consider myself half-and-half. I don't know how it does." The only time she acknowledged effects of her Asian half was when she wrote in journal two about being "proud to see an Asian-American success story" after an Asian doctoral student shared his dissertation research.

Karen reveals that she's never had a teacher who was not European American. She relates: "I've had all White teachers and I have never felt really discriminated against in class. I can't compare to any experience I've had because I've never been rejected because of being half Asian." Though Karen states that she doesn't think ethnicity makes a difference, her journal entry about the Asian doctoral candidate illustrates that perhaps she didn't know it would make a difference since she had never seen a positive Asian role model before this experience. Given her biracial background and experiences in the European American society, why would she have any reason to explicitly question the role of ethnicity before now? Karen asserts: "I feel that if you really want something and you try hard enough you get it." Karen perceives that achievement, success, and access to schooling are all a matter of merit, and have nothing to do with an individual's ethnicity. Yet her positive response to an Asian academic role model belies that assertion.

To her friends in the bilingual education program, Kelly is an enigma. After four years of undergraduate courses and active involvement with the Latino group on campus, few even knew she was Native American. She is half European American and half Native American. Yet she identifies and involves herself with neither of those. Instead she chooses a third identity—Hispanic. "I don't get it either," she explains. "I feel more comfortable with the Hispanic population than I do with my Native Americanness."

Something in her past keeps her from knowing, but simultaneously wanting to know her Native American identity. She explains: "When we fled the reservation, my dad was sorry he had involved us in that life because it almost destroyed us. . . . They [her parents] have a respect for it [Native American culture]. It's weird. Even though I'm afraid of it I still want to know." Kelly writes that applying for the OD program gave her "the opportunity to quietly say yes, I am Native American. I am. For once now I will not let my *white* features deny my *red* blood."

However, once in the program, Kelly was not sure that she was ready to acknowledge her Native American ethnicity. She explains:

> Maybe it is the ghosts, Terry, but you see, I'm sorry I came here. I knew I should have thought more about it when I filled in the application. No one thinks of me as Indian. That's okay now. That's one thing I've learned, that it is okay, despite what other people of color might presume. Let me take their misunderstandings, let me take that pain, let me be White. Because the ghosts only haunt me as an Indian, Terry. Do you notice? I cannot talk about living on an Indian reservation. I cannot personalize anything. I can't talk for long about any of it. I just want you to know that I can see that in myself, that inability to deal with it. This inability to deal with it is even worse now.

Kelly is unable to find any inner peace between the opposing forces of her "red blood" and her "white features." Through interactions with the OD participants who question her "Native Americanness" because of her very White skin color, she is unable to reconcile her dual ethnic identities even when she strives to. During her college years it has been easier to keep those struggles hidden and dormant within her, or not to let the "ghosts" of her past rise to the surface to haunt her. But within the OD program, where she began with the perception that this was a context where she could begin to acknowledge her Native American past and culture, Kelly found she was incapable of dealing with the pain from the past.

In her autobiography Michelle stated that she was "in search of herself." Up to this time, she felt she had no knowledge of Africa, racism, or prominent African American figures such as Martin Luther King or Malcolm X. Her relatives were not into the "culture thing." But in her seeking a cultural identity while being in the United States the past ten years, Michelle's Jamaican upbringing resulted in cultural tension. She is Black by race, but she is not African American. Her ways of thinking, acting, and interacting are not the same as her African American counterparts'. Growing up in Jamaica, she did not face the same oppressive struggle of racism and discrimination faced by her U.S. peers. Thus, she does not view the "problems" of racism from the dominant European American culture the same way as African Americans do.

Conflicts arose on several occasions that illustrate how the other African Americans in the group tried to socialize Michelle to their way of thinking. For instance, discussing a scenario during one class session resulted in a conflict for Michelle. The scenario that Karma, Deirdre, and Michelle were given involved a European American male English teacher correcting the Black dialect of two African American boys in the hallway. After arguing over whether or not language is cultural, Michelle became frustrated at being cut off by the other two.

DEIRDRE: No, but it says, "in helping them to adjust to institutional,
     educational requirements," so to me that says that I want
     to know. . .
MICHELLE: But what—
KARMA: I think that culturally aware is in every aspect of life.
DEIRDRE: Yeah, but that may not have anything to do with the
     educational requirements.
MICHELLE: But I also think so, but listen -
DEIRDRE: I'm talking about. . .
KARMA: What requirements do you mean?
DEIRDRE: The ones that they're talking about here in number three?
MICHELLE: Will somebody listen to what I have to say?
DEIRDRE: Wait, wait, wait . . . I know that, I'm just saying—
MICHELLE: I'm responding to what you're saying!

This incident was not the first nor the last time that Michelle was cut off because others disagreed or misunderstood her position. The most poignant illustration of the African Americans trying to socialize Michelle to their perspective takes place during the at-risk planning session. In this ethnic grouping, with five other African Americans (Paul, Rochelle, Charles, Lisa and Karma), Michelle is repeatedly cut off every time she offers an idea. Michelle wants to focus on solutions, while Lisa argues that not everyone agrees yet on what the problem is. Michelle suggests that they list teenage pregnancy as an at-risk factor. The following exchange took place:

LISA: I don't think that has to do with color.
MICHELLE: Well, I'm not saying it does have a color.
ROCHELLE: Yeah, but . . .
MICHELLE: But, I think, though because of the culture, because of
     more religious background in Blacks they are more -
LISA: I disagree. No.

MICHELLE: Yes, well this is my opinion. Because of more cultural upbringing -

LISA: But you can't say that is everybody -

MICHELLE: Well, I'm not speaking for everybody, of course not!

LISA: But you're saying Black people -

MICHELLE: In general. I did say in general.

LISA: That's not a fact. That has no color.

MICHELLE: But this is my opinion.

LISA: Well, let me tell you. . .

MICHELLE: When I'm done! When I am finished, please! Please!

LISA: I just don't think we should say it.

MICHELLE: Why not? But this is my—you're saying I'm not supposed to say what *I* think?

LISA: But Michelle, you're very -

PAUL: (interjects) I think what she's trying -

MICHELLE: Listen!

PAUL: Can I say something kind of as a mediator?

MICHELLE: Oh, go ahead.

PAUL: I think when you're making some of your comments and stuff, you're just, like, saying, "Black people as a whole." I mean, and you did say just now, "Yes, this is my opinion," but when you're making your statements and stuff you should say, like, "I feel" or something. Because when you make a statement pertaining to the whole Black race, then other people might want to express their opinions.

MICHELLE: Okay.

PAUL: So maybe you should just say, "I feel this way about this."

MICHELLE: Al.right. Okay. Let me say it this way then. I feel this way about Black people, *in general. In general,* about the way we are brought up more religious, we tend to think that children probably shouldn't have sex till they're married. We tend to want to think our children shouldn't have sex till they're over twenty-one or things like that. Even though we may see that children do have sex from age, probably thirteen, fourteen or fifteen, we really don't accept and deal with it the way it ought to be done. So we, *I* think, *in general*, Black parents don't educate their children the way they ought. Or I should say the way we ought to cause I'm a Black mother, too. And that's one of the reasons why Blacks are more prone to get pregnant. Girls are more prone to get pregnant at a younger age, and the boys are prone to get another girl pregnant at a younger age. And that's what I'm saying. It doesn't have to be, we don't have to disagree to agree.

PAUL: In speaking of at-risk children, that's a topic, it's a problem with overall society itself. I don't think it's narrowed down to Blacks.

MICHELLE: Okay.

Michelle is silenced after this exchange. Her peers tell her she overgeneralizes, and that it's not what she says but how she says it that is offensive. She listens for the next twenty minutes, during which time Charles talks nonstop for twenty minutes without being interrupted. It's only after Charles's soliloquy that Michelle speaks again to share her view on how she has been treated.

MICHELLE: You know one of the things that I've confirmed even more as we've been sitting here talking is that. . . Before I say that, let me say this. Since I've been in America I've become more prejudiced than anything else. And it's prejudice towards certain things. But I realize Black Americans, and I'm not taking about White, we all know they are prejudiced against everybody else. But out of all the minority groups, you guys are more prejudiced against people like me, different Blacks from other parts of the world, including Africa, than anything else. Than anything else, and I've seen it all the time. Black Americans are more prejudiced as a minority group than any other minority group, against their own, other Black people that come from anywhere.

CHARLES: You see that goes back to the media. We have never been, and I don't say this for a lot of people either. I don't. . . . It's true we got folks that say, "I don't care about the South Americans, I don't care about them Jamaicans, or them Africans." There's a lot of people, yes I know that. But have they ever been that—

MICHELLE: I'm not talking about a lot of people. I'm talking about you five right here. For instance, they let you talk for twenty minutes. Twenty! And I was the only one interrupted to say do you know any Africans here, right? If I had opened my mouth, which many times it happened, you guys just wait until I open my mouth and you jump down my throat! Even if I'm agreeing with you!

From these encounters Michelle internalizes what she needs to change in herself to be more accepted by her African American peers. In her interview she reflects: "I've always done self-evaluation. But being here I've done so much more in a short time. I'm more aggressive than I thought I was. The way I word my sentences, trying to turn the volume down on my voice, be more aware of my aggressiveness even in friendly relationships." For Michelle, being Black, and in America doesn't mean she has the tools necessary to be ethnically called "African American."

Internalized Racism

Debra came to the *Opening Doors* program as a first step in search of the Asian identity she has ignored and been ashamed of until now. Coming to *Opening Doors* was an initiating step toward accepting and appreciating herself. She relates:

> I'm amazed that I feel comfortable around another Asian person. I don't say this degradingly, I say this interestingly, because all my life I've been embarrassed to be associated with other Asians. I wanted so badly to be White. It seemed disgraceful to be a member of the Asian group. As a child, what was honorable about it for me? I saw no positive role models. Who the hell wants to be part of a group people laugh at?

It's interesting to me that I am racist towards myself. I negated myself because I am Asian. I didn't want Asian friends because I was ashamed. I only began healing my internalized racism after I realized that I was a racist.

Debra explains further how hatred of her own ethnicity affects her life:

> This past year at college I was working on internalized racism. My whole life, ever since I was adopted, I put myself down cause I was Chinese. I didn't really realize I was doing it. How could I admit I was doing it to myself? . . . A lot of self-esteem is wrapped up in ethnicity. I was hating myself for so many years, from age six to twenty-two. That's a long time to hate yourself. My race and ethnicity is such a big part of me that it's really hard to like the other parts. . . . My self-esteem is caused by so many things, and a big chunk of it is hating my ethnicity, and that will effect my self-esteem.

Carol reacts to Debra's search for knowledge about her Asian self with questions and signs of her own internalized racism. Carol's self-hate is compounded by her move to the United States late in her life, at age twenty-six. She wants desperately to get a teaching degree, to be able to contribute to making classrooms for children a much more comforting environment than what she experienced. But she is kept from reaching her goal by university officials who suggest that her English is not "good enough."

It is more than just language, however, that contributes to Carol's feeling of anger, resentment, and shame. Simple differences she encounters daily with her own family cause her anxiety and feelings of shame. She explains:

> I was brought up to fit in, to compromise. If there's no rice, I eat hamburgers. I'm not happy. You never hear my side of the story. I'm a good girl. You eat hamburger, I eat hamburger. And you don't ask, and I don't make noise. You assume, you don't know to ask. I'm not really happy. I don't get my rice, but I don't speak up so you can't know. It's not your fault. I have to speak up. I feel weird serving rice because you don't eat it. When I first came here, I hide my food. People in China don't say "gross" or "ick." Whatever you served, you eat it. You appreciate it because your parents work hard and mean well. And all you say is "yuck!" I feel terrible. I feel ashamed. I hide my stir-fry in the oven when people come over to the house. I'm ashamed to be different.

Ethnicity Identity Construction from Schooling

The degree of pride in cultural heritage, and whether or not contextual settings allow for the expression of that personal ethnic identity, is the focus of this section on schooling experiences. For some, a strong sense of ethnic pride and understanding that is developed in the home and community may cause greater conflicts and frustration when the same sense of belonging and importance is not shared at school. For others, the same firm grounding in cultural heritage and pride provides the strength needed to endure daily the hostile environment of school. For those who enter school with ethnic identity conflicts from the start, school may become the context where cultural heritage and lineage are forgotten, misplaced, or ignored in hopes of fitting in with the European American mainstream. Either way, past schooling experiences shape ethnic self-identity. Specifically, OD participants had three views of ethnicity: (1) ethnicity as an obstacle to be overcome, (2) ethnicity as a burden of responsibility, and (3) ethnicity as neither positive nor neutral, but something that just is.

Obstacle to Overcome

Facing a second-language barrier is a salient experience of schooling for Fabian, who speaks Spanish as his first language, and for Carol, who speaks Chinese. Though Fabian expressed hesitation at how his ethnicity influenced his schooling, he was sure of the impact of the language difference. He relates:

> I could have focused on language at the beginning as being a deterrent. I was placed in an immersion rather than bilingual program. I missed so much and I didn't realize until I was a sophomore in high school what I'd missed. I was in immersion until fifth grade, it was all in English. I must have missed so much because most students were saying how they'd read this book and that. I felt, where was I? I missed out.

Carol is adamant about the effects the language barrier has had on her. She writes: "With Chinese background, I'm a devoted student. However, being not born in the USA, I face communication problems. And that create a lot of anxieties." Carol explains how language creates a double bind in schooling:

> They [non-English-speaking college students] can't be a student 'cause they can't speak English. But when Chinese man came here to work on the railroad, they can't be manager type cause they can't speak English They can't go to school. You must have a chance, but they don't have a chance to try because they have to know some English to go. I'm a four-point student. You give me a test, I flunk every one of them. That won't stop me from learning or being an A student. Sure I have my problems. I don't understand biology or whatever, never mind, I will. Suppose I want to be a math teacher? Those tests I can't pass are the words that I don't know. Yet I am not going to if I fail. They [college officials] say I don't like it, but I pass everything else. They say, "You're minority."

Carol elaborates further on her linguistic double bind. On the one hand, the school officials tell her she can't teach because she doesn't have enough language. But when she asks for help with language, she's told she doesn't need it because she's a 4.0 student. The result is negative. Thus, an obstacle of language differences (which she was willing to overcome) is transformed into a discouraging, defeated view of her self-worth. She explains:

> It's negative because I want to be a teacher and they won't let me in because of my language. If I don't pass they don't let me in, rather than saying what else can we use Carol in some other place. They can't draw from that perspective, that the language isn't all. You guys in education, you know what it takes to teach people, so why you treat me like this? I'm not American, but what can I do about it?

Carol is left helpless because she is not American. Not only is she helpless, but she now has internalized a negative view of her self-identity based on her experiences with linguistic differences.

Debra's internalized racism is entrenched even further in her identity in the context of schooling. She explains how having bad feelings about her ethnicity is "multicause":

> Everything is multicause. When I feel bad about my ethnicity, I'm going to feel bad about a lot of things. Having bad self-esteem in that way affects my school. . . . I think if I would have grown up feeling proud of being Asian, being Chinese, having an accent, that would be one less thing to feel bad about, and I'd have that much more room to succeed and make friends, because I can't be friends if I feel bad about myself. I've leaned what a great influence a person's feelings about their ethnicity can have, how so many things are affected.

Driving Lisa's passion for historical truth from an African American perspective is her own suffering through school and the negative effects schooling had on her self-esteem. She relates:

> They [African American children in the public school system] don't see themselves. Why should they pay attention? I was that way. I didn't drop out, but when they talked about history I didn't see myself there. And when they skimmed over the slavery part I was under the desk! I was so embarrassed because of the way they told it.

A positive self-esteem can be damaged through the stress of the perceived need to overachieve. Lilia explains: "I'm afraid to ask. Afraid to not know. I am the first one on both sides of my family so I have more pressure. My family says, 'You're in college. You graduated.' I do feel I have to work harder."

Laura also talks of working harder to fight the need for sensitivity. For her, overachieving comes in the form of having to work to break negative stereotypes. Laura says, "Because of my color and my last name, I've always been marked before I open my mouth. Teachers have had perceptions, and I feel I've had to be super outwitted to be noticed more in a positive light. Working against negative stereotypes."

Paul also feels he's had to work against negative stereotypes. He writes: "My ethnicity forces me to work harder in the classroom. The reason I say this is because most people assume that African-Americans are not as smart as whites. This attitude pushes me harder to prove this stereotype to be wrong."

Tonya's father spoke little English. The little he did speak he didn't speak "properly," so he was always made fun of. This transferred into his stressing the need for her to learn English properly, having no accent whatsoever. Tonya's father pushed her to overachieve to overcome language, and Karen's mother instilled in her the need to "be better than everyone else" because she's half Japanese and living in America. Kelly also expresses her complications of an overachieving attitude:

> I am *white girl, school girl. That girl, you know, off the res.* I felt it necessary to overachieve. I wasn't able to do it immediately and was excused with, "Well, she's a res kid." When I moved off the res to go to college I felt overwhelmed. The campus was bigger than any town I had ever lived in and so . . . white. I was an overachiever without the skills, socially or academically, to succeed let alone overachieve.

Lisa writes that her African American ethnicity caused her to "find the strength and determination to go into a situation/system on a daily basis, knowing, I was not welcome. An experience that has made me more determined in all facets of my life."

Rochelle sums up the feeling of all OD participants when she says, "I feel like, as a student of color, I have to work at least twice as hard as nonminority students just to be comfortable from day to day."

Burden of Responsibility

Being one of a kind in daily situations means having to explain yourself over and over again to others who do not share the same views or experiences. Miguel explains:

> In classes here at this university I'm often the only minority. So I feel it's part of my duty to represent my perspective into the class. Being Mexicano-Chicano brings a different perspective to the all-female, mostly White women classroom. It gets me more sensitive to minorities in different situations. It also gives me an advantage because I can think in different perspectives. I think in the White male point of view because that's where I grew up. But in me I also have my minority point of view. So I think I have more points of views. I'm bilingual and biperceptual. . . . Many times I have to disagree with the White male point of view because it doesn't bring in other points of view and so I have to go to the minority view and bring that in.

However, as Rochelle elaborates, shouldering the responsibility for *the* perspective when you are only *one* perspective is a heavy load. She says:

> I can't speak for every African American in the world! I can say for me personally, but you need to be aware of all different views. I used to say, "*I don't know,*" when they would ask me, "Well, what do African Americans think?" But I didn't want to give the impression I didn't have a view. But at the same time they weren't looking at anyone else in the classroom and I resented being singled out. I still don't know which way is best.

As the burden becomes heavier, day after day, one gets weary. As Celia states, "You have to carry that responsibility with you to always educate people. It's not going to go away, unfortunately. But you have to know it does get tiring."

Walter shoulders the responsibility of teaching in a different way. He doesn't have the attitude that it is an added burden, perhaps because he perceives his role in life as a teacher. Walter very patiently and matter-of-factly explains parts of his culture on several occasions. He is the constant teacher. When beginning his five-minute oral proposal to the group, he began by having everyone close their eyes. Once all eyes were closed, he said, "Now open them." When he saw everyone's eyes open he questioned, "How did you know when to open them?" When the group responded, "We heard you tell us," he replied, "So when you ask a Native American to listen to you, they don't have to look at you because we hear with our ears, not our eyes." With this very simple demonstration, Walter dispelled the myth that people have to look each other in the eyes to be heard.

On another occasion, Walter explains to his small group the origin of the stereotypical term, *Indian giver.*

> Okay, I'll explain *Indian giver* to you. First thing is you need a favor. Okay, I'll help you with the favor. When they say Indian giver, they didn't mean you wouldn't give it back to you. But when I helped you, it is your obligation to help somebody else in need. Not necessarily me. It might be a long way off. But to return that favor to me, you return it to somebody else. And so that's the Indian giving that we talk about. But there's a misconception that if I give something to you, the next minute I take it back.

Rochelle is very sensitive to the double-edged-sword of opportunity and manipulation. She states:

> As an African American graduate of this university, I've seen a great deal of things I haven't liked when going up against the majority. I've tried to use this system to the best of my ability. I've taken advantage of many opportunities that have brought me a long way. But, at the same time, these experiences have disillusioned me. Sometimes I feel like a broken record talking about it so much! I have come to feel as though I am the one who is being used in the name of this establishment's commitment to diversity. This is something that I really resent. Oftentimes it just seems like students of color don't matter, except to serve as proof that this university is truly committed to diversity. To me, this is a joke, and it's frustrating. Sometimes, I just want to close myself off from everything and everyone. It makes me tired.

Laura also expresses feeling like a used token:

> I've been the token minority person in different programs. In the orientation program here, there was a photographer and you could tell

she was looking for a minority for the picture. There were four Anglo students, one sorority, one athletic, and all were White. Then she was looking for people of color to round out the picture. The first year I tried to hide, but the second year I just accepted it.

Just Is

Whereas others express a tension, a struggle between their ethnic identities and the European American mainstream classroom, Diane and Deirdre recognize that two views exist but they do not see them as necessarily competitive. Diane writes: "My ethnicity does not influence my learning experience. My learning experience is influenced by other forces." In fact, she thinks ethnicity does not and should not play a role in her schooling. "I don't think, how is this related to my ethnicity. I think I learn things I want to, that are new. I think learning should be school oriented, and not associated with ethnicity. But outside of school, that's a different story."

Deirdre uses her age to explain why she thinks ethnicity is not positive or negative, just a fact of life. She writes: "Being a senior in college, I know there's more than one way to look at anything. Ethnicity is just that additional perspective, another side to look at things from. I don't think of it as positive or negative. Everyone has ethnicity." She also writes how ethnicity is just a matter of perspective. Not a right or wrong perspective, just a perspective. "I think I, like most people, view anything from my own perspective. My perspective as a African American female will determine what I believe about any information that I am given."

While Diane and Deirdre both acknowledge ethnicity as an influence, they do not believe it determines success or failure in school. Karen denies that ethnicity has nothing to do with schooling, or even achievement for that matter. She says: "It's never really dawned on me, you know? I've just never really felt different. I know I'm half-and-half, but so what? As long as I'm good at what I do, what difference does it make? I mean, isn't the dream world that we can still get by on your merit, regardless of who you are?" Karen believes in the American dream. She believes that all obstacles can be overcome if you set your mind to it, and apply yourself. Ethnicity does not play a part.

Community experiences, mediated by forces such as family, religion, and cultural gender expectations, affect schooling experiences.

OD participants may have similar cultures and languages but they have very different personal histories. These differences in their personal histories create differences in school learning and academic success. Fabian speaks of problems encountered in school because of the language barrier. Jesus also came into the country speaking only Spanish yet had no language problem after first grade. Having a strong sense of ethnic pride and cultural history can be an integrated sense of self even in the school setting, as it is for Diane, or it can be a burden of responsibility, as it is for Rochelle and Celia. Self-hate from internalized racism can cause an even greater sense of negative self-esteem in the context of school, as Debra describes. Negative self-esteem can also be transformed into the strength to succeed against all odds, as Lisa has done. The Opening Doors participants brought perceptions of themselves, and of themselves in relation to others in school, to the OD context.

Pinar and Reynolds (1991) explain that "deconstruction shows how a discursive system functions, including what it excludes or denies" (p. 5). Deconstructing the past experiences of the OD participants reveals the repeated exclusion and denial of ethnic self. Perceptions of achievement ability, cultural pride, and self-esteem, and cultural responsibility constructed from past experiences in communities and in schools influenced expectations, and ultimately the interpretations of OD learning events.

EFFECTS OF ETHNIC IDENTITY
ON LEARNING EXPERIENCES

> *As I think about each of our life stories, I realize*
> *that even though we all came from different ethnic*
> *backgrounds and have different life experiences, the*
> *things we hold in common outweigh our differences.*
> *What makes our lives so intertwined is that most of our*
> *life experiences have been influenced based on who we*
> *are. We are all people of color. We are people who are*
> *on a journey through life in search of identity,*
> *acceptance and respect. Our struggles are similar.*
> —Adrianne

Strength, gained through adversity, is the underlying common bond shared by the Opening Doors participants. These individuals came having suffered and endured varied life experiences. Though they came not knowing what to expect about graduate school, they did come expecting to be in a social setting with a group of people like themselves. They expected to be welcomed, understood, and accepted as opposed to their past schooling experiences of being ignored, left out, and alienated. Some came with the primary goal of learning about graduate school with diversity issues a second priority. Others came expecting to bond and find support with a group of people of color as a first priority, with learning about graduate school as secondary. Still others combined issues of diversity with academic goals, considering both goals mutually important. Whatever expectations each OD participant had prior to actually beginning the Opening Doors program, the expectations, formed from self-perceptions of ethnic identity, influenced the individually constructed interpretations of the OD learning events. The effects of ethnic identity include (1) self-doubt, (2) seeking untold stories, (3) intense emotional bonding with people of color, (4) ethnic identity role models, (5) academic role models, and (6) staff role models.

Self-Doubt

Participants came to the program filled with high hopes, expectations, anxieties, and self-doubts. They came with a mixture of excitement and thrill of the opportunity, tinged with skepticism of programs and ability to access the perceived European American world of graduate school. Lisa, now thirty-eight years old, writes about her joy and excitement at being given the opportunity she missed as a youth:

> I thank God for answering this prayer (uttered years ago), and allowing me to have this experience I thought I'd long ago missed. . .. When I received the letter of acceptance I was thrilled! My first thoughts were; who should I tell? Who would care? Should I tell anyone? Will they think I'm bragging or putting on airs? And so what if they do, maybe it's time I did a little bragging on myself, I mean, this is a once in a life-time opportunity for me. In other words, this is definitely something to shout about!

Michelle expresses how the joy of acceptance was tainted with fear and self-doubt:

When I applied to the Opening Doors program I had some doubts if I would be accepted. It seemed so out of my reach, so upper class, and I did question myself, was I ready for this, or do I have the qualifications to come here and make an impression through my writing or my participation in class activities?

Lilia, even though she was a successful undergraduate at the same institution, also writes explicitly of the mixed reaction of excitement tamed by self-doubt brought on by her perception of graduate school being for "White people":

When I first received my letter of acceptance. . . I jumped up and down with joy. Then I found myself thinking, am I cut out to do research, and for that matter cut out to go to graduate school? Who do you think you are setting yourself up thinking you will make something out of yourself, graduate school is for the White people. I was angry at myself for even thinking of this self-doubt. But it wasn't me. Tears rolled down because I have always known that God wanted to do something special with my life. And that something was Education. Why this self doubt, I told myself. . . I've always known that there is racism and hate in our surrounding world. However, I'd always believed that old saying, *sticks and stones may break my bones but words will never hurt me!* Well I was wrong. And I was angry that racism and ignorance of some individuals had affected me to the point where I felt self-doubt in myself.

Celia came with skeptical perceptions of why she was chosen. She wanted to know if the decision was based on her personal qualifications of being good enough for the program, or if the program needed one of her ethnicity. She is very sensitive about filling quotas versus acknowledging her own self-worth as a capable human being. She explains:

I did not expect to get in because of my grades. I had misconceptions of the program. I thought it was going to be directed by a White person, and White people are always doing this. It was a good surprise. . . . In my application I didn't know if I was going to make a good impression. So when I got the letter I was glad to think they looked at another level, they just didn't look at grades. . . . *I* knew I was capable. *I* know I can do this. But the thing is if people give me an opportunity to do it. I guess I always put myself down. I don't think I can get there.

The need to overachieve, to prove to European American counterparts that people of color can also academically succeed, was an overshadowing force throughout the program. Feelings of wanting to do better than others caused tension, stress, and performance anxiety. Wanting to overachieve, and feelings of having to work twice as hard to do so, created perceptions of self-doubt of being able to compete in the European American mainstream of graduate school.

Seeking Untold Stories

Even though there were doubts and anxieties, participants came to the Opening Doors program ready for an educational experience that welcomed rather than excluded their experiences. They came ready for the attention, recognition, and basic acknowledgment of their very existence. They came seeking knowledge. They came, as Pinar (1991) suggests, eager to remedy the distortions and reform the deformities created by the absence and denial of their ethnic identity in their past schooling experiences. Lisa's area of study is African American history. Often the weekly group discussions she was in focused some on exchanging knowledge of people and versions of historical stories that have traditionally been left out of the school curriculum. In one small group discussion Diane, Karma, Lisa, and Wes shared their under-standings of historical events from their African American and Native American perspectives:

KARMA: Just like in that book I found. We need to weed out all these things. The guy that did the first heart transplant was African American.

WES: Yeah, Daniel Williams.

LISA: Other facts like that contributed to the well-being of all the United States were done by somebody other than European Americans.

WES: I've found a lot of inventions by Black people. Like the straightening comb and stuff like that.

LISA: You know, . . .one of the things is that the Indians helped us escape from slavery.

DIANE: The Indians played an important role leading escaped slaves through the territory.

LISA: Right. They knew how to get away and they helped us get away. . . . I think the number of Indian slaves are minute because Indians knew the land. It was their land.

WES: That's right.

LISA: It wasn't happening, you know? So they helped us in return. See, people of color have done these things you know. Welcomed people with open arms, . . . you know, and when they [African Americans] met another people of color, it was still, "Let me help you." So that's where you have African Americans and Native Americans helping each other.

Celia's political science background gave her the opportunity to share different views of the same old stories. She writes:

Right now I am thinking of the significance of the coming holiday. The fourth of July is supposed to be one of the biggest days of celebration in this country, but what does it really mean? People don't go to work, banks and many businesses close for that day, people buy fireworks, it's summertime and everything seems to be perfect for the celebration of the independence of the United States of America from the motherland England (That kingdom that would not let the 13 colonies do what they wanted to, and they felt so oppressed). The founders of this country were foreigners to this beautiful land that belonged, and still belongs to the Natives of the Americas, the whole continent (Spanish took care of the other part). The thing is that the Englishmen that came here and the Anglo people that live today refuse to realize that they stole the land they live in. To me, this celebration of the independence of this "Great democratic country" signifies the slaughter of the Native Americans, the greed that drove the newcomers to disrespect and destroy everything that was in their path. The newcomers' ambition to build a great nation not from solid foundations, but from dark, false, illusive foundations, that were supposed to glorify freedom, equality and justice. As many know this was not so. Too many people were forgotten, repressed, enslaved and stripped from their cultures to benefit those great founders of this United States.

Bonding with People of Color

Factual, or what OD participants call "book knowledge," wasn't the only affirmation sought. OD participants also came seeking recognition and attention as people of color. The anticipation and high expectations of finally being able to be surrounded by people like themselves intensified the emotional bonding experienced through the autobiography sharing. Not only the act of sharing itself, but what people risked to share had a profound effect on everyone in the group. The voices of pain and struggle, the injustices endured, and the tenacity and determined will developed to overcome those injustices, produced an emotional and spiritual high that provided a common ground of bonding. Describing this process, Tonya writes:

> As I listened to the different autobiographies, I found myself conducting an inner search and making connections between my life and theirs. I had so many different emotions surface. I cried and laughed, felt happy and sad, angry and sympathetic, strong and determined, and very proud of who we all are. Examining each emotional experience, I came to realize that all of us shared similar feelings and experiences, and upon probing our inner selves, a very special bonding process was automatically occurring.

Having a forum to share these experiences was a welcome relief of pressure for Rochelle. She writes:

> I am so thankful to have a chance to talk about how it feels to go through this hell [being African American on a predominantly White campus] with other people who know how it feels. I have learned a lot from everyone's autobiographies. . . . Everyone has been so giving of themselves, and this has definitely had an impact on me. You see, it has been a long time since I have wanted to open up to a group, and be part of something. It is so important to be able to be myself while those around me are being themselves, too. It should feel right for all of us!

Participants opened up and shared pain with others they only met the day before. This suggests, as Celia writes that "there is something very special about this group that makes us all work together and share each other's experiences." She goes on to name what they all came seeking: "This group has shown me love, caring, comprehension, understanding, and most of all honesty."

In her journal, Adrianne describes what she perceives as the common bond between them.

> What makes our lives so intertwined is that most of our experiences have been influenced on who we are. We are all people of color. We are a people who are on a journey through life in search of identity, acceptance and respect. Our struggles are similar. Most of us have experiences of being excluded from our pluralistic, democratic society, simply based on our race. Despite obstacles, we as people of color have struggled and survived.

Adrianne later explains, knowing others' struggle also provides a self-affirmation not felt before, "These past few days have been a time of bliss, sense of affirmation, relief, having all my needs met, being valued, fitting in, being understood."

The OD participants were thankful for being given the chance to have a "normative" schooling experience with people like themselves and with people who dress, think, and talk about strategies to enable others to have the same opportunity. As Carol says, "I have been inspired so much by everyone of this program. I feel very close to them because they are my type of people—minority."

Many of them had never been given the opportunity to come together as people of color in an academic setting. Debra relates: "It is interesting for me to look down our lunch table and see only people of color at it. This is my first experience of being an active member of a people of color group. It feels different. It feels good."

Laura writes about her own revelation concerning just how good it really feels to interact daily with a group of people of color:

> On Monday I had this really trippy experience. As I entered the library, I noticed a large group of students working on research. They all seemed to know one another. Maybe they just finished class and had started working on their research much like the Opening Doors group had done the previous week.
>
> It wasn't like these students were any different than other groups of students I had seen working in the same library during other college days. As I walked into the library, it was like this sudden surprise. "Wow!" I exclaimed to myself, "All these people are so

light." Wait a second, I thought, "big deal." I had seen the situation before, it never made me do a double take.

As I looked around to find a table to work at, I realized that the situation was nothing new. But somehow, working a while with a group of minorities had suddenly become my norm. You know what? I love it! I love looking into their deep dark eyes and feeling that I am welcomed. . . accepted. . . understood. . . a comrade.

Deirdre tells of how being with people of color instills a sense of self-confidence in her:

I will say what has made this week a good one. I have, through several experiences, come to find out how much confidence and faith some of my peers, coworkers, and others have in me. Just to know that people think that I can do things helps me to be able to do them. I am not saying that I did not already have confidence in myself and my abilities, but it does my heart and ego good to know that others express faith in me as well. It gives me renewed strength and adds to my endurance; this boost of encouragement also helps me to feel closer to those that the words of confidence are coming from.

Ethnic Role Models

The sense of bonding, comradeship, and acceptance from being surrounded by people of color fulfilled a personal need for social interaction with others like themselves. Having twenty-one ethnically diverse individuals together to create a supportive community provided a social sense of belonging that individuals had not experienced in their previous schooling. In addition, individuals also sought particular ethnic models on a personal level.

Having been stripped of her cultural identity when coming to the United States at an early age, Debra wanted to know more about her Chinese heritage. She writes:

Identity. Would it have made a difference in my self-esteem if I have had Asian role models in my primary school years? I had few role models. There was one Asian teacher in my elementary school and she only spoke to me twice. There were few other Asian kids in my school, but why would I want to be associated with them if they were being made fun of?

Debra came to the program with the predetermined notion to "learn what my people are all about and interact with other Asians. I want to stop pretending I'm White." Thus, it was no surprise when Debra chose to spend time interacting with Carol. She relates:

> I especially enjoy talking to Carol. She tells me things from a Chinese woman's frame of reference. It intrigues me to hear about my culture and heritage through her eyes. Carol says that she sees Chinese body language in me. I talk excitedly as if I'm angry. She says Chinese people do this. I'm surprised that I'm still Chinese in some ways. But I guess I'm not really surprised, I lived in the Asian culture for the most significant years of my life (The first six years).

Carol found camaraderie with the other Chinese students in the dorm who were not part of the OD program. She explains:

> There are a lot of Chinese there and they are very helpful. I like it. We're all students so we have lots in common. We share Chinese newspapers which is very good. It gives me an opportunity to learn more about this university. They're the old ones who have been here and can tell you what you want to know.

To Adrianne, having an African American role model was explicitly one of the reasons she chose to apply to Opening Doors. She states:

> I was attracted to this program because of the title and because I heard of Celeste's reputation of being an excellent African American instructor and her work with multicultural programs. Additionally, the opportunity to research minority issues in education under the direction of an instructor who was not only knowledgeable about these issues but also had life experiences of being a minority was appealing.

Having learning experiences from an African American viewpoint made a difference for Adrianne, who asserts:

> Like Lisa, I have never had the experience of having a minority teacher or professor until I enrolled at [the college she presently attends]. [There is] an Afrocentric curriculum and African American

instructors therefore, the African American viewpoint is not infused into the curriculum. It is The Curriculum—along with regular studies. It has made a difference in my attitude toward learning. I have role models who are sensitive to my needs, I am in a more supportive and comfortable learning atmosphere, where my concerns are not based on my race.

The sense of comfort and support Adrianne feels from not having to justify her race to African American instructors stems from her view that African Americans have a similar experiential knowledge. Being in an atmosphere where the teachers are of African American ethnicity, she does not have to spend time and energy defending or explaining her African American view to European Americans who do not acknowledge the types of experiences she has endured. When asked why she chose Celeste for her interview, she responds, "I think it's the role modeling, the experiences. I guess I signed up to interview with you because I felt more comfortable. I didn't feel that I had to explain."

Academic Role Models

It wasn't just a matter of having role models that mattered. It also mattered that there were ethnic role models who had achieved academic success. Wes describes how the panelists, Kunjufu and Akbar, in the *The Rise of College Campus Racism* video, viewed in the first week, were a source of inspiration for the African Americans in particular:

> You know, I was just thinking. You remember the African American guy? Kunjufu, was it? Him and the other guy [Akbar]. I wanted to get books. I mean anything that they've written because it seemed that they've done a lot of research on African Americans. Especially African American males. And I just wanted to like read anything that they have. You know, just find out. I mean, this is all fine, like graduate school and you have to have this to get ahead, you know, the American dream, to get what you want. But I still want to get that left-out knowledge I'm missing about my people. So I can be a stronger Black male and educate my brothers and sisters.

Charles also gleaned inspiration from the African American scholars. In his final journal entry he writes:

I love this video [The Rise of College Campus Racism] because for once educators are speaking out against the injustices that occur on predominantly White campuses across the US. Finally someone at the top agreed with what I feel as a student of color! Dr. Naim Akbar, and Dr. Jawanza Kunjufu, my soul brothers—they are on it!

Though questioning what she viewed as an "African American emphasis" in the activities the first week, because both the video and the article read were by African Americans, Karen was more able to relate when an Asian American doctoral candidate came to talk about his experiences with the dissertation process. Karen writes:

I was very proud to see an Asian-American success story. Mr., I mean, Dr. W. serves as a positive role model. I now desire to achieve more. Seeing the reality of his position and education makes me reach for even more. I always knew I would get my master's degree, but maybe I am also meant to earn a doctorate. It would be a dream fulfilled. It truly is wonderful to see ethnic diversity and positive role models on our campus. *If only more diversity were here it would be that much more apparent of what minorities have to offer the world.* (emphasis added)

Karen's final statement is particularly poignant in response to the original intent of the Opening Doors program, namely to provide encouragement and support to ethnically diverse undergraduate students with the intent of those students becoming academic role models for students of color in the future. It is also poignant given her resistance to acknowledging that race or ethnicity matters.

Staff Role Models

Each of the four staff members came in with differing levels of academic experience, teaching experience, and role expectations within the program. Having teaching experience that the other two did not have, Celeste and I fulfilled instructional roles. Kristy and Wes served primarily as research assistants, taking field notes and being participant-observers. Yet each staff member in some way was a role model to participants. Charles writes:

This brings me to a point of discussion about education and our role as educators. Celeste, Wes, Kristy and Terry have all been examples of true educators. I say and mean this because each one of them understands the process of learning and are currently working on mastering some particular field. But, another asset that they bring is their ability to relate to others. I feel that they take time to understand us and help us understand our research, and at times, ourselves.

Celeste

Being African American and the director of the program was of significant importance to all participants. Celia and Adrianne expressed that usually the directors of these kinds of programs are European American. So to have someone of color be the person in charge rather than a token representative within the program was vital. However, the event that best illustrates the complexity of the importance of Celeste's value as a role model of color was the C. Conference.

The C. Conference is a yearly conference for public school administrators in the state. The focus of this year's conference was "Restructuring: What It Takes." Celeste's role was to be one of three respondents to the keynote speaker. The first respondent was an elementary school administrator. Celeste was the second respondent. A local middle school teacher was the third. The keynote speaker, a research specialist from the Bay Area Research Group, began her presentation, "Puzzle of Structural Change," making the restructuring of schools analogous to fitting pieces of a puzzle together. She provided overheads and a description of the components necessary for restructuring schools, which included (1) critical linkages, (2) balance in a performance-based system, (3) four questions to ask when restructuring, and (4) four components needed to restructure.

However, as the Opening Doors participants noticed, and as Celeste pointed out in her response, nowhere in this twenty-minute overview of restructuring schools was there any mention of multicultural issues. The only comment the speaker made regarding multicultural issues was an overgeneralization that our schools are doing a good job of meeting the needs of all students. Celeste's "bold rebuttal," as Adrianne names it, questioned whether or not we have done a good job of meeting diverse needs of students. Adrianne writes:

Celeste's voice was needed in the conference today. She gave
participants a fresh outlook on the need for restructuring schools—
adding the most significant piece to the puzzle—multicultural
programs based on respect for and celebration of cultural diversity. I
also like her idea of teachers being learners. . . . Also I liked Celeste's
bold rebuttal to the statement that "schools do a good job of teaching
a diverse group of students."

Celeste challenged the speaker to add a vital missing piece to the
total picture of restructuring education. But what OD participants
noticed was that she did so in an academic manner. While some
celebrated and felt relieved that Celeste was there to provide the
missing voice for people of color, others reflected on the reality of what
would have happened if Celeste had not been there to bring up the
forgotten issues. Rochelle reflects on how Celeste's comments made her
even more aware of the importance of having a voice in the system:
"The comments Celeste made at the C. Conference were totally
missing. It made me really think, how do they view us when none of us
are here? What's going to happen to us? We need to get in the system."

Along with importance of providing the voice of missing
perspectives, Celeste was the positive image of a successful, academic
person of color that exhibited strength in character, as well as
knowledge. Lilia was particularly struck by Celeste's image, and shares
how the image personally affected her:

When you spoke on restructuring, just looking at you, and seeing
myself in you one day—that really mattered to me. It made me feel
good that you were up there and that I would be up there one day. . . .
You were so professional and you knew who you were. The Kente
cloth that you had was so cool because that showed that's who I am.
And as far as being a Mexicana, that's what I want to do. You go up
there and you're really voicing who you are and what you believe in
by being that professional.

Celia also shares with Celeste how her poise and scholarly attitude
provided a model for others to look up to and to strive to follow. She
relates:

Seeing you in a different role—Dr. Celeste D.—in the outside world.
Being able to respond in such a powerful way. Subtle yet assertive

and truthful. You were so diplomatic! I just loved it. You were very
political even though you didn't sound like that. It was just like a role
model. I could be in that place. If there would be more people like
you, things would be able to change. . . . You gave us an example of
what we could be and that impacted me a lot. Especially being in a
group where it was so obvious. And not showing being nervous.
There were all these White people, and saying what you were saying,
and just being able to say it like that.

The only time OD participants referred to Celeste as Dr. D. was in
the context of the C. Conference. It mattered that she was African
American and therefore a role model for people of color. It also
mattered greatly that she was a person of color who was articulate,
scholarly, diplomatic, and deserved the "alphabets behind her name."

Kristy and Wes

Kristy's presence was very quiet, contemplative, yet attentive and
personal with students. After their first meeting, Lisa writes: "I sensed a
spirit of caring and kinship with Kristy not long after our introduction."
  Kristy was assigned as Diane's mentor. Responding to her
impressions of mentoring after the first week, Diane writes:

I felt really comfortable talking with her about my project. After our
first official meeting, I left her office anxious to start my research.
The guidance that I have received has been just enough. Any
questions or concerns I have, my mentor has been able to address
satisfactorily. The communication and the ability to share information
has been very positive.

Celia shares her feelings that even though Kristy is quiet in large group
settings, "she does show interest. She's always asking."
  Wes's interaction with OD participants was much more social and
outgoing in contrast to Kristy's quiet interaction style. Often, Wes
participated as an active learner in the group discussions, especially
with the African Americans. Wes's social style created a jovial
atmosphere for some. Lisa writes: "Meeting Wes was like finding a lost
brother. Once he came into the lobby and joined us, all my negative
energies took a hike! We sat there and hooped and howled, then we'd

gather our thoughts and discussed some issues of the day, and hooped and howled some more. It was fabulous."

However, even though the OD participants enjoyed Wes's personal nature and willingness to socialize with them, several of the African Americans became particularly disappointed with his lack of seriousness toward academic responsibility. This issue was of particular importance during the fifth week because Celeste had to be out of town, and I was assigned the responsibility for directing the class sessions. In journal discussions the fifth week, Lisa, Karma, Rochelle, and Charles, all African Americans, discussed the issue, wondering why it was that I led the class in Celeste's absence, and why Wes and Kristy didn't play greater roles. Unlike other small group discussions, when Wes would join the African Americans, Wes was not participating. Both Lisa and Karma asked Wes point-blank why he just sat there and didn't contribute to the class discussions, to which he replied, "I don't have anything to say." Charles adds his frustration to Karma's and Lisa's comments about Wes's weak academic modeling. Charles has firm convictions about the responsibility African Americans have to one another that he believed Wes was not fulfilling. Charles asserts:

> He [Wes] sits back. And that's like me, as a Black man in the sciences, and there's not that many, and we have a science program for students of color and I sit back and don't even talk to them but just come in and laugh. True that's fun, we can *kick it* all the time, but I'm still not doing anything. That's leaving me out, when I've been asking. Where are those Black role models? Where are those people of color who understand me? We need to sit down and have an intellectual conversation. I don't want you to just laugh with me. Yeah, I like you, but I need you to share something with me that you've been through because you are in graduate school. You have made it over there. . . . And you should get into some deep conversations so that you can make an impact on others instead of just joking around. I mean, you know social issues, that's cool, but if we could talk about research, where I could talk about microbiology to you and sit up here and explain my proposal to you, I know that I better be able to do that. . . .And when it comes to comments about our speeches, don't just sit there and say that everything's good. Have some criticism for me. Because, you know if we don't do that to ourselves it's going to be hard when somebody else does it to us. That's the way we take care of our own people. We're always saying "that's cool." Why are we

saying that's cool when we know somebody is going to be saying "that's negative"? I'd rather get it from you. Tell me now so when I go out in front of others I don't mess up. And that should be your responsibility.

Terry

I was concerned about whether or not I could or even should try to be a role model for the Opening Doors participants. I was very aware of my European American presence amid the otherwise all-people-of-color experience. After the first week, I wrote in my journal to them:

> *I want to talk, and ask questions. But then I stop and ask myself, should I? I think to myself, it's your interpretation, your experience, and I don't want to intrude on it and I wonder if you think I am . Yesterday in listening to the group discussions I stopped myself several times from jumping in. I guess I'm asking you, would you feel it's an intrusion?*

As could be expected with twenty-one individuals, I received twenty-one different responses.

Miguel was one of my former students who knew of my experience teaching Latinos in the same part of the state where he grew up. Because of our past interactions, Miguel didn't have a problem with my being there. He wrote back: "I admire you very much for the efforts you do in educating future teachers about being sensitive to their students regardless of race, gender, and economic status." Although Rochelle and I had never officially met before the program, we both knew Celeste. For Rochelle, trusting me was enabled by sponsorship. She writes: "If Celeste trusts you, you must be ok!"

Celia was very skeptical of my presence until she read my journal. She wrote back: "I must say that, I have been surprised by you. You really put yourself on paper as you are and expressed your thoughts and fears. I must say that I'm glad that you can understand your position as a White person in our group." Karma had a similar response after the second week when I openly participated in the research discussion about objectivity. In response to my speaking out in the discussion, Karma writes:

Thanks for being a part of it. This is fascinating because I thought
you were a *stick in the mud* and here you are this person with
thoughts with issues. Okay, let's deal. I 105% agree. Your energy
inspires me this week. (Did someone put something in your coffee?)
Please keep it up. In order to keep this diversity happening we do
need you. Thanks for your input.

Sharing my honest reactions, thoughts, and feelings with the group
enabled lines of communication to be opened. Diane writes: "Your
openness and desire will allow you to seek out more. I would feel
cheated if you did not participate more because you too have a lot to
offer us." Charles expresses how important honesty is to him as a
student of color:

> I would first like to say thank you for sharing your feelings and I
> would like to add that it is important to me as a student, researcher,
> and person of color that you share your feelings with us because if
> we're all in this together then we must be able to share freely.

My willingness to open up and share my feelings of hesitation and
insecurity, and the fact that I voluntarily chose to interact with them
daily to gain firsthand knowledge about people of color from people of
color, also helped to establish credibility. Lilia writes: "I applaud your
research in this area!! If the majority was more like you wanting to
learn from me/people of color, things would be a lot better!" Celia,
Carol, Rochelle, and Charles each wrote comments in support of my
efforts, also. Celia's comments best illustrate their thoughts. She states:

> I really hope you understand us and learn as much as you can from us
> so that you can take this knowledge to your colleagues and share with
> them your experiences. . . . I would like for you to say comments
> from time to time, because you as the rest of us have valuable and
> intelligent comments to make. . . . I'm glad that you decided to learn
> about other people's culture. That makes one less ignorant person in
> our world of confusion and misunderstanding.

Along with honesty and research pursuits, my public school
teaching experience with Mexican/Latino youth gave me credibility
with some of the participants. Tonya, one of the Mexican participants,
shares: "The Hispanics are the only ones not represented in the staff. . .

and I'm happy with the fact that you [Terry] are able to relate to some of the needs because you worked with them."

Familiarity (either through direct contact or by mutual acquaintance), honesty and openness, initiating action to show sincerity in wanting to be interpersonally involved, and past teaching experience in diverse settings gave me credibility as a role model for OD participants.

The personal histories of the OD participants detail the experiences from which they constructed personal perceptions of self as object, the ways in which those perceptions influenced self-worth and self-esteem, and finally, the influences of those personal constructions on the social constructions within the Opening Doors context.

Communities, family, religion, gender roles, and schooling affected the degree of positive or negative ethnic identity construction. Charles and Michelle both illustrate the differences the historical relationship with the dominant culture creates. As Kincheloe and Steinberg (1993) argue, "Culture cannot be grasped outside the history of culture" (p. 302). Neither spent their childhood years of primary socialization in the United States so had not encountered the racism and discrimination on a daily basis as described by Lisa and Karma. The stories of Deirdre and Adrianne illustrate how explicit teachings from parents can act as a counterbalance to the negative experiences of living as African Americans in a Eurocentric country. The explicit details of schooling experiences depict, as Pinar (1992) suggests, how schools "distorted by deletions and denials" (p. 32) perpetuate the perception of self as object. Lack of positive images in the curriculum materials and ethnic role models for teachers, coupled with stereotyped images, are among the ways OD participants described experiencing the distortion of culture.

The OD individuals internalized the reflective appraisals of self as object from their lived experiences. Following the personal meanings of these ethnic identity constructions into schooling experiences shows how the context of school objectified the self. For those without an already developed positive sense of ethnic self, school can cause greater alienation. The inability to express personal self in the schooling context leads to internalizing the view of self as object. Ethnicity becomes an object to be overcome. Fabian and Carol still struggle with language differences, and even Jesus and Tonya described making conscious efforts to overcome the language barrier in order to fit in. They give up the personal self in order to be accepted as a social self.

The Eurocentric curriculum creates a perspective of diverse ethnicity as an object of invisibility. No role modeling in teachers and only negative stereotypes in books led Lisa to perceive that she could not succeed in school because no one else like her was in the system. Lisa was also objectified to thinking of herself as a slave, which was something to be ashamed of. Karma described how the few images present in the textbooks were not positive ones to identify with. As she says, she would rather not be associated with looking raggedy. Participants also explained ways in which being the only one in their culture among Europeans constructs them as an object of "the perspective."

The experiences of constructing self as object influenced the initial expectations and subsequent interactions in the Opening Doors context. The desire, the personal need for social interaction among people of color, was intensified in view of the personal histories they brought to the context. Debra came especially to find ethnic role models to alleviate her self-hate. The need to share the untold stories of historical contributions, the intense emotional bonding, and the importance of ethnic role models in the program illustrate the need for addressing the personal self that had been denied in the European American mainstream.

CHAPTER 5

Deconstructing Self as Object

*In reconstructing the traumas behind the images, I make
"sense" of them, and once they have "meaning" they are
changed, transformed.*

—Anzaldúa (1988, p. 34)

The past experiences of the OD participants illustrate how their lived
experiences have created personal perceptions of self as object. In order
to achieve the grounded self illustrated earlier in Figure 2.1,
deconstruction of self as object is necessary. The grounded self is
similar to the concept of self as subject (Brown, 1988; hooks, 1990;
hooks & West, 1992; Cliff, 1990). Michelle Cliff (1990) explains why
it is imperative that turning self as object into self as subject is the
crucial starting point for a multicultural perspective to develop. She
writes:

> Object into Subject. What does that mean? We live in a society
> whose history is drenched in the philosophy and practice of racism,
> the oppression of Black and other Third World peoples. This is the
> point at which my definition begins: If you study racism—if you
> understand the history of the United States—you will find that under
> racism the person who is oppressed is turned into an object in the
> mind of the oppressor. (p. 271)

Turning people into objects represses the emotions of fear, pain, guilt,
and shame that come from interpersonal interaction with a fellow
human being. Objectifying or grounding beliefs in stereotypes rather
than interacting with actual individuals keeps human beings from

relating to one another on a personal level. It keeps us from knowing, and more important, keeps us from understanding one another. However, one must first understand oneself as subject before one can understand, relate to and appreciate another as subject.

Understanding oneself as subject begins with the past experiences that shape or construct the individual in a particular context in the present, hence the importance of sharing the direct experiences, the symbolic meanings, and the self-identities constructed from those experiences and the reconstruction of those identities in the present situational context. One must personally be able to reflect on and socially discuss the obstacles of the past in order to understand the present. Or as Cornel West (1992) suggests, "breaking bread" through social sharing of reflections on past experiences enables a reconstruction of past events leading toward transformation for the future. "There are tremendous impediments and obstacles, very difficult circumstances and conditions, but the breaking bread that could lead toward our critical understanding of the past and present and our transformation of the present into a better future seems to be so very important" (hooks & West, p. 2).

Self-knowledge is crucial for understanding self as subject and involves both self reflection on past remembrances and critical questioning of those experiences in the present. For those ethnically diverse from the dominant mainstream culture, reflection on constructed meanings of the past often reveals a view of self as object. Ethnic identity within the dominant mainstream culture became, for OD participants, a barrier to overcome, a source of negative self-esteem, and a responsibility to represent all of one's ethnicity. Each of these internalized, objectified meanings of ethnicity assigned by the dominant European American mainstream culture are an impetus for self-hate or internalized racism. As Audre Lorde (1984) writes of her growing up as an African American child, "Children only know themselves as reasons for the happenings in their lives. So as a child I decided there must be something terribly wrong with me that inspired such contempt. The bus driver didn't look at other people like that. All the things my mother had warned me not to do and be that I had gone right ahead and done and been must be to blame" (p. 146). Racism, stereotyping, and overgeneralized, objectified views of the individual causes internalized oppression, racism, hate, and anger for individuals ethnically diverse from the dominant mainstream culture. Ethnic and cultural identity becomes something to fear, to hate, or to hide from, just as Lisa described in her reactions of wanting to crawl under the desk when slavery was the topic in the classroom, rather than an integral part of self-identity to respect. Achieving respect for self, for self as subject is the basis for a grounded self.

Simply put, having a grounded self allows one to answer the questions, Who am I? What am I? Where did I come form? Where am I going? For whom am I going? What is my purpose in life? All OD participants voiced at one time or another during the eight weeks that "you need to find yourself first. All other issues are secondary." Jesus explains how for those diverse from the dominant mainstream culture, one's ethnicity is crucial in the search for self: "My own ethnicity is enhanced by dealing with people from other ethnicities. Knowing others' perspectives helps you become more comfortable with who you are." He goes on to describe how he personally makes a conscious effort to do just that: "Knowing who I am, where I'm coming from, helps me to look at other people's cultures and what brings them to where they are." Walter states quite simply the importance of knowing oneself: "How well you get along with other people depends on how well you understand yourself."

Though the OD participants agree knowing oneself is the first step toward getting along with others, all would say that the task is not an easy one. In some cases, individuals have been systematically kept from knowing. However, the Opening Doors program provided an opportunity to reflect on self and on self in relation to others. Focusing on the pedagogy of the OD context, the autobiography activity began the reflection process. The weekly journal writing allowed for reflections to continue and for others to question. The at-risk planning session, where OD participants were grouped by ethnicity, provided a particularly salient opportunity for critical reflection on past experiences. OD participants reflected on their past experiences in order to suggest changes for the future in the televised at-risk session.

REFLECTION ON PAST REMEMBRANCES

Grounded Practices

Participants came to Opening Doors in various stages of self-development. Several participants exhibited a very grounded sense of self, while others had a focus on searching for self. Walter exemplifies someone whose experiences and reflections have enabled him to become truly grounded. Comments he makes begin with "In our culture. . . ." Walter knows and accepts that there are two cultures in the United States he must balance, "because that's the way it is." His ten years of studying the oral history of the old ways enables him to pinpoint and articulate the differences between his Native American culture and the European American mainstream. He states: "In our culture we judge you by generosity. In the mainstream you're judged by greed, what you have in material goods." He doesn't view the differences as combative or competitive, with one needing to replace or overcome the other. Instead, he describes it as a balancing act: "I think I've done pretty good at balancing. I've done what I've had to for home, and I've done what I had to for the mainstream. So it's kind of a balancing act." When asked about trust and truth he continues: "Another cultural thing is you don't judge a person either way until you know. So I could say you get to know them first, the character from the inside, not first impressions. So that's what I do."

Diane is also very secure in knowing exactly who she is, and who she is in relation to her Native American culture. "Yes, I have a proud culture" she writes. "However, the culture is a part of me; I am not the culture. I am an individual who just so happens to be Native American." While other Latinos construct their identity from particular labels (Chicano, Mexicano, Latina), in reference to her ethnicity Tonya exhibits her own self-knowledge when she relates, "I don't make an issue of it. I know who I am. I know where I'm going. I know what I want. It doesn't matter what I'm called: Hispanic, Latino, etc. If they ask me, I say I'm Mexican. But I know who I am. I don't feel I need to correct anybody."

In College

Rochelle has a strong sense of positive self-esteem gained from her family support and encouragement while growing up. However, her college experiences gave her a reason to be explicit in her pride and celebration of being African American ("on a predominantly White campus," as she says often) instead of being marginalized or trying to overcome her ethnicity. Her response to the autobiographies illustrates this newfound importance of cultural identity for her:

> When we did our autobiographies, I saw numerous different cultures.
> I loved how people were so in touch with their cultures and open

about their experiences. At this stage in my life, I'm an identity buff. . . . Everyone should know about who they are and stay true to themselves.

Though Miguel had a sense of positive self-esteem while growing up, he also mentions how his sense of self did not include his ethnic heritage until he came to college:

The last two years I've found myself here at college. In high school I had mainly White friends and I was trying to find myself. In the Valley the Mexican population is looked down upon. So when I got to college I found myself because of students I hang around with, people who have been proud of themselves. They had the attitude I needed.

Jesus, like Miguel, grew up being able to fit in by surrounding himself with White friends. Jesus tells in his autobiography how it wasn't until college that he was able to fuse his two marginalized lives together:

My culture is also important to me. I belong to a folklore dancing group on campus. It was hard for me because I was enculturated into the White school system. During high school, I had two lives. I had my home life and then my school life. My school life was White, and my home life was Mexican. The dancing now is a way for me to bring the two together.

Charles recounts his difficulty beginning his college career: "I wasn't strong when I came to school. I knew the Black people wouldn't accept me because I was so different. So I lived in the international dorm for three years." After three years of near anonymity on campus, Charles's brother encouraged him to get out and meet people. "By getting involved, " Charles describes, "I started realizing the strength and leadership I had in my African pride." Charles's strength and leadership from his African pride led him to become the president of Student Minority Affairs and a member of the College Knowledge of the Mind, a group of college students who visit high school students to recruit ethnically diverse students.

Charles's decision to get involved resulted in new degrees of self-pride as an African American male. His teachings (or sometimes preachings, as exhibited through his oratory style) include knowing who you are, actively finding out and seeking to know who others are in order to contribute changes for the future. Charles proudly proclaims his African heritage through everything he does. His ethnicity is an integral part of who he is and cannot be separated from his grounded self. Therefore, when asked about the effects of his ethnicity outside of school he was articulate in explaining how he has interpreted the way he can personally operate in the world for positive change:

> I try to talk more with cultures outside of school. Just talk. There may be racist undertones, but I've learned to be cautious. Things may not be the same for them. But I don't let that stop me or get to me. I know that there are things we can do as doctors, as graduates, that we can come back and still give back to our [African American] people. So I say you got to stay with it. The more angry you are, that's going to keep you out. You have to get over it. Me being there is angering somebody else. If you think like that, then . . . if you get yours, you will be the boss. Turn the struggle into power. Otherwise you're just another person on the side complaining. I'd rather not complain, but do something about it.

College in Later Years and the Present

Whereas Rochelle, Miguel, Jesus, and Charles were able to find themselves while still in their teens and early twenties, other OD participants had to wait another ten years, until they were in their thirties, to experience the same self-discovery process. In her autobiography, Adrianne talks of how her academic pursuits arose from trying to raise her own African American children with positive self-esteem. Searching for ways to assist and support her children led to her self-discovery. She relates:

> In being sensitive to the needs of African American people the importance of culture and identity should be stressed. In my search to help my kids have positive self-esteem, I also discovered myself. In discovering myself I realized that I had lost something that was very precious. In discovering myself in the literature and examples . . . I realized that I had a rich legacy.

The cyclical process of finding herself and passing on the legacy of knowledge to her children drives Karma in her efforts to be a teacher. She, too, was not able to search for herself until the age of thirty. But she wants to ensure that other African American children do not have to wait as long as she did. She states: "To me, this is who I am and who I want to be, an inspiration to kids. That's why I'm going to teach, so I can help children be who they are from the age of five, rather than from the age of twenty. This experience is something I needed when I was eighteen!"

Lisa, similar to Adrianne and Karma, also sensed an urgency in finding herself as the first necessary step before being able to meet the needs of her own children. After schooling experiences that did nothing but deflate her self-esteem as an African American woman, it wasn't until the age of thirty-eight that Lisa had positive African American role models at school. While she was enrolled in a four-year college with an Afrocentric curriculum, two female African American professors helped Lisa find pride in her African American heritage. These women helped propel Lisa's drive to restore historical truth in the curriculum as a means of restoring self-esteem and pride in African American youth. Lisa explains to her African American OD peers:

> We need to start reading about, and finding out, about ourselves. You see, it all starts here. [points to her chest] I can't do anything until I'm set in here. You know what I'm saying? I don't have anywhere to go because I'm dealing with me. So what I do is reading about me and people like me. That is how I am able to give to my children self-esteem, a sense of pride and cultural heritage.

Searching Now

OD participants possessed various degrees of grounding in knowledge of self as subject. Some came to Opening Doors with a fully developed sense of grounded knowledge and exhibited a secure sense of self based on knowledge of self as subject that enabled a sense of ethnic pride and self-respect. Walter best illustrates the concept of a grounded self. Knowing that he has spent over ten years actively seeking that grounding attests to the reality that finding oneself is not an easy task. Several testified to finding themselves during their college years, in their late teens and in their early twenties. For others, those college years did not come until later in life. Only after experiences of marriage, divorce, and children did Adrianne, Lisa, and Karma have the opportunity to attend college as an action to discover a positive sense of self. They did in their thirties what other college students are able to do in their teens and early twenties. Thus, these three women endured ten more years of struggle before being able to ground their sense of self as subject.

Last, there are those who seek in varying degrees, to find a sense of cultural and ethnic self in the present. Debra and Carol both struggle with internalized racism. Debra is more conscious of her effort because of her academic coursework as a psychology major. Michelle announced in her autobiography that "I am in search of myself" and readily admits that she is working to figure out who she is, not only in relation to her African cultural heritage but also as a Black Jamaican woman living in the United States among African Americans.

Kelly came to the program with hopes of being able to "not let my white features deny my red blood." However, in facing her own Native Americanness, she also faces the "ghosts" related to her Native American self, the ghosts that "only haunt me as an Indian." Though admitting she is not personally able to cope with the pain of these ghosts from the reservation, she believes in the importance of self-knowledge and self-identity as the first step in helping children in the classroom. In response to a journal question about what can be done in education, she writes:

> We need to begin with the individual who establishes their own identity. Begin at the beginning with the education of the individual. We need to know where we come from and where we are going Students should have the opportunity to teach to help them understand themselves. When asking a child who are you, what does that mean? They should be able to tell you.

Kelly acknowledges that ethnic identity and knowing oneself are important, and her struggle indicates she is unable to "deal with it." Karen, on the other hand, does not acknowledge that culture or ethnicity has much to do with her sense of self-worth. Karen has internalized the American dream work ethic. For her, as long as you work hard, you can achieve and succeed at whatever you choose. She reasons that if there are no Asians in particular positions such as school teachers it is because they did not want to be there. She does not identify with the struggle expressed by other OD participants. In talking with Debra and Carol, she explains why: "See, my thing is, I never felt out of place, really. . . .See, that's how I'm idealistic. I think if you treat somebody nice they will be nice to you. If you're qualified for something, you're going to get it. I've never encountered outright, 'No, you're not getting it' [because of ethnic discrimination]. . . . I've always gotten what I want."

CRITICAL SELF-REFLECTION THROUGH OPENING DOORS

Regardless of the degree of grounded self for individual participants, Opening Doors enabled a process of continuous critical self-reflection throughout the eight-week period. From a symbolic interactionist perspective, critical self-reflection is the way in which a self communicates in order to establish an identity. Charon (1992) explains: "As we communicate toward self we are able to see our selves in the situation, to recognize who we are in relation to others and vice versa, as well as to evaluate our own action in the situation. We are able to judge our selves and to establish an identity" (p. 87). Two related but different kinds of critical reflection enabling identity formation emerged through the Opening Doors learning events: critical reflection on past experiences in relation to the present and critical reflection on self.

Critical reflection on past experiences in relation to the present is demonstrated by the discussions during the at-risk planning session. These discussions not only addressed past experiences, but critical questioning of those past experiences in order to suggest change for future educational practices. Weekly journal writing also afforded OD participants the time and the structure to question themselves and their actions in relation to others.

At-Risk Planning: Questioning the Past

The discussions from the At-risk planning session show why something that is so important (finding/grounding oneself) is also very difficult to accomplish. To provide guidance for future generations in addressing issues of at-risk students, the place to start is knowing, and then questioning that knowledge about the past. The at-risk discussions illustrate how difficult it is for people of color not only to find themselves, but also to keep their ethnic selves in a society dominated by European American ideals and values.

Addressing African Americans in the group, Charles articulates how the Eurocentric curriculum in schools has been so detrimental in preventing African Americans from grounding themselves:

> Because that's something you missed out on, especially African Americans here in the U.S. We have missed that part of our culture. We should learn from our African brothers when they had been oppressed by British colonies and all of that. . . . Because only when I can know myself can I better deal with other people, I can better work in society, I can make it.

Lisa explains the obstacles standing in the way of African Americans being able to ground themselves in this country and the consequent ramifications of not getting along with others:

> So the problem, the reason why so many African Americans don't respect themselves, is that the historical truth has never been taught. We've been maligned in the history books, and on the screen. In the day-to-day living we've been maligned. So we're still trying to recover from that. . . . Being an oppressed people makes us act outside ourselves. . . . I'm not trying to say that Africans, that we, did everything good, everything right. But there's some things that we've done that so many of us just don't know. There's still much I don't know, and it's going to take some time. You know, take the responsibility to find out. . . . We've got a lot of disrespect amongst ourselves. We don't appreciate who we are. And I don't think we can get that before you have a sense of pride.

What Lisa explains here is actually an often expressed concept in popular psychology: you have to love yourself first before you can love others. However, the difficulty lies in loving yourself in a society that has maligned your heritage and stripped you of your dignity and sense of pride.

Lilia explains to her Latino group (Tonya, Fabian, Miguel, Celia, Laura, and Jesus) how the difficulties of one ethnic group are not like those of another. She asserts in group discussion what she considers to be very different problems suffered by Mexican Americans and Asians:

TONYA: And there's a language barrier. They [Asians] have a language barrier, too.

FABIAN: I think they have the same [language difficulties as Latinos]. I may be wrong, [but] Asians will assimilate. Latinos, we're still going to maintain our culture.

LILIA: See, where's China compared to us? Mexico is down here on the border, we can almost go every day. . . . That's the hardest thing for me. [People say] "Why do you guys want to keep your language? Why do you guys want to do this or that?"

TONYA: "Why do you want to keep going back to Mexico?"

LILIA: Yeah, it's like when everybody else is assimilating. That's how my friend, I call her a mutt, because she doesn't even know who she is now. There's no heritage there anymore. I go, there's a big difference. First of all, they [Asians] came over here on a boat. They wanted to come. Some of us were already here, and Mexico is just right down there. There's not an ocean in between us.

CELIA: Our border was moved for us. Land was taken away while there were people there.

LILIA: And then on top of that, they put barriers for us, you know? And they weren't allowing people to go to school.

TONYA: I get disgusted thinking about what they did.

LILIA: It was not like it is now.

FABIAN: Going back to the school system, the border's so close to the U.S. we'll always have this influx of Mexicans. They [Mexicans] will not know the English language. So when they go to public schools, to some extent the language barrier will and does affect them, and they will not do well due to that.

LILIA: That's why I'm saying it's so ironic that the United States has this thing that there is one way, because we're a pluralistic society. There are so many of us [Americans with different culture] and so different that I don't understand how they could possibly fit into this one [point of view].

Continuing the discussion of barriers blocking the ability to keep one's own cultural identity, Lilia adds, "It's not prestigious to learn Spanish in the United States." From this statement come stories from five Latino group members to illustrate not only that Spanish is not prestigious in the United States, but to be monolingual in a language other than English also labels one as stupid and damages one's self-esteem.

MIGUEL: When you [Latino children] come into a school and you're not bilingual, you're monolingual Spanish. That's why they [school officials] think we're stupid. They don't think they're [Latino students] stupid because they're bilingual, they think they're stupid because they are monolingual Spanish.

LILIA: They're [the European American school system] not going to go out straight and tell you. But . . . they're pulling out my kids [in my student teaching experience] from the regular classroom because the teacher doesn't speak the language and she's not willing to work with him, and [she] put him into a language resource room, or a Chapter I or migrant or bilingual. And they're not teaching them what they should, they're doing these little dumb things. They're not teaching them content. Instead of teaching in Spanish the stuff they need to learn, they're not looking at it that way, they're saying okay, we're going to go back to third grade and give you a first-grade book, and we're going to stand up and see if you can read these words. That kind of thing. That's telling me they think this kid cannot do the work.

CELIA: . . . Just by the fact that you come from another country, even if you have graduated from a high school in your country, if you attend a university, they will still put you, like they did to me, in remedial mathematics. Just because I did not know how to speak English I was put in these awful classes where they wouldn't teach me anything! I felt like I was in the second grade. I had learned that [what was being taught in the remedial math class] a long long time ago. And they put me there because I didn't know how to speak English. They assumed because I didn't know how to speak the language that I wasn't going to be able to perform.

LAURA: Like my aunt, she was one of the first Mexican families over here and she was put in a special education class for a year and a half. Her mother didn't know that was happening. Her mom went into the school, her mom was from upper-class Mexico, she came over here because she was friends with an ambassador for Mexico, I mean she was very well educated. She came in and kind of ex-plained herself [to school officials]. She didn't know English very well but she was a very intelligent lady. And they had her daughter in a special education class just because she doesn't know English.

JESUS: Several of my brothers and sisters were held back just because . . . they didn't speak English. Even if they were at the level [in content understanding] of everyone else.

CELIA: My brother is a good example of that.

The African Americans discuss the lack of historical truth, and the Latinos focus on the damaging effects of language differences on self-esteem. In the Native American grouping, Walter talks of how historical continuity is intrinsically linked to the language. When the language is lost, so is the meaning in the Native American culture. He says:

> You know, it's different back home. I live in the Sioux community called Little Eagle, where I was working. There's a town not far away. They're not Native American. In the morning, eight o'clock, all these teachers pull in and at four o'clock they all go home. So they don't know the people they're trying to teach. This is a Bureau of Indian Affairs school. . . . And see, Indian enculturation was their main goal. Their goal was to get people so that when they lose their language, they lose other things.

Later in the conversation, Diane asks about identity. Once again, Walter responds with the integral nature of identity, self, and language in the Native American culture.

DIANE: What about identity?
WALTER: All that's covered in the culture. The language, the value system, the identity are all there.
DIANE: You know how some [Native Americans] are really traditional and some are inbetween?

Historically, Walter argues that the loss of language also symbolizes the loss of culture, and why efforts to restore lost Native American culture cannot be regained easily because of the integral role of language in the Native American culture

WALTER: See, that's happening in the Indian studies. Okay, there's the time, like in the nineteen sixties, when I went to school where it wasn't cool to be an Indian. And there was this group who was off the reservation. They didn't want to speak the language. They didn't even want to associate with us. Then, in the nineteen seventies it was cool to be an Indian again. So those people who were out there turned around and they tried to learn everything that they should have learned. . . . They were going to the extremes to try to prove that they're an Indian.

KELLY: What do they call that movement, uh, Born Again Indian? [All three respond in laughter.]

WALTER: Yeah. [laughs) Anyway, those are the people that are writing about our information today, and it's not accurate. . . .See, it's all that shallow, superficial understanding. That's all they understand. To them, that's all it means. Whereas if you talk to real old-time Indian people, they are the ones that truly understand.

KELLY: Then isn't there something with the language, too? Not specifically culture, . . . where there's an old dialect where it was more pictures, talking about more with pictures, and now it's a little bit less than that?

WALTER: Well, here's a key example. Like *Okisewa*. If you ask, like, this group over here, the one I was talking about, *Okisewa* means to remember. But if you ask an old man, what does *Okisewa* mean? What this guy is talking about is real petty stuff, like yesterday and stuff like that. But ask a real old man the same question and he'll go back and it's a state of relaxing. Like old people that have gone back to the spirit world and will come back and talk through you, and that would explain things. So there's a big difference between just remembering stuff and going way back. Now, you ask someone and the only thing they know is pretty words. So they don't know the true meaning of remembering. There's a big difference, like in that group that came back and tried to learn things but did not. So the language is the key to everything.

KELLY: Because the language ties in to all the spiritualness.

Walter continues to illustrate how it's not only the meaning of the language that is being misinterpreted and misrepresented, but the meaning of the spiritual ceremonies that is also lost. He says:

What's really funny is every year, thousands of people go on vision quests. And they don't speak the native language. And the old people that come visit you speak it. So, it's funny because you can't say you can't do this, so they get up there for four days and come back. Most the time they talk about what they saw. They don't know what people said to them. There's a lot of people coming from all over, from New York, LA, all over. . . .That's why we call them *wannaBes*. Whatever they say, fine. But down deep inside we know that there's no way that they could have, because of the language. And even this group here today, some of them still don't speak Indian. Like the guy that used to be the keeper of the pipe. He stood up and told all these young guys they were going to sun dance. He told everybody they were going to smoke the pipe, and that language was the key to everything, and when they finished one guy stood up [and spoke in the native language]. He didn't understand what this guy was saying. Anyway, he went on and on about how he went on a vision quest and the old people gave him this and this and this. And everybody was just surprised because they [the old people] only give you one thing. Like the right of healing, the right of sun dance, and this and that. And some people are given the right just to earn a sweat lodge. And whatever they give you that's okay, because that's where you're needed. But he wanted his star way up on top. So there's a set pattern of the way you do ceremonies. And if you don't understand those, then you're going to mess it all up. . . . So it's really funny when they come down in the ceremony. They're mixing everything up so much that it doesn't mean anything to anybody anymore.

The Asian grouping discusses a difficulty of another kind: stereotypes.

DEBRA: There are a lot of people [Asians] in Chinatowns who are poor. That's a myth that they're doing well. I've read many articles in my research about Asians living in Chinatowns in real severe conditions.

CAROL: How about at-risk then? Since it's assumed we can be smart or bright kids. But if we do have problems like when I go to my teacher and say I have a language problem, and he say,"You don't have a problem, you're a four-point-oh student." And I tell him I do have a problem. They don't believe me.

DEBRA: That happened to you?

CAROL: Yeah. I mean it's not bad. But I do have a language problem. He says, "You talk nice and everything. What's the problem?" I say, "Well, I do have vocabulary problem." I mean, I have, but it's not very serious and they're not listening. What does that mean?

DEBRA: That goes under the stereotype, do you think? You know, the teachers have a stereotype that Asian people do well and [so they] don't listen to your problem.

CAROL: No, they don't. It happens all the time. Even now at college. I want to be a teacher. I told them I got a problem. They say, "What you worried about? You got a our-point-oh." But that don't mean I don't have a problem, cause I do. He says only one quarter and my problems be all gone.

KAREN: What about the assumption that all Asians are good at math and science? You know? You think, seriously Asian, you assume math! Science!

CAROL: Are you good at math and science?

KAREN: I was fairly good, but it's never been a comfort range. It's always been, oh, I hate this.

CAROL: And they all come to you for help? Like your friends assume that you know everything. They come to you, and that make you feel bad.

KAREN: At times, yeah. Because I had to go to my teacher and say I hated geometry, I hated trigonometry. Algebra was good. I felt it made sense. It was easier, but my friends were like, oh, you're Asian, you should be a whiz at this ! And it's like, well, I'm good at English and history. Sorry. I'm one of those liberal [arts] kind of types. But don't I know, of course I'm going to *love* [sarcastically] chemistry and physics?

CAROL: [Brief pause] So patience has been a threat to me, to us. We want to succeed, but we don't want to, because if we do it will be more pressure on us and it won't be fun.

The ethnic groupings articulated four ways the dominant European American mainstream causes ethnically diverse individuals to internalize ethnic identity of self as object and makes it difficult for ethnically diverse individuals to know themselves as subjects. First, Lisa discussed how the Eurocentric curriculum excludes the cultural heritage of individuals ethnically diverse from the European American mainstream. In turn, the exclusion, or invisibility, leads to the personal inability to appreciate and respect the diverse cultural heritage needed to perceive self as subject when that cultural heritage is something that mainstream society marginalizes and denigrates.

Second, the Latino grouping discussed how the lack of political prestige the European mainstream assigns to the Spanish language creates negative self-esteem. The interpretation within the dominant school system of language differences being deficits creates the image of oneself as not being good enough, or damaged in some way. For those in the school system to assume students need special assistance such as remedial math, special education, or retention because of speaking a different language suggests that the language itself is deficient and inferior. Therefore, the individual speaking the language must be deficient and inferior.

Third, the loss of language also results in loss of cultural meaning and significance. Walter explained through the example of the wannabes participating in the vision quest how without knowledge of the native language, the symbolic meanings of rituals, ceremonies, and spirituality of the Native American culture are misunderstood.

Fourth, the discussion in the Asian grouping illustrates how stereotypical meanings applied to culture or race causes fear, stress, and frustration when the individual does not fit the stereotypical norm applied. As an Asian, Karen does not fit the Asian stereotype of being good at math and science. However, her peers perceive her as being the one to consult for help because she is supposed to be good at those subjects, according to the stereotype. Carol describes how the pressure to succeed becomes a double-edged dilemma: patience enables success, yet success leads to more pressure to perform successfully.

The European American mainstream defines diversity by the ways in which it differs from the mainstream perspective. Audre Lorde (1984) names this European American mainstream perspective the *mythical norm*. She writes: "In america, this norm is usually defined as white, thin, male, young, heterosexual, christian, and financially secure. It is with this mythical norm that the trappings of power reside within this society" (p. 116). There are numerous ways in which comparison to the mythical norm succeeds in rendering the ethnic identity of individuals as something outside themselves, or objectified from the dominant European American perspective. Internalizing the objectified view of self as defined by the dominant culture creates a negative self-concept to be overcome. Even for those who consciously attempt to find out more about themselves as subjects, the search for self as subject is a struggle in the Eurocentric mainstream society of the United States.

The Opening Doors Experience: Questioning Self

An integral component of the struggle is questioning not only one's own experiences, but one's own self-concept as a result of those experiences. Symbolic interactionists assert that the ability to look back at self is defined as self-perception or self-concept (Charon, 1992, p. 78). The activities of the Opening Doors program enabled OD participants to question the constructions of self as object in order to reconstruct themselves as subjects. Charles writes in his journal how the OD program assisted his search:

> The Opening Doors experience thus far has given me the opportunity to make my own decisions and ask questions that pertain to me and will benefit me! To me, the better I know myself, the better I can assist others. This has forced me to find out what my strengths and weaknesses are and to live with them and try to improve myself!
>
> I would just like to say that I am continually learning about myself, and someday, I know I'm going to make a great professor and look back on this time of my life and say, "Those were the days of trying to find myself." (Smile)

Charles actively seeks to know himself as subject, but at the same time he actively seeks to know others also. An important part of Charles's self-knowledge is actively finding ways to better relate to others. He writes:

> To pass on something for you to think about which is related to what I just said, how can I effectively share myself with others to where we have a genuine understanding and not one where we must walk on eggshells, but one where we can feel comfortable together? I think this is somewhat difficult, but not so difficult if we are true to ourselves, and that's what I am seeking to do for myself (smile)!

Several participants talk of learning more about themselves through the *Opening Doors* experience. Jesus reveals:

> I learned a lot more than I thought I was going to about myself! That's what surprised me. I wasn't expecting to look into myself and evaluate. It was important in that it allowed us to get to know others as well.

Explaining why she trusts people, Carol grounds her belief in reflecting on herself. She relates: "Perhaps by looking at myself and my reasons for doing something. Perhaps it's not a good excuse, but if I have mine, others must have theirs too. Basically people are good." She goes on to explain what she has learned by looking at herself, through the help of role modeling from the African Americans in the group:

> I've learned in this program it's OK to be who you are. To show right, wrong, or whatever, it's OK. It's nothing to be ashamed of. I've been trying to tell myself you shouldn't be ashamed. But I wasn't comfortable with myself. I didn't have the strength to do that. But now, being with them [African Americans] I see I can be brave being with them. It takes courage being different

Karma describes a self-reflective process in learning to deal with others: "You have to think, 'Am I handling this right?' A lot of times we don't listen to ourselves enough. And when we don't follow that inside ourselves we always come up wrong. In dealing with people you need to do that."

Kelly provides an example of someone who, in reflecting, has not yet come to terms with her past. She states:

> I have a lot of feelings about my life on the reservation that I haven't wanted to deal with for a long time and that I still have some things I haven't dealt with. Some things have come to the surface but I just don't want to deal with them.

Whereas Kelly was able to realize she wasn't quite ready to deal with the past, others realized that healing only comes through self-reflection. Witness the painful self-reflection in the following journal entries. Many OD participants came with wounds that first needed to be healed before seeking to understand themselves. The process is as much an inner, personal struggle as it is an outer, social struggle. The first week was a week of pain and struggle for Debra, who writes:

> I've felt like crying since our discussion about the film, *Rise in Campus Racism.* The talk brings up feelings of pain for me. It hurts thinking about the times I've been a racist. Life was a great deal more comfortable when we weren't thinking about such hard issues. I do know that these feelings are part of the struggle. I also know that through pain I grow.

After the first step of recognizing and acknowledging the pain, Lisa writes how self-reflection and acting on that self-reflection are part of an ongoing struggle.

I am trying to work on many character defects lately. I'm feeling spiritually bereft, so I know that I am not being true to God and myself. I have to try harder to position myself to continually do and say good things about the people around me. Negative energy seems to have invaded my space!

Rochelle's entry illustrates further the ongoing nature of self-reflection. She reflects on how her perceptions and actions in one context were not appropriate in the next context. In turn, her reflection enabled her to question and critically examine her actions and thoughts in relation to others. She writes:

Whereas my view was a plus last week in a culture sharing setting, it hasn't necessarily been a positive this week. I let myself fall into the trap of setting the standard of how others express that they are being true to themselves. And my standard isn't necessarily appropriate for others. The thing is to realize that my attitude could be considered very similar to the attitudes of those who I claim judge me unfairly by their standards. Everyone expressed themselves differently, and I know I need to be more sensitive to this fact. It's almost embarrassing to admit such a thing about myself.

Sometimes I wonder if I'm wrong to feel the way I feel about certain things. Sometimes I wonder if I'm too hard on others. Perhaps I expect certain things from people, and then I feel let down when they respond differently than I expected. I know I'm wrong to do this. I know that it takes time to learn about others. I just need to have patience, and take the time to understand.

The weekly journal writings provided a structured opportunity for the critical self-reflection process to take place. At one time or another throughout the eight weeks, OD participants used the journals to focus on issues about themselves. However, the most illustrative example of the reflective process can be seen in Karma's journal entries. Each week, she addressed issues in herself, and herself in relation to others. Excerpts from four of the first five weeks demonstrate the ongoing nature of her reflections and the critical questioning that evolves from them.

Journal 1

This program at this point has given myself an awakening far beyond what I ever imagined. There is a vast amount of feelings that need to be released and focused on. The pain one feels when dealing with cognitive feelings can have a profound effect on one's thoughts and actions. This can definitely erupt and allow one to release a dramatic expression of him or herself. This feeling can be very painful, but through pain we can start to heal. The healing is essential to growth as human beings.

In order for myself to make a difference in my own life I must be able to see within my own heart, my own pain; it is only then I will be able to heal. How would one know if something is wrong if we are not able to feel the pain of our own realities? The battle is half won when one admits there has been unjust and/or harm done and with humility we are able to begin to heal. The battle is never won if one cannot admit again that there is a problem.

I have been enlightened to reiterate the respect that is needed to come to the forefront of every individual culture. We must first love our own being, and happiness you will not get from the other, happiness comes from within. When one can love him/herself then and only then one can find peace.

Journal 3

I do feel that throughout the past 3 weeks we have, as a group, we came together, drew apart and came together again. The reason not being so clear I must keep reminding myself of my purpose. My purpose as a mother, father (sometimes), sister, aunt, friend, student, mentor, creator, and most of all who I am to myself. I feel, at times, what am I doing? Where am I headed and why? The answer is not always immediate but it appears in forms that, in some cases, needs reflection. For example, last year I had no idea that the accomplishments I made were applicable to the self satisfaction I feel at this very minute. I'm wide awake, alert and am blessed with full mental capacity .

Journal 4

I have to admit I am just getting around to accepting my own people. Let me explain, for a long time I used to be very apprehensive toward Africans. Not because I did not accept them as part of my heritage. It was because they were different. They talked different, they acted different, they dressed funny and they are very aggressive people. But I realized they are wonderful, sincere people who are just different by the way they were raised [not] because they are these bad individuals. I feel I really missed out on what I could have received by way of education of their culture because I am connected in many ways and I am very proud to be or have an attachment to that lineage. . . .

Being in this group I see . . . all of us are attracted to his/her culture. I am not saying that people do not want to be together within their own cultures. I am stating that even when people are in familiar territory they separate. I am far from perfect but I am really trying to understand myself and [my] reaction to unfamiliar surroundings. Your culture is just as important to me as mine (at least I would like to grow enough to be sure of that). Life is so wonderful that we as people, as human beings, can be able to add or say that I will try to do my best to understand and appreciate those who are not like me. I will try to humble myself to the knowledge that I am ignorant with regard to others. I will be who I am and allow you to be exactly who you are without judgment or criticism. I will let you and will allow myself to be the best I can be.

Journal 5

This week unlike other weeks I have spent the majority of the time in silence and alone. This time has allowed me to focus not only on what I am doing with my project but to be with myself. I feel that I am a people person but there are times when seclusion is a must for my well being. With seclusion do you disregard your friends? And the question comes to mind, who really are your friends anyway? This is why knowing who you are is so important. Loving yourself and being who you are without fear of rejection can transcend the physical limitations you put on yourself.

Karma's journal entries illustrate the integral combination of self-knowledge coupled with self-examining questions. In Journal 1, she shares the realization of pain as the essential first step in the healing process. This realization leads to her questioning, How can one know if there is wrong if there is no ability to feel pain? In Journal 3, the questioning continues as a result of interactions with others: What am I doing? and Where am I headed? are questions posed to refocus the self to stay aligned with personal purpose and function. Journal 4 is another entry of personal realizations. Admissions of growth and ignorance of others are written in order to guide future actions with others. "I will be who I am and allow you to be exactly who you are without judgment or criticism." Journal 5 illustrates the critical questioning of self once again, elicited by personal actions taken in dealing with others. Again, the questions posed result in another self-realization: "Loving yourself and being who you are without fear of rejection can transcend the physical limitations you put on yourself."

As Pinar (1981) asserts, the "understanding of self is not narcissism; it is a precondition and a concomitant condition to the understanding of others" (p. 186). The varied aspects of self-knowledge possessed by OD participants illustrate the varying degrees in which knowledge of self as subject is a necessary prerequisite for establishing self-identity for these individuals who are ethnically diverse from the European American mainstream. Being ethnically diverse from the dominant culture creates a salience for cultural/ethnic pride as part of the identity. Ethnic culture becomes a salient aspect of identity formation because in the Eurocentric mainstream it is the feature that is not valued and in most cases is rendered invisible. Therefore, to reconstruct self as subject one must deconstruct self as object through critical reflection on the past.

Whereas the first part of the chapter described the ways of defining the grounded self, the second part of the chapter examined the importance of self-knowledge as an ongoing reconstructive process. The ongoing nature of the process is propelled by critical reflective questioning, as illustrated through Karma's journal entries. In the at-risk planning discussions, OD participants, through the critical questioning process, revealed distinct factors ethnically diverse individuals endure to keep their ethnic identities in the United States. These factors serve as the mechanisms for constructing the objective view of self, and are the barriers to be deconstructed. As Audre Lorde (1984) describes, "america's measurement of me has lain like a barrier across the realization of my own powers. It was a barrier which I had to examine and dismantle, piece by painful piece, in order to use energies fully and creatively" (p. 147). Questioning past events also facilitates questioning the self in the present. In the Opening Doors program, the assigned weekly journal writing was a structured learning activity that provided an avenue for critical questioning of self to emerge.

OD participants explicitly state the necessity to know oneself before being able to know others. To know oneself more specifically means knowing oneself as subject rather than object. This necessitates the dismantling of self as object through the process of critical self-reflection. The degree to which individuals can reflect, or deconstruct, past experiences to reconstruct the meaning of those experiences is the degree to which self as subject can be known. The better one knows oneself as subject, the more able one is to know the other as subject.

(Re)Presenting Self as Subject

*The feast of Kwanza, the African-american festival of
harvest . . . begins the day after Christmas and lasts for
7 days. There are seven principles of Kwanza, one for
each day. . . . Today is the third day of Kwanza, and the
principal for today is Ujima—collective work and
responsibility—the decision to build and maintain
ourselves and our communities together and to
recognize and solve our problems together.*

—Lorde (1984 pp. 42-43)

According to Mead, the second stage of self-development "marks the
construction by the individual of the generalized other" (Bush &
Simmons, 1990, p. 140). The social consciousness that emerges, and is
often referred to by critical, social critical, feminist, and post colonial
scholars, is similar to the concept of the generalized other in social
psychology. Mead used the term *generalized other* to describe the
culture of the group. "A generalized other is a set of rules that develops
in interaction and which individuals use to control themselves in that
interaction. . . . It is the conscience of the group that individuals are
expected to follow in interaction" (Charon, 1992, p.172).

The OD participants developed two foci of social consciousness:
in-group others and out-group others. In-group refers to the particular
ethnic group to which individuals identify and act according to the
interaction rules of that particular ethnic culture, whether it be African
American, Asian American, Native American, or Latino. Social
consciousness of the out-group refers to the individual's broadening

focus of the generalized other to include rules of interaction within their own ethnic culture as well as rules of others outside their particular ethnicity.

For ethnically diverse individuals in the United States a sense of collective responsibility to their own group must develop before they are able to broaden that responsibility to others outside their group. Hooks and West (1992) describe why this is so: "When Black people come together to celebrate and rejoice in Black critical thinking, we do so not to exclude or separate, but to participate more fully in a world community. However, we must first be able to dialogue with one another, to give that subject-to-subject recognition that is an act of resistance that is part of the decolonizing, anti-racist process" (p. 5). Referring back to Figure 2.1, after deconstructing self as object, through the process of critical self-reflection, the first stage of (re)presenting self as subject is social consciousness and active participation toward the in-group.

One of the guiding reasons OD participants were interested in graduate school was that it was an avenue for them to give back to their collective, generalized other in one sense or another. The focus of their research projects illustrates this point. Table 6.1 lists the OD participants' research projects. Motivation for topic choices is described briefly, and categorized as serving either a personal sense of self, or an interest for a social, collective sense of self.

Five OD participants chose research topics to serve a personal nature, while the other sixteen chose topics to serve the needs of others, perceiving their personal experiences within the scope of a social, collective sense of self. Previously, Karen, Kelly, Michelle, Carol, and Debra were described as examples of individuals not yet having a grounded self. Thus, it is not surprising that Table 6.1 shows these same five women as the ones pursuing personal topics. Debra states from the outset that she wants to recover her Asian self that has been alienated from internalized racism. Kelly's interest in violence is a means for her to deal with what she acknowledges as her own violent experiences. Both Michelle and Carol choose topics to enable their understandings for dealing with the immediate needs of their own children. Karen, though having no children, also focuses on her immediate family situation. Her choice to research mastery learning is a result of her sister's recent experience of failing a course with 79 percent where 80 percent mastery was required for passing.

Table 6.1. Opening Doors Research Projects

Participant	Research Title	Motivation for Topic	Focus of Giving Back
Laura	The Needs of Multicultural Adolescent Students	Personal Experience	Social *Out-group*
Lilia	Re-evaluating the Label "At-Risk"	Personal Experience	Social *Out-group*
Diane	The Academic Counselor's Role from the Native American Student Perspective	Personal Experience	Social **In-group**
Karen	Philosophical Assumptions and Implications of Mastery Learning	Family sister	Personal
Walter	Teron/Hunkpapa: A Way of Life	Personal Experience Preserve Culture	Social **In-group**
Miguel	Shaping Tomorrow's Future by Recruiting and Retaining Mexican Americans in Higher Education	Personal Experience	Social **In-group**
Tonya	Can We Bridge the Gap? Factors Relating to Credit Accrual Contributing to Migrant Dropout Rate	Personal Experience Job	Social **In-group**
Michelle	How are Children Affected Educationally, Emotionally, and Socially During Parents' Divorce?	Family children	Personal
Charles	Microtubules: A Demonstration of Their Function and Location in the Fungus Mucor Racemosus	Pre-existing Research	Social **In-group**
Carol	An Alternative: Montessori Method in Public Schools	Family children	Personal

(continued next page)

Table 6.1. *(continued)*

Celia	A Latin American Perspective on Content Illustrations: What Do U.S. Textbooks Tell Us about Central America?	Political correction of stereotypes	Social **In-group**
Rochelle	Communication between African Americans and Anglo Americans at a Predominantly White University	Personal Experience	Social **In-group**
Deirdre	A Status Report of Washington State Community Colleges' Orientation Programs	Job	Social *Out-group*
Fabian	Factors That Contribute to Code-Switching in a Bilingual Classroom	Personal Experience	Social **In-group**
Jesus	Cognition and Language Acquisition: The Bilingual Connection to Mathematics Education	Personal Experience, Pre-existing Research	Social **In-group**
Debra	What Contributes to Cultural Pride? A Two-Step Interview for Qualitative Study	Search for Ethnic Self	Personal
Lisa	Back to the Drawing Board: A Strategy for the Education of African Americans	Family children	Social **In-group**
Adrianne	Equity Diversity: Concerns of African American Students and Parents at a Predominantly White High School	Family children/Job	Social **In-group**
Karma	Cognizance of African American Success/Failure in Academia	Family children	Social **In-group**
Kelly	Students' Perceptions of Violence in School	Personal Experience	Personal
Paul	Correctional Education as a Means of Rehabilitation	Pre-existing Research	Social *Out-group*

Of the sixteen remaining topics chosen based on serving a social self, twelve chose research questions focusing on the in-group, or their own ethnicity. Four dealt with out-group issues. Whether the focus of their research study was the collective in-group or collective out-group, each social choice was predicated on the notion of giving back to a larger community as a means of constructing the future from a view of self as subject. The in-group focus was perceived as necessary in order to enhance societal change so future generations would not have to struggle with the socialization of self-as-object.

IN-GROUP RESEARCH PROJECTS

Five of the eight African Americans chose research topics as a means to specifically give back to the African American community. Each research topic resulted from critical reflection on past experiences of schooling which fostered a perception of themselves as objects. Through critical examination of past schooling experiences they diagnosed what they perceived as missing in their schooling experiences, all experiences which created a sense of self as object. As Pinar (1992) asserts, "knowledge enables us to see who we are and what the world is" (p. 233). Therefore, they constructed what they perceived as the necessary conditions to provide the missing knowledge which would enable future students to see themselves as subjects rather than objects.

Karma researched the effect of social studies curricula on fourth-grade African American males. Her "passion," as she frequently described it, is grounded in her own schooling experiences in the past, as well as those of her children's schooling experiences in the present. Of her own education, she reflects:

> I think of history and I think, I don't want to be in social studies. I would take math to get out of social studies. By being here and diving into African American issues I feel I've been cheated. I had to do social studies to graduate. But there are so many things I don't know. I feel like I didn't get anything out of it. . . . We need to understand the essence of their [African American ancestors] importance in our lives. These people made significant walks through our life and they are beautiful people. . . . And know that darker does not mean ugly. . . . It's respect. We can't change the images, but we can change what it means.

Karma takes the "lack of respect" for her own African American ethnicity she has internalized from own experiences to fuel her passion for more education so she can help future generations experience better schooling situations. She asserts:

> I'm going to push toward my master's. We need more intellectual understanding to instill power, pride, confidence, and self-esteem in our babies so they won't be thirty-two years old looking for themselves. That's a horrible place to be! Knowing that, I need to keep going. I think, Go! I need you, we need you, die trying, but do it!

Lisa's passion for educating African American youth is a direct result of her own past objectified experiences. She states: "At first my passion came from being treated badly by both Blacks and Whites out of ignorance. That energy came out in self-destructive behavior, in alcohol and drugs. But then I had children." She dedicates her energy to keeping her own children from experiencing the destructive and negative effects of low self-esteem she suffered from her internalized objectified view of self. She wants to spare her own children the suffering of the objectified view. She explains:

> I want to teach, to be there for African American children. They concentrate on males in my opinion. My son's a little genius and they're [Eurocentric school curricula] out to destroy him. I'm not going to trust those not interested in my son. My son's grown up happy, being nurtured, and next year he's going to kindergarten.

Lisa's fear is that when her son goes to kindergarten he may not experience the support she has been able to provide at home, in which he can internalize a positive African American self-concept. However, from her own experience she projects that the Eurocentric curriculum in schools will objectify her son's sense of self as it did her own. Lisa wants her son and other African American children to have the role models in their schooling she did not have. "I never thought I could go to college," she explains. "I'm thirty-three and I always thought I was too Black to go." Thus, Lisa views her individual efforts as an integral part of a larger collective self identified in her African American community, her generalized other.

Charles shares Lisa's and Karma's goals of giving back to the African American community. However, where Karma and Lisa aspire to teach in order to actively contribute to their collective selves, Charles looks for ways to be an African American leader through his scientific research. He states:

> Last year proved to be better for me, because of the fact that we began to open up more to one another, we studied more together, and as a result we felt more comfortable being there. This education program has been helpful for me. I used to think that lab is jail and I am missing part of my life. When do I get to the people part of this? I'm a people person and this is teaching me a social use for my discipline as a scientist, and now I can see how important I am as a person of color in the sciences and what I can give to other people of color.

Walter and Diane perceive themselves as part of the larger Native American collective self. Walter came to the OD program with intentions of doing research to serve Native Americans. He relates:

> The teachers didn't understand us as Indian people. I looked at a school where they said, Okay, we'll leave it up to you as teachers to incorporate their [Native American] culture into their everyday studies. And they [European American teachers] didn't. Because it was left up to them they kind of swept it under the rug. But I figure with this program I would write a research paper and accompany that with lesson plans so that when you were doing a lesson about history, or geography, or science you could take part of it and use it.

In discussing his research topic, Walter explains: "It is something I always wanted to do. It's my culture, my background. I've been through all the ceremonies. I speak the language. So I can see a lot of mistakes others don't." He continues to reflect on how his personal schooling experiences influence his interests now, in the present. He retells me the same story he told during the at-risk planning session (recounted in the previous chapter), about the continuing struggle with those who do not know the language, the ones who are attempting to write the information about Indians, and are causing misinterpretations.

Though Diane does not share Walter's trials of losing a first language, she perceives her capability to give back to her Native American collective self in a different way. She writes,

> Ever since junior high school, I knew that I wanted to be part of the educational system. It wasn't until I started college did I decide that I wanted to be a teacher. I may come up with several different reasons why I chose to pursue the teaching profession, but I only have one. In today's society, the young [Native American] people are not taken seriously. Consequently, they are not given the support or confidence to achieve anything. I find this true on the reservation. My purpose in education is to instill confidence and trust in the students. I don't want to sound like I want to save the day and bring these students out of the closet. For the most part, young students are hopeful. As they grow older and encounter different teaching styles, their perception of learning is affected. Many times these students are affected in a negative way. What I want to do, in a subtle way, is be a positive impact.

Miguel explains that his reason for wanting to be a teacher stems from his personal search for positive ethnic role models in school. He says: "That's why I'm going back to the classroom, knowing they need positive role models and being proud of who they are."

Fabian's own struggle with English as a second language provides the impetus for his research project on code switching. His choice is based not only on his own past experience learning English in the United States, but also on a recent experience in his efforts to help others. He explains:

> When I was doing my student teaching one of my master teachers discouraged me from speaking Spanish and English within a sentence or phrase. She felt that it was more advantageous for the student to start and finish a sentence with the same language. I don't see anything wrong by code switching, especially if I'm conversing with a friend that speaks and understand both languages. Most of my friends I grew up with are educated and they use code switching a lot. I think code switching goes hand in hand with the environment one grows up in. In Texas, where I grew up, many "Texanos" or Chicanos use code switching. Code switching is part of their language. They call it Spanglish. As a bilingual teacher, I will not discourage my

students from speaking "Spanglish" but I will make them aware that in all Spanish-speaking countries and in some parts of the United States, people will not understand them if they combine or switch from Spanish to English.

For these individuals, their actions in the *present* (immediate research project in Opening Doors) are directed toward personal aspirations of making social change in the *future*. However, the motivation for change in the future is grounded in critical examination of the *past*. The past experiences of internalizing the objective self provided from the dominant European American perspective necessitates the social interaction and consequent personal action for the collective in-group. Interaction for and with the in-group is crucial for acting toward self and toward others as subject. The generalized other, the rules and perspectives by which actions are guided, have been dominated by the Eurocentric perspective of self as object. Therefore, in order to change the governing rules of action and interaction to self as subject, it is necessary for the individual to change who is viewed as the generalized other. For these individuals, the salient group of generalized other becomes the in-group of their own ethnicity.

OUT-GROUP RESEARCH PROJECTS

The majority of OD participants share a perspective of a collective self primarily focused within their individual ethnic groupings. Some have a view of collective self that broadens the in-group perspective of collectivity which includes those outside their own ethnicity. Lilia expresses this all-inclusive view of giving back to the out-group generalized other when she writes:

> I think about the hundreds of ideas and dreams that never came to be because of the self-confidence that's been stolen. This is why I've made it my responsibility to always encourage young and old to be the best they can be and that the sky's the limit, regardless of race and gender.

Laura also perceives her aspiration for the future as serving the collective self of all. As an education major, she perceives her teaching role as a way to bring multicultural understandings about *all* ethnic groupings to *all* students. Laura exhibits her active involvement in multicultural education in the way she responds to her group (including Charles, Paul and Kelly) in discussing *The Rise of College Campus Racism* video:

> Okay, so we do see a problem with that [African American heroes being left out of the Northern European curriculum]. We all know there's a problem in education with history. Then, I think the next step is looking for the solution. I'm encouraged that I do see the solution in future educators. We are going to be educators. We are sensitive to multicultural issues and we're going to change it. For instance, when I went into my student teaching I told my master teacher I would teach ancient Black history. I would teach ancient India and China, and I'm going to let the students know different perspectives of historical happenings.

Deirdre also seeks to disrupt the status quo of the dominant Eurocentric perspective of the past (and present) in order to facilitate the needs of All students in the future. She states:

> I do not want to become like the "America" that I know, the one that my classmates have encountered, and the one that I grew up in. The experiences of those in OD have reinforced the commitment that I have made to myself—to effect change where I can and to become a voice for those who might not be able, for whatever reason, to speak for themselves. I do not want to become part of the status quo or be comfortable with it. I want to acquire the tools I will need to be "credible," and that is what I will learn more of here.

Deirdre recognizes that seeking education today for herself as an individual is the first action needed to create social change for the future. She relates.

> With each dose of power [education] that I receive, I feel the desire to extend it to those I touch and can touch on a daily or less frequent basis. "Those" includes my family, friends, colleagues, and those students I currently serve as well as those in the future.

BUILDING BRIDGES BETWEEN IN-GROUP
AND OUT-GROUP

Individuals whose focus is primarily the generalized in-group collectivity do not necessarily exclude the out-group. However, focus on the in-group generalized other suggests a necessary progression in (re)presenting self as subject before being able to (re)present self as subject to the generalized other of the out-group. In other words, ethnically diverse individuals who have constructed a concept of self as object from internalizing the social rules, norms, and values of the Eurocentric dominant society must refocus their sense of generalized other toward their in-group in order to reconstruct a concept of self as subject. They have already internalized the norms of the dominant out-group, and those norms have resulted in internalized self-hatred and anger for not being able to match the "mythical norm," as Audre Lorde (1984) names it. This hate and anger directed toward self as object is then projected into interactions with others, often resulting in conflict. Therefore, in order to better understand and interact with others as subjects, individuals must first learn to respect and value themselves so that they may come to value others.

One example of the importance of perceiving the in-group as the generalized other in order to further relationships and understandings with the out-group is Adrianne's view of her research. Even though Adrianne's research and personal commitment are focused on her African American in-group, she perceives her in-group focus as an active commitment to further relationships and understandings between her African American in-group and the broader, out-group community of all students in the education system. She explains:

> Until that day when equality prevails throughout our society, our struggle will continue. Until the day of Martin Luther King Jr's Dream, our challenge as educators is to work toward promoting the Dream. Do we have equal opportunity for all of our students in the school environment? In the school curriculum? In our expectations that all students can learn?
>
> I am encouraged by the desire and commitment of those who are involved in the Opening Doors program to be agents of change. We are the warriors needed to infuse a new vaccine into a decaying school system. Our battle is against Eurocentric school systems which are not only robbing students of color, but Anglo students of

knowledge of each other which will help us to get along in a global multi-culturalistic/ethnic society. We should be teaching our students to be citizens of the world, not just citizens of the United States.

The focus toward the in-group is not an act of exclusion, but rather an act of democratic inclusion of those who have been historically excluded and rendered invisible in the Eurocentric school system. In-group consciousness gives voice to the silenced and visibility to the invisible.

Celia suggests a perspective similar to Adrianne's, focusing on the betterment of all individuals when she writes: "We must remember where we are and what we have, reflect and act accordingly to change the world and make it a better place for everyone and not just a few privileged people." Celia's academic background is political science rather than education. The research she chose was a content analysis of Latin American images portrayed in social studies textbooks. She relates how her research, which focuses on Latin America, is an effort to assist all individuals:

> Doing this I'll be able to be more sensitive to every other ethnicity. I'll probably be able to tell people what I find, and it will be useful to show we must be on guard. What we read is not always the truth. We need to read between the lines.

Learning more about oneself is a beginning step toward learning more about and understanding others, which is the essence of being multicultural. The more self-knowledge we acquire, and the more consciously explicit we make this knowledge, the more we are able to see ourselves in others. Audre Lorde (1984) describes this process: "When we define ourselves, when I define myself, the place in which I am like you and the place in which I am not like you, I'm not excluding you from the joining—I'm broadening the joining" (p. 10). The more we can see ourselves in others, the more able we are to interact out of value of and respect for others. Walter has a clear notion of interconnectedness between self and others. He states:

> I came to a conclusion we're all related whether we like it or not. Everything in this universe is related one way or another. The plants are here for a reason. The sun is shining for a reason. So the sooner we accept that and live by that, the sooner we can get along.

Charles also values and acknowledges the interconnectedness between self and others. Though he repeatedly states his personal aspiration is to give back to the African American community, Charles also actively seeks to know and understand the cultures of other people because he believes human beings are interrelated. He asserts:

> I believe that we are here for a purpose and that everything we as humans do is interrelated to others and our surroundings. For example, if a particular group of people is hurting then that hurt is transferred and affects those in the surrounding area in one way or the other. Either the pain is felt by others or it is others who are inflicting the pain. All things are tied together and I believe that it is imperative that we collectively cooperate and collaborate to make our existence long lasting. Our future depends on us working together to achieve common and different goals.

As educators and as people of color we must find ways to collectively work together yet still keep our individuality. We must allow ourselves to feel comfortable when we associate with those of our own culture and not let the majority culture influence our feelings and thoughts when they choose to label us as separatists, militants, and isolationists. We must also allow ourselves to freely experience and enjoy other cultures and not allow our own culture to hinder us from learning and understanding others. With a better understanding of others, much more improvement in today's race relations will be accomplished.

Charles exemplifies someone with the perceptions and actions of being multicultural. This includes a process beginning with knowledge of self. Next in the process is knowledge of self in relation to others. This social consciousness of self includes the responsibility to generalized others within the same ethnic grouping (in-group) and awareness of the interconnectedness of the in-group to the out-group.

Developing an in-group social consciousness is a necessary step toward developing a social consciousness of the out-group, a perspective of subject to subject interactions. An in-group social consciousness must be developed to enable the individual to dismantle the objectified self before reconstructing self as subject. Efforts of ethnically diverse individuals within the dominant European American culture to seek out socializing situations among their own ethnic in-group must be conscious and deliberate. The deliberate actions grounded in a particular view of self and perspective of reality will be actions toward the particular view of the individual. All actions enable or inhibit the perspective of one over the perspective of another; therefore, all actions are political.

CHAPTER 7

Lived Truth and Distorted Honesty

Our words are not without meaning. They are an action.
—hooks (1989, p. 28)

Thus far, we have viewed the self from the individual's personal meaning-making construction. As stated in Chapter 6, the social self remains the individual's own view of his or her social self. Now our discussion moves to the ways in which individuals choose to act on constructions of their personal and social selves, as well as the results of individual actions from the view of the other. In Mead's terms, this chapter focuses on the Actor: the social self (or "me") as it acts toward the "I," the impulsive, spontaneous self unsocialized by society (Charon, 1992, p. 69). Blumer (1953) describes the interaction of social selves as "a moving process in which the participants note and gauge each other's actions, where they organize their action in relation to one another, and where they inhibit themselves, encourage themselves, and guide themselves as action unfolds over time" (p. 197). How the Opening Doors participants noted and gauged one another's actions is our focus.

All actions of the individual, including talk, are defined here as political actions. Political in this sense does not refer to government, but to a feminist view of one's own underlying beliefs, perspectives, and intentions and to their interpretations of others' actions. As feminist theory suggests, all individual choices of what to say and do, as well as the intentions motivating the action, support a particular view or perspective of the individual's constructed reality and the place of the constructed self within that reality. In this way, all action is political.

157

Choices to act, not to act, or how to act are decided from the individual's perspective of his or her grounded self.

LIVING AND LEARNING DIVERSITY

When asked to name the most important thing learned from the OD experience, thirteen participants answered they learned much about other cultures, and the differences among members of their own ethnic cultures. However, these understandings were not reached without social conflict and personal struggle. As Rochelle writes, "I've made some good relationships. But I've also learned that it takes time to do this. We, as people of color, are VERY diverse. Our differences are to be appreciated and respected. Sometimes this is easier said than done."

Lilia adds to Rochelle's observations that this OD experience was another reminder of the difficulties that arise when faced with differences. She states:

> We tend to think as minorities it's all going to be easier coming together. We tend to forget the differences. This was another reminder. Just because we're all minorities doesn't mean we're the same. . . . As minorities we tend to be ignorant of each other. We tend to feel our experience is the experience and everyone else's should be like mine. But if you're not as sensitive to what the Anglos have done then you haven't felt it the way I have.

The two major learning events of the first week, the autobiography sharing and the video discussion of racism, revealed a tension between two forces that continued throughout the remainder of the program. The heightened tension was the balancing between the personal self and the social self. The autobiography sharing provided an avenue for individuals to voice their personal, lived experiences. However, as each participant took a turn to share personal histories, the others were asked only to listen, watch, and observe from a distance. No interaction followed; no cooperation was required; no differing opinions needed to be worked to consensus. One view prevailed, and rightly so, since it was the individual's self-portrait that was the major concern. However, *The Rise of College Campus Racism* video discussion, as well as the remaining learning events (small group presentations, scenario discussion, Behind Closed Doors, and at-risk planning session), required that multiple voices and opinions be shared. Interpersonal interaction was necessary. Social interaction and negotiation strategies needed employment.

The difference between the autobiography activity and the learning events that followed can be compared to the difference between one merely watching a movie or play on stage and being the actor who must create the performance. The viewer sits safely in his or her seat, watching, perhaps agreeing or disagreeing with what takes place on stage, but still remains relatively passive, taking in the presentation on the screen or the stage. The viewing experience remains a singular, personal process. The actor, on the other hand, must interact, cooperate, and coordinate with others to create the performance. The actor socially interacts with others, negotiates by necessity, and sometimes compromises. The viewer need not negotiate. Whatever meaning he or she creates remains a personal construction. The actor, however, must actively construct his or her performance in tandem with others.

As individuals, each of the Opening Doors participants agreed that mutual respect of diverse perspectives and providing a place for those voices to be expressed was essential to broadening understanding of themselves and others. However, the personal desire for equal access for all views becomes compromised and even threatened when others view a particular perspective as intrusive or offensive. Once individuals voice diverse perspectives, which by definition will pose conflict, a new challenge arises. How might respect for others' views be maintained even while one's own views are threatened with misunderstanding, misinterpretation, or even outright disapproval or disagreement? Celebration of diversity from a spectator's view came easily while listening to autobiographies of personal struggles and triumphs. The willingness to act with a similar magnanimity was not as quick to surface when interpersonal interactions resulted in disagreement and discomfort.

When only minimal conflict from interpersonal interaction occurs, individuals may attain the personal consciousness of the grounded self as well as the social consciousness of self in relation to others. OD participants celebrated all efforts equally as individuals shared their autobiographical experiences and their personal passions. No one questioned that Lisa sought to give back to the diaspora by concentrating on including the African American history left out of traditional curricula. No one questioned Adrianne's search for her historical legacy to pass on to her own children. Debra, who came to heal her own internalized racism through being in a group of people of color, received sympathy and compassion. OD participants treated each person's individuality with respect. The group celebrated the common bond of their differences—from a distance. However, the celebration became harder to maintain once individuals engaged in interpersonal interactions to express and advocate from social consciousness. The Behind Closed Doors and scenario learning events best illustrate the conflict created as personal knowledge grew into social consciousness and resulted in statements of political action.

Behind Closed Doors, Session 1

Bell hooks (1990) asserts that the academic field of cultural studies is

> rapidly becoming one of the few locations in the academy where there is the possibility of inter-racial and cross-cultural discussion. Usually scholars in the academy resist engagement in dialogues with diverse groups where there may be critical contestation, interrogation, and confrontation. (p. 125)

The intended structure of the Behind Closed Doors (BCD) learning event was to be a place where "dialogues of critical contestation, interrogation, and confrontation" could be voiced. Even though Celeste explained on the first day that these sessions were "a time to talk with people that you trust. . . a place for issues that don't have a place to be shared, without worrying about who says what," not all OD participants attending the actual events left the first session with strong feelings of trust.

The first BCD session, during week two, did not exhibit any interrogating, contesting, or confronting dialogue. Most of the discussion concerned the clarification of procedural and managerial issues within the program (such as reviewing directions and due dates of assignments). Participants were more concerned about asking about the program (object) than asking about the people (subject) involved in the program. Participants engaged in little to no interpersonal interaction. Only when Karma voiced her irritation about what she considered the "immature behavior" of another individual in the group was the objective distancing of discussion on programmatic issues broken. However, Karma only alluded to the behavior and the individual, not mentioning any names or the specific events. Therefore, several participants left not knowing whether they were the ones to whom she was referring.

Despite Karma's attempt at moving the discussion away from programmatic issues to interpersonal ones, some OD participants interpreted the lack of interpersonal discussion in the open forum as a lack of honesty on the part of the others. This lack of honesty from the group disturbed Lisa and Rochelle in particular. Lisa writes:

> I can't seem to get away from the thought that many people are here for everything except the learning experience (again, I know I judge harshly), and I say this because I don't sense a very high degree of honesty, and support. Our first *Behind Closed Doors* session to me, was a farce! I've heard so many complaints and petty gripes, and even some real and justified questions. But somehow, none of these issues came forth. Instead we talked about people being homesick and someone [referring to Karma's comment] had the nerve to broach someone else's personal problems before the group (that was totally out of order), and yet not say one word about herself.

The BCD sessions affected Rochelle the most. Though Rochelle was "for the record, generally disappointed in the Behind Closed Doors experience," her reflections of the experience, written in her weekly journal entries, illustrate self-reflection, critical reflection, and the tension of balancing the needs of her personal self with the needs of accommodating her social self. After her disappointment with the first session, she writes:

> I sensed that everyone wasn't being honest about how *they* perceived experiences. It's not that there always had to be a complaint, but everything isn't always rosy, as some lead us to believe. For example, small group work is taxing by nature. It's hard to reach consensus on what to do, and to get colleagues to understand ideas that you're trying to convey when they have ideas of their own. It's natural to get frustrated or to have some conflicts. But in *Behind Closed Doors*, all groups were supposedly in total accordance....NOT! Can we just be up front and straight for a minute? I mean, truthfully, it was refreshing to hear Karma's account of her experience to date. She told the well-rounded truth! I'll admit that her comments made me step outside myself and examine my behavior over the last week. I seriously wondered if I was guilty of the immaturity that irritated her.

But, at least it made me reflect and think! Isn't that what *Behind Closed Doors* is all about? Instead, it resembled an evening class session. I felt as if I should've brought my pen and notebook. I was disappointed. I question how much I can really learn about someone who is different than me if they aren't honest about who they are [and]what they think and feel. We'll never see that happen if people continue to say and do what they think is "most acceptable" or "good," regardless of their true feelings. I have been guilty of calling such behavior "White." Now I'm not so sure that's accurate. I have to be more careful of such labels.

Obviously, Lisa and Rochelle have differing views about the comment raised by Karma during the session. Lisa perceived Karma's comment as out of line, while Rochelle perceived the comment as the only fresh voice of honesty, an impetus for critical self-reflection on her own actions as well as an indication of how others perceived her actions. Jesus and Tonya add two more perceptions of Karma's comment. Jesus writes about his need for clarification of the comment:

> I was also bothered by the fact that Karma thought that some of us were not acting like adults. I think everyone in the room could not help but think whether it was them she was talking about. I know others feel the same way, and it would be nice to get a further explanation in order to solve the problem, if in fact there is a problem.

Whereas Jesus looked for someone else to settle the confusion, Tonya initiated her own action to settle the confusion by going to the source:

> I was a bit confused about some of Karma's comments during our *Behind Closed Doors* session. She mentioned something to the effect of growing up and behaving like adults not like children, which made me examine myself and the others I have been around. Yet I was unable to make a connection. How could anyone be acting childish and I not notice it? So I just asked her about it and she clarified for me. I wanted to address it at the session, but did not feel comfortable doing so right then and there.

Behind Closed Doors, Session 2

The second Behind Closed Doors session took place the fourth week.
Those who found no benefit from the first BCD session chose to use
the time to work in the library on their research projects. Others,
disappointed with the first session, came with a mission to make this
session more beneficial to their personal needs, or promote what was
termed a "deeper" conversation (deeper meaning discussing and
debating interpersonal issues that affected their personal rather than
social lives). Topics of conversation that night centered around
controversial and salient issues of ethnic identity. The two primary
topics were interracial dating and labeling (who uses labels, who
creates them, the political and personal connotations of labels, and
personal meaning constructed from labels). The scheduled one-hour
session dispersed two and a half hours later.

Heated, pointed, and intense talk filled the room. Acting on her
personal need to know, Michelle directly pointed her questions of why
Black men date White women to Paul, Charles, and Wes, the African
American males in the room. The Latino group members (including
Laura, Lilia, Miguel, Tonya, Jesus, Celia, and Fabian) each shared their
views of the labels and their differing connotations. Celia gave a
historical analysis of why *Latina* is more appropriate for her and why it
is offensive when others assume she is Mexican. Tonya and Jesus
counter that labels didn't make that much difference. Miguel suggests
that he agrees with Tonya and Jesus when he states, "I don't care what
you call me, you can call me Miguel." Fabian added that even though
he was born in Mexico, which makes him a Mexican American, he
identifies more with the Chicano culture of the United States than the
Mexican culture of Mexico.

In the midst of the serious and heated fray about labels and their
meanings, someone turned to Walter, who was sitting silently during
the discussion, and asked, "What do you want to be called?" Not
changing his relaxed posture, sitting back in his chair with his arms
folded across his chest, he hesitated a moment, then very flatly stated,
"You can call me Chief!" Everyone in the room, including Walter
himself, broke out laughing. The next morning, Walter explained to me
that his comment was a deliberate action to lighten the atmosphere that
he perceived had become too heated.

The OD participants attending the second BCD session left with
mixed reactions. Those who came into the program with expectations

of being able to share and discuss important personal issues with other people of color (Lisa, Karma, Rochelle, Charles, Michelle, and Celia in particular) left this discussion with a sigh of relief and exhilaration. Finally, they felt that people were being "honest" and revealing their "true selves," as well as offering a learning experience. The participants who were the most vocal during the discussion (Rochelle, Charles, Lisa, Michelle, and Celia) and the most animate in their talk and actions during the session were also the ones most inspired by the interaction.

The following journal entries from Rochelle, Charles, Lisa, Michelle, and Celia illustrate how these individuals view the importance of political action, of acting on their beliefs and convictions, and encouraging others to do the same. They argue that only through individual action and willingness to act on their personal passions can understanding and celebration of differences be reached. They recognize that it is not only beneficial but imperative for individuals to act on their own convictions within a social, public setting to achieve subject to subject understanding. Only through "engagement in dialogues with diverse groups where there may be critical contestation, interrogation, and confrontation" will change result.

ROCHELLE: My sincerest thanks goes out to all of those who attended the last "BCD"!!!!!!! It's about time that we opened up and shared ourselves with one another. I was beginning to seriously doubt that it would ever happen with this group. . . . I learned so much! I really appreciate the opportunity I was given by everyone who participated to see other points of view. Only then can we begin to grow together, genuinely respect each other, and most importantly, CELEBRATE THE DIFFERENCES!

The thing I want to stress is that what took place at BCD was positive. My fear is that some of us may be turned off by the expression of different opinions or points of view. This is confusing to me because it contradicts what (I think) we all advocated for in the beginning of OD . . . the right to be ourselves, whatever that entails. It doesn't mean that we should, or that we do, belittle that which is different. Don't we view America as a "Salad Bowl" with all ingredients providing a variety of unique flavors, as opposed to a "Melting Pot" where everyone is the same? This isn't to say that we don't have similarities, too. We have several! But, each of us is unique because of our culture and individuality. It is our right to be that way . . . rich with culture and individuality, as long as we are open to others claiming that right for themselves as well. . . . I just want to reiterate that I think the OD group is richer for having shared and learned about each other, and I look forward to more of the same in the future!

CHARLES: Some exciting things have happened! The main thing was *Behind Closed Doors*. Finally, we were able to get into some deep conversation about each of our cultures, and the idea of multiculturalism. To me, this discussion was one of the most exciting learning experiences that I've had during the OD program. It felt really good to see what other people go through, feel, and how they responded to different issues we discussed during *Behind Closed Doors*. I think that it was good for the group to engage in this type of discussion because we began to discuss the issues which we so often discuss amongst those in our own cultures, with others. Through this type of interaction, change will come about in the future.

MICHELLE: "Emancipate yourself from mental slavery, none but ourselves can free our mind." The words of the late Robert Nesta Marley were the thoughts that kept going through my mind, since the discussion at the *Behind Closed Doors*, Wednesday evening.

LISA: This has been an interesting week mainly because of the last *Behind Closed Doors* session. Here it is, we're four weeks into the program and it wasn't until this past Wednesday night that I was able to feel a little close to the people that have occupied much of my life lately.

Some felt that it was a negative experience, but I wonder how they expect to get to know who people are if they don't get a good sense of their passions.

I noticed a closeness the next day. Everyone seemed content with what had been discussed. I hope that level of honesty is prevalent in all the sessions to come.

CELIA: I honestly believe, that this was the most honest discussion we have had as a group together. There were many topics covered and all of them were of great importance. I have to say that I was very glad that we touched upon the topic of labeling. Labels happen to form our everyday lives. Everywhere we go we have to say what our names are, what we are and what we represent. There are always those questions such as, *What are you? What ethnicity are you? Where are you from originally?* and so on. Therefore I was glad that we talked about this as a whole group. Not only that, but I was able to speak my mind and at least try to explain my views about how I call myself and my culture. The labels, Hispanic, Latina/o, Chicana/o, Mexican and so forth. I really hope I was able to get my point across. On other topics that we covered, I really liked our discussion on racism and the different types of this human phenomenon we have to face almost every day as a people of color. I think it helped in the sense that we are aware that, if not racism, a type of discrimination occurs within our own cultures.

Not all OD participants shared the view of the need for confrontation to act politically as expressed by Rochelle, Charles, Lisa, Michelle, and Celia. As with other interpersonal situations, the place where the right to be oneself and where that individual right impinges or infringes on others is a very fine line to discern. Paul, in particular, felt personally challenged concerning the issue of interracial dating. He writes:

On the subject of interracial dating . . . I feel as if I am the bad person when it comes to dating White women. At least it seems to be like that in the eyes of Black women. First off, I don't feel I should have to defend myself for dating White women. In fact, I have dated Black and Asian women also. I must agree that there is a problem with Black men marrying or dating White women for reasons other than love. . . . For me I know a lot about both sides of the Black/White relationship. And I do not see it as a color thing, its a caring and love thing, and we should all understand that. So, before people put labels on Black men for dating White women, they should think about why they are doing it, and it's not always negative. As for me, I don't think so, because every Black woman I see is a reflection of my mother in a cultural sense and I love her and would not do a thing to hurt her.

Other OD participants attending the second BCD session observed and learned from the animated interactions. Diane is one who viewed the gesturing, raised voices and intensity of emotions exhibited by others, yet said nothing herself. Even though she did not verbally participate in the discussion, she formed an interpretation of the others' actions in her journal.

The *Behind Closed Doors* session was pretty interesting. It's good that people want to talk to each other and I'm glad that we have that opportunity. To me, it seems we do a lot of talking in the dining hall. Maybe the conversations don't get as heated as *Behind Closed Doors*, but the issues are there. . . . I felt like a lot of arguing was going on for no apparent reason and nothing was being solved. Sometimes I felt that no one was being heard.

While Diane perceived the session as heated and filled with unproductive argument, Walter, who tried to lessen the tension in the air through his "You can call me Chief!" comment, writes about how he perceived the behavior displayed as evidence of insecurity and immaturity:

The event that amazed me the most was *"Crashing Behind Closed Doors."* Some of the issues that were brought up were a few that really reflected insecurity and immaturity. What people do within their personal life should not be everyone's concern. The issue of dating people from another race won it all. I think it's a personal choice! We should broaden our own horizons so we can understand these issues instead of viewing things with tunnel vision. I truly feel that we could use this period wisely by planning and talking about issues that will benefit *Opening Doors* in a positive way.

Walter was in the classroom early with me the following morning, and I took the opportunity to ask him what he thought of the events the night before. After looking around to see that no one else was in the room, he recounted his observations that most of the discussion resulted from individuals lacking a grounded self. He interpreted the conflicts as a result of personal insecurities, of not knowing who they are. "If I don't know who I am by now," he said, pointing to his chest and shaking his head, "all those labels are a result of not knowing who I am, inside here." Walter based his interpretation on his religious training, which had taught him that the four races were put here at the same time—all equal—all brothers.

Other participants responded less emotionally and more academically, assuming a matter-of-fact perspective on learning from the views expressed in the BCD session. Karma acknowledged being able to reflect on her own personal limitations and having the opportunity for personal growth through sociopolitical interactions when she wrote,

I am so narrow-minded at times it is hard for me to believe I am actually saying this. I had no idea that Mexicans, Mexican Americans, Chicanos, Hispanics, Puerto Ricans and all Spanish speaking people had a line (invisible as it may seem) to separate themselves from each other. I guess I am so wrapped up in the African American plight that I fail to see what goes on in the world around me, it not being my immediate space. Growth is a wonderful thing to do.

Karma, an African American, learned something new about Latinos during the controversy, and Miguel, a "U.S.-born Mexican," learned more about how African American views differed from his own. Miguel writes:

The topic of what to call each other was one that has been battled many times in the Chicano/Hispanic student center. I don't mind what people call me. Mexicano, Hispanic, Mexican American, etc. But what does bother me is when people are nasty about what you call them out of ignorance. What I mean by that is that it is very hard to tell a Latina. . . from a Hispanic. I don't feel that person should get mad or upset just because I could not tell them apart. That person should politely correct me. I would do the same. The second topic of interracial relationship during dating or marriages. I noticed that it is a lot hotter . . . subject between African Americans than it is between Mexicans. I guess I felt that the subject of love was left out. However, I didn't like the fact that it sounded like some African American males just used White women. Hot topic!

These varied journal entries in response to the second BCD session illustrate the interpersonal conflicts that emerge when individuals act politically from the personal self. When individuals act toward different referent groups (in-group or out-group) as their generalized other, the political action of one individual often conflicts with the amount, degree, or intensity of political action by others. Rochelle, Charles, Lisa, Michelle, and Celia represent individual selves who actively seek interpersonal engagements to enable their understanding of others. Diane and Walter appreciate individual differences in a subtle way, but do not go looking for it. Karma and Miguel both perceive the experience as a learning one: learning more about themselves as they learn about others. Left out are the voices of those who felt threatened, intimidated, and offended by the whole affair, and were unwilling to write about it or talk openly in the social forum of the classroom.

For Rochelle, the excitement and exhilaration of a good discussion became clouded by hesitation and fear of offending after personal reactions from the second session were shared with others. In her journal the fifth week, Rochelle discussed how her personal reflection on her actions, and the meanings others placed on those actions, lead to this change in attitude:

Well, this week I don't have much to say (I think). The reason for this is that it seems that every time I do say something, there is *someone* who finds it offensive. It is not my intention to do so, but it seems inevitable. So I am choosing to keep my thoughts, feelings, opinions, or whatever, to myself. Let me explain.

Last week, we had a *Behind Closed Doors* session that I found quite invigorating. I felt that we, as a group, learned some things about each other that perhaps we hadn't thought about before. We debated and argued and challenged ourselves to examine what's inside of us (by the way, through my research, I have learned that "debate" and "argument" have different connotations in various cultures. This could explain why most of us African-Americans considered this a positive thing, while numerous other individuals thought very negatively of it). I honestly enjoyed it. . . . The point is that what I took as a good experience, was offensive to someone else. And I looked back at the whole thing and realized that someone may always be hurt or feel wronged. This realization really disturbed me! I haven't just experienced this in OD or BCD, it happens everyday outside of our workshop, as well. . . . The problem is that we can't understand each other's pain. If you don't believe that someone's pain is valid, then don't you think you will continue to hurt them over and over again? If you belittle someone else's feelings, how can you say that you respect or value them? All you can do is accept their feelings, and do your part to stop causing them pain. We sometimes even experience this reality with our own people, devaluing what we have inside. I think it's even more devastating when it comes from your own people. Yet, this is something we *demand* from Anglo-Americans everyday. "Don't tell me my pain is *not justified!* Instead, do your part to make it better!"

All of this goes to say that I have decided that I don't want to offend my colleagues in this way, and I apologize if I have offended someone. But, I can't apologize for how I feel because that is denying myself to please someone else. That is a direct contradiction to my belief that our individuality is important. I wonder if I should stop attending *Behind Closed Doors* and focus my "debate tendencies" on informal discussions with other interested parties instead. This way, *Behind Closed Doors* can be what it needs to be for others without disappointing me. On a more personal level, I wonder how this will pan out with people I encounter everyday. I can't withdraw from the world so as to not hurt anyone without denying anything to myself! I don't know. This is something I've battled with since we discussed last week's journals.

Rochelle's journal entry clearly illustrates the tension that arises between the personal self and social self. She reflects on her personal need to speak her perceptions, yet understands that her need may offend others. Rochelle also is consciously aware of cultural style differences that may account for varied interpretations of events. By analyzing her own actions, and others' responses to her actions, Rochelle comes to understand that offending one while voicing the perspective of another will inevitably offend or hurt someone. However, she also comes to realize that the pain of conflict is not something to be avoided, but voiced and worked through to enable taking the role of the other. Her statement that the problem is we cannot understand each other's pain is her way of explaining that if one cannot role take, one is unable to view the other subject to subject. Rochelle's actions, and the responses her actions elicited from others, in the present context of Opening Doors, enabled her to critically reflect, generalizing this specific interaction to implications for other life situations.

Celeste was absent the fifth week, and the third BCD session took place week six, after she returned. Because Celeste's absence and the scenario activity, which took place while she was absent, directly influenced the events of the third BCD session, it is important to describe the interactions resulting from the scenario activity before describing the third BCD session.

Scenarios

The scenario discussions took place the fifth week of the program when Celeste had to be out of town. Before she left, the staff (Celeste, Kristy, Wes, and myself) discussed responsibilities during her absence. Because neither Kristy nor Wes had teaching experience, the staff agreed that I would lead the class sessions, while Kristy and Wes would respond to journals and transcribe tapes. In the scenario activity (described in more depth in Chapter 3), each group was given a different education scenario to read, and asked to record responses to the questions provided and to discuss their individual responses. Then, each small group reported their responses and discussion to the whole group. During the small group discussions it was apparent from the loud voices and dramatic gestures that the African American table (including Deirdre, Michelle, Karma, and Lisa, who was sitting on the side, not participating) was in conflict. Specifically, the conflict occurred between Michelle and Deirdre, who could not agree on their clashing interpretations of the intent of the exercise. It ended in a standoff with Deirdre saying, "I'm not going to say anything because my opinion isn't being heard anyway!" The conflict, left unresolved between the individuals, caused pain and frustration between the African American women. However, for Michelle, the experience also served as an impetus for self-reflection. She writes:

> Is it only my thinking, or only my observation, but are we as Black people destined to tear each other down every chance we get or in any manner we see fit? Is it because we were slaves in the early centuries? Or is it because even today in Africa, Blacks are being used to fight and kill their own people? After all, the Chinese were also slaves then, and still today don't regard human rights for their own people. In this small group, it happens ever so often, we try to tear each other down with our tongues, and I don't mean speaking about something you are against. We don't respect each other's opinions, (in some cases don't respect the other person), and sometimes feel we are so right, we have to put down others' opinions in order to make our own look good. I am also aware that other ethnic groups, within this group, may not voice their opinion truthfully, for fear of offending one another. Or, are they voicing their opinions, but so tactfully that it is not offensive to anyone?

Literally I'm hurting inside. I understand the situation up to a point, that maybe because we were oppressed and in some ways still are, we may take it out on our own people subconsciously. I will be trying to correct MY ways, and can only hope, that others will see a need to correct their own ways.

The session also caused a conflict for Lisa, but she chose to express her distress covertly. She sat silently throughout the whole class discussion, only whispering occasionally to those in her proximity. Kelly, sitting at the table adjacent to Lisa, reports observing the way Lisa chose to exhibit her displeasure by writing her thoughts on a sheet of paper and showing it to others. Kelley recalls: "Lisa in class was waving the paper saying, 'Here we are again under White oppression.' She was flashing it back and forth during class, tapping at it." Tonya also saw the paper Lisa had with the note written about being under White oppression, and recounts her whispered conversation with Lisa during the class session:

> I asked Lisa why she wasn't saying anything and she pulled out this notebook with a paper saying, "Why must we once again have a White person take control of us and dictate to us? I'm really angry about this." But she never said anything.

Though obviously disturbed that a European American was managing the classroom during Celeste's absence, Lisa chose not to write anything that week in her journal about her disturbance. In fact, she distanced herself totally from the situation by copying a spiritual passage for her journal entry that week. Tonya provides an explanation for why Lisa did not confront the issue of her discomfort:

> I said something to her later about, "How do you know Celeste didn't set it up that way?" That's the reason why she didn't write about it in her journal. After I said that, she decided to wait and find out. She also thought that was a problem of "forgetting your own" and bringing White people in when you have or get the position of power.

That fact that a European American conducted the class while two assistants of color (Kristy and Wes) sat in the background was troublesome for both Lisa and Karma. Though Lisa chose not to write about the issue, Karma did choose to write in her journal about her perceptions:

I believe the staff did their best in trying to fill Celeste's shoes. They provided activities that were stimulating but for the most part degrading. I would appreciate more participation from the roles that Kristy and Wes play. They seem very distant in activities and this does not feel right at times. Terry is fine but so is President Bush when he stands in front of the television and speaks. I would have really liked, in Celeste's absence, more participation from them [Kristy and Wes as graduate students of color].

Three journal entries that week expressed discomfort from Lisa and Karma's reactions to a European American taking charge of the class:

LILIA: This weekend I was bothered by a comment that was made in Celeste's absence. It was to the fact that a student was bothered with the fact that Terry who is very much WHITE had conducted Monday's class. This individual would have preferred one of our minority TA's. When I heard the comment it was not being addressed to me though I started to respond and then caught myself and stopped. I wanted to say that although it would have been nice to have a minority teacher conduct the class, due to the circumstances it was not possible. Wes to my knowledge has no teaching experience, Kristy who is very bright, in my perception, tends to be a little on the quiet side. To be a little objective, I guess Wes and Kristy could have had more input in the class presentation.

KAREN: Rumor has it that an individual or individuals were not satisfied at having a White teacher on Monday. I find this a bit hard to take. In my opinion, the teacher should have been the next ranking person after Celeste and in this order I believe that Terry would have come next, hence this is why she taught. I watched a CNN program a few weeks before I came here this summer and I listened to a brilliant African American scholar expound on problems of hyper-sensitivity. I think the aforementioned illustrates this idea. I am not at all happy with some of the attitudes displayed.

KELLY: I would also like to comment on a conversation I had with someone concerning the idea that they did not like the fact that Terry, who we all know is White, led the class on Monday. If people were going to get so bent out of shape about it, they had the opportunity to say something about it to Celeste when she first announced that she'd be leaving the class for a week with Terry in charge. I know that this announcement was made at least a week in advance. This sort of pettiness drives me crazy and is part of what contributes to my unhappiness here. From now on, though, I'm going to say straight out in class or wherever that someone sounds ignorant when they do. I feel like my silence has been in part because of intimidation, but also because I like to give folks the benefit of the doubt and to have their own opinions . . . but some of their opinions are unfounded and detrimental, such as that concerning Terry leading the class on Monday.

Upon her return the following Monday morning, Celeste began the class as in the previous weeks, by having each small group discuss the common themes in their journals that week, then share their small group themes with the whole class. Though Karma and Lisa disliked the European American leadership the previous week, and three (Lilia, Karen, and Kelly) wrote about their discomfort with that view, none had verbally mentioned the controversy by the time all groups finished reporting to the whole group. Then Celeste turned to Kristy and myself, and said:

> We didn't give the TAs time to say anything. And you all need to speak because I wasn't here. So I can only talk about what I heard here this morning. Comments? Thoughts?

Kristy and I both hesitated, looking at each other. Finally, I decided to speak up and mention the unmentioned controversy:

TERRY: Well, there were definitely varying opinions in journals this week, and there always are. . . . Now, I think one of the things that people politely, or whatever, did not bring out was that one of the things people overheard others saying is the problem with me doing it was because I'm White.

TONYA: [quietly] That's exactly right. [looks over toward Lisa]

TERRY: And no one said that. I think that does really need to be dealt with, that it wouldn't have really been a problem if I were African American or Asian, or anything else. At least from my perception. My perception is that I'm White, I ran it, and I shouldn't have.

After my comments, Carol and Rochelle asked for clarification about the journal I wrote that week. Carol wanted to know if one of the groups had said something to me personally about not liking my being there because I was European American, while Rochelle assumed my journal comments came from the scenario discussion. I reassured her my comments did in fact stem from that class discussion, not from any personal encounter. After I clarified Rochelle's question, Lisa responded:

> Given this is a minority program, when I looked up and saw Terry and I looked back and saw Kristy and Wes in the background, my question is not a personal one, but a structural one. If this is a minority program, it seems like an ideal opportunity for minority TAs to be more active than they are. And it's not a personal thing, Terry. I don't know if you want to believe that or not. But when I see two people of color that to me can teach me something that I don't know since they're going through something that I haven't experienced, my question is, Why don't I hear them? I wanted to wait until Celeste came back to find out exactly what the structure is. Everybody has made assumptions about that being the order. Well, I didn't want to make the assumption. And I didn't want to write anything out of anger in my journal to you [Terry] until I found out exactly what the structure was. My frustration here is that I see two people of color, even in a minority program, sitting in the background while the White person has control. We have the same structure. It always comes back to the status quo.

At this point, other participants engaged in the discussion to share their personal interpretations of the event with Lisa:

KELLY: Celeste before she left said that Terry was.
LISA: I don't care what she said. I'm telling you what I saw.
CELESTE: She's talking about the structure.
LISA: I'm telling you what I saw, and how it made me feel. I know what she said. But I'm telling you it bothered me.
TONYA: I personally feel like I learned, I mean, we had the scenarios. But I didn't think Terry gave us any feedback that was coming from herself. In fact, that was my question, What were these for? I wanted to know what experience she's had dealing with some of these issues. She's been a teacher out there. You've been a teacher.

[looks at Terry] Some of these scenarios, I want to know, what have the outcomes been? What has happened? That's what I wanted to know. And I felt like, she was just facilitating.

KAREN: Well, I also feel that since we are people of color and minorities we need to know how to get along with White people.

LISA: But we do that *every day!*

KAREN: But I mean, I don't see, I mean, just things I've heard though.

LISA: I've had it with this multicultural attitude in here! It's driving me crazy! We do that every day. We need to deal with who we are. And try to deal with the fact that sometimes we don't get along as people of color. There are many differences amongst us in here that nobody's dealing with.

CELESTE: Let Karen speak.

KAREN: So, are you saying that we don't need to see different views? I mean, like Whites? I mean, I really feel like we react hyper sensitively to a lot. Big-time!

LISA: I think that for thirty-eight years of my life I have been taught by teachers that look like Terry. I thought I had the opportunity to be taught by somebody else.

KAREN: But we have that here, and I don't see how one day.

CELESTE: Yeah, but.

LISA: It's not just one day.

Lisa's interpretation stemmed from a historical, structural view of the hundreds of years African Americans have struggled with the "White oppressor" in the United States. For her, the issue had nothing to do with me as an individual. Rather, she directed her reaction toward what I symbolized. However, the views of Kelly, Karen, and Tonya all stemmed from a perception of the immediate situational context, rather than the historical frame of reference from which Lisa perceived the event. Kelly's issue was one of pre established rank and expertise, which she did not question. Karen reacted out of interpreting Lisa's response as hatred toward all Whites. Finally, Tonya's comment represents an interpretation of an academic search for knowledge.

More important than knowing how these four views differ, is that each represents a failure to take the role of the other, to understand views not their own. One must be able to role-take, as described by symbolic interactionists, to understand the other. Charon (1992) explains: "To understand the other demands taking the other's role in order to understand where the other is 'coming from,' to see the meaning of the other's words and acts. Meaning is obtained through determining what a word or act represents—to the other" (p. 113). Lisa's constant interruptions illustrate that her major interest is having her views understood. She did not engage in knowing or understanding the views of others. The inability to role-take in this situation was not characteristic of Lisa's actions alone, but of the other three as well. Each counter argument proposed by Karen, Kelly, and Tonya demonstrates how they tried hard to convince Lisa that she was wrong in the given context, rather than try to understand her historical position.

Through this brief discussion of the scenarios learning activity, participants did not reach a mutual ground of understanding. Instead, the result was for some participants to take sides. It was through the interpretive lens of taking sides that participants came to the third BCD session.

Behind Closed Doors, Session 3

Between the fallout of the scenarios learning activity and the last BCD session, OD participants were formally interviewed. Seven of the ten participants who chose to interview with me deliberately made their choice because they wanted to talk specifically about the events unraveled through the scenarios, as well as hear my opinion on whether they should attend the next BCD session. Their concerns centered on interpretations of the previous session in which these seven individuals in particular felt uncomfortable. Diane characterized this tension-filled atmosphere:

> The views people are expressing are pretty bad [in Session 2]. They seem judgmental and close-minded to me. I thought some of the comments were racist. Like the kids being zebras [in reference to the discussion of interracial dating and children of interracial marriages] comments really bothered me. I don't like the heated talk. When other people try to give their opinions, and they can't do it they just shut down. . . . People are edgy about tonight [Session 3] because things have built up and it's taken this long for people to express themselves and tonight they want to do it.

One of the "things built up" is that individuals perceived Karma and Lisa as speaking for them even though individuals had opinions different from the ones Karma and Lisa voiced. The fallout of the scenario activity disturbed Jesus. After completing the formal interview questions, he proceeded to share his insights with me. He began by explaining how he thought the reactions from Karma and Lisa were overgeneralized in that they assumed everyone in the room felt the same way they did. "We weren't complaining [about the scenario activity]. It was more specifically their own group than in ours." Jesus expressed the same concern in his journal entry:

> I also did not appreciate being spoken for when no one asked me for my opinion. This happened during the discussion on Monday when one of the two women stated that "everyone" was unhappy about the scenarios that were given to us by Terry, and that they were distributed. It was stated that everyone was arguing about the scenarios and that no one appreciated them. I felt that this was very inappropriate because there were groups, mine included, who did not feel this way about it.

Even though he did not appreciate being spoken for, Jesus found himself in a position of not knowing how to proceed in the interaction. He shares:

> I found myself between a rock and a hard place. I didn't want to create a snowball effect. I wanted to protect everyone in the room from being in an uncomfortable situation. I also find it hard to argue with them [Karma and Lisa] sometimes because I just don't know where they are coming from.

Karen, who was involved in the stand off discussion with Lisa in class, was another who came to the interview to share her distress about not being able to express her thoughts in a way that would be heard. She states:

> I learned about myself I need to speak up more. I keep my feelings, thoughts, opinions inside. I felt like if I'd said something on Monday it would be interrupted. And it was. If I can't make a couple of sentences before they interject that's when I figure, I don't know how much you're listening anyway. So that's why I've chosen to be quiet. . . . I was too angry to say something about the scenarios.

Though Karen felt she was unable to take the initiative on her own to say something about her displeasure, my opening up the discussion encouraged her to further explore ways she could act in the situation. She told me:

> When you finally said something, I thought, Good, maybe we could break through to the truth. I thought, Be realistic! Be honest! . . . At lunchtime we talked about being shocked but pleased that you said something. . . . But you seem to be fine with it. How do you do that? You deal with it. I feel like I'm going to cry all the time. It feels like Lisa just does not like Whites.

In response to Jesus, Karen, and the others who asked whether I thought they should attend BCD, my response was the same:

> I can't tell you what you need to do. However, if your concern is that your views are not being heard, your views will remain unheard if you choose to stay away. The only way we can help each other understand our views is if we voice them.

Jesus decided to attend so he could ask Lisa and Karma to explain and thus better understand their views. Karen also decided she would attend, saying, "Although I don't want to go to BCD, I don't want others to think they're right. Also, how am I learning to be more culturally sensitive if I don't?" Karen wrote part of her journal before the BCD session. In explaining her decision to attend she writes:

> I want to try to understand people, although I do feel that some will never change in their attitudes. I will attend *Behind Closed Doors*, for I will no longer allow those who voice their opinions more loudly and more frequently than others to allow themselves to believe that is how everyone thinks because it is not. Although I will not come away comfortably and although it will be difficult to voice my opinions, I shall attempt to do so because I am growing tired of listening to a few select individuals cut others, such as myself, off. I will not tolerate those who have the indecency and rudeness to interrupt what I would like to say after I have politely listened to their opinions.

Thus, as Diane previously stated, edgy people came to BCD Session 3 because issues had built up and people were ready to voice their views.

Though several OD participants came to BCD Session 3 with intentions to talk specifically with Karma and Lisa, Karma and Lisa chose not to come. However, this did not stop those who came from expressing their feelings. What took place ended up being an attack against two people who were not there to respond to the criticism. Whereas in previous sessions, Celeste tried not to interfere with people's expressions, this time she did redirect comments, explaining that it was not appropriate to be discussing issues about people who were not there and a more appropriate way of solving the conflicts would be to speak with the individuals themselves. About Celeste's advice, Karen writes:

> I was unhappy at *Behind Closed Doors* because I felt I didn't get my chance to express my irritations and feelings of distress. Lisa and Karma did not show up and I really wanted to tell them about me and how I feel and perceive the way that they act at times. I was unhappy that Celeste did not want me to address my particular problems with that subject and I was happy to have shared my concerns with her after class. She listened and gave some insight as how now I must attempt or at least should try to address the situation in a constructive manner. While I don't really feel that I must make a disclaimer in order to explain I do agree that I should be willing to go ahead and take that step toward peace.

After the second session, the OD participants who spoke the most left feeling good, and the ones who said little or nothing left feeling threatened. However, in the third session, the ones perceived as threatening the second session were either silent or absent this time in efforts to accommodate the feelings of the others. Though Rochelle debated whether or not to attend the third session, because she did not want to offend anyone further, she did attend. However, she remained quiet the entire session. She did not contribute verbally, but listened intently to what others were saying. She writes:

> For a group of people who had previously expressed so much disappointment about folks getting "attacked" at BCD, some of us seemed to have no problems attacking people who weren't there to defend themselves. The ironic thing is that their absence was an attempt to spare the accusers from hurt feelings. Never in my life have I seen such a blatant display of cowardice. Now I think I've seen it all!

Fabian writes how he agrees with Celeste and Rochelle that it was not appropriate behavior for people to speak out against those not present, and reiterates the implicit social rule that individuals should handle personal issues in private, not in public:

> To me this session is getting worse and worse. I was astonished to hear some of my colleagues complain about someone else from the program. I realize that we are all entitled to express our own concerns or ideas, but to bring these comments up when the other person is not there to respond to the comments made against her (them) is not right. I really hope that these people that had some concerns bring them up when Karma and Lisa are here to defend themselves. . . . If certain individuals have concerns about someone else, they should express these concerns to the other individual personally.

Miguel, who was absent for the scenario activity, returned to hear versions of what had transpired from other OD participants. He was present the following Monday when Celeste returned and Lisa explained her reaction to the entire group. Acting on hearsay, not having been involved himself, Miguel engaged in attacking Karma and Lisa during their absence in BCD session three. However, his own reaction forced him to do some critical self-reflection on why it was he responded in that manner. He writes:

> I am a very open-minded person. I don't prejudge people and try my hardest to respect their ideas and beliefs. However, I was very quick to judge the reactions that took place on Monday. Not taking into consideration different backgrounds and reasons for that kind of reaction. Even more important different styles in expressing one self. I hope to have learned from this experience.
>
> It all comes back to why did I react in that manner? Why did I myself prejudge Lisa's reaction? It was for two reasons, they are not excuses but I am human. First, I saw a person [Terry] that I respect and admire being judged because of her skin color. Not for what she has done for us as students and minorities. Second, I saw a person [in general] being judged for their skin color. That is something I would not allow to happen to anyone. I hope that next time I am faced with this kind of situation I will allow for people to explain themselves before reacting and allow for discussion of the situation.

TRUTH, TRUST, AND HONESTY

When conflicts arose in interpersonal relationships, the source of the dispute was named truth, trust, or honesty. Who was judged as being honest or was deemed as being truthful at which time were regular themes that emerged in the journal writings, class discussions, and informal talk during the program. After BCD Session 1, Lisa and Rochelle both used the term *honest* to judge others. Charles and Celia both claim people were finally honest in BCD Session 2. As defined by Charles, *honesty* means that a person shares "deep. . . personal feelings, thoughts, emotions in order to encourage change in the future." Rochelle writes how honesty comes from critical self-reflection: "We debated and argued and challenged ourselves to examine what's inside of us." For these individuals, honesty and truth stem from the inner, personal self and the willingness to risk sharing personal self as subject with others.

Participants were asked to describe the criteria they used to judge another as honest, truthful or credible. How do they know whether another individual is telling the truth? When asked about credibility, Celia responds:

> I can see in their eyes that they're honest. I can see that they are self-determined, self-assertive, and when they say something it's not empty talk—like politicians! Be serious yet friendly, have fun, be willing to talk to you; getting to know you shows respect. . . . Like when Terry spoke. She's blunt and honest about what she thinks. I like the honesty part of her. She admits there's a problem and says wait. It takes a lot of courage to say that. Just that gives her a lot of credibility.

Lisa describes those with credibility as "folks that do what they say. They walk the walk, not just talk the talk. I can easily discern those who talk *to* or *at* me instead of *with* me. I *watch* and *listen*. That's how I know." She further explains that a combination of academic knowledge and experience is needed for credibility:

> You can become focused on the [educational] degree by the *passion* of experience. . . . A lot of African Americans haven't gone back to deal with their experiences of being African American. Not the text-

book African American, but the *real* African American. And I can tell.

When probed about the direct experiences with OD participants that were the basis of honesty conflicts, Karma revealed a difference between actions in the dorm and actions in the classroom:

> People want to be the center of their own attraction. They say things and don't express them to who it needs to be expressed. My experience in the dorm is when we have a chance to be alone with peers they express anger with the situation, but when there's an opportunity to express that [in the group setting] they don't do it. Makes life hard to live with in that respect. . . . This has been a vast learning experience for me . . . knowing that people are going to be this way. In respect to knowing you're *not going* to get a real person all the time.

From Karma's perspective, not being honest has to do with others who do not say and do the same across contextual situations. Not being honest is not saying the same things in public and private. Adrianne also describes a difference between the dorm self and the classroom self of others:

> When I look at dorm life and I look at the classroom, the issues that are going on in the dorm are extremely different. The relationships there and in the classroom are completely different. . . . People put on a lot of fronts. People keep to themselves in the dorms. I don't think they are willing to confront the issue. Not willing to confront a concern that someone else has. A lot of issues that have been brought up in the class could be resolved in just day-to-day contact.

Lisa was particularly disturbed by the different "faces" people donned in and out of the classroom. She relates:

> Truth is being who you are when it's not easy to be who you are in a setting. Being truthful about who you are no matter who you're with. Some of the young African Americans are militant when we're in our own African American group and bring up issues of their own. But in the classroom either they say nothing or are very multicultural. And

to me, that's a *lie*. Others won't bring up any issues at all. They talk
about day-to-day issues that have no consequence to *who* they are.

Though Lisa herself recognizes her own judgmental and critical attitude
toward other African Americans who change their tune from
Afrocentric to multicultural in different contexts, her judgments come
from direct interaction with her in-group OD participants. She describes
herself as the "Midnight Sister." She is there to listen, to speak up, and
becomes the lone martyr. She explains:

> They'll do it in the midnight hours in my room. They'll say we need to
> pull together and gain control of education. That we should have
> pride and not be controlled and tied by White people. I take very
> seriously what you say to me. But what you say to me you better say
> in public. Don't put me on the line and see if I fall. They'll come to
> me at 6:00 in the morning and talk, but you never hear it. . . . I'm tired
> of them [other African American OD participants] playing games
> with me. Using me for your Midnight Sister to get frustrations out
> and playing multicultural with all these other people. I'm struggling
> with that because I feel I'm judging them. But how much do I have to
> put up with? My back is going to be straight no matter where I am.
> But is that too much to ask of you, to do the same thing?

Karma, Lisa, and Adrianne would like for others to change their
behavior to be what they view as more consistent and honest with
themselves. However, Walter sees that change needs to happen within
those who are doing the judging. He states: "I see some real personality
problems going on between people that don't see eye to eye." When
discussing issues of truth, trust, and honesty, Walter reveals how well
grounded he is in his cultural beliefs:

> Another cultural thing is you don't judge a person either way until
> you know. You get to know them first, the character from the inside,
> not first impressions. So that's what I do. . . . You can't base it on a
> short-time encounter. I base it on how well I know them. I have
> friends I trust, and others I don't. Everybody deserves a chance to be
> trusted. . . . I listen to everyone. But that doesn't mean I have to
> remember what they said. [Smiles] I base truth and trust on
> experiences I've had and a lot of common sense, too.

Rochelle and Charles both describe why issues of trust and honesty are vitally important to understanding others. Rochelle asserts: "It's important to be yourself. To have a meaningful relationship we have to be able to relax and be ourselves. If you're walking on eggshells with me you're probably not interested in getting to know me." Charles insists that persistence is necessary in understanding oneself, as well as understanding others. He explains:

> I want to understand my Africanness. I want you to share yours [individual culture and ethnicity], too, but let me share mine. I don't try to get into nobody's business. But people are pulling apart. They're shying away instead of dealing with it. I'm stubborn and bullheaded. I want to get through it because that's going to make me so much better. If I'm running toward you, and you're backing up, it's like, Okay, I won't talk to you then. You don't have to be loud. Just express your opinion. Just say it. At least you get to that point.

Charles also recognizes that the key to resolving conflict involves dropping the social rules that prevent the self as subject from acting. He states:

> In conflict you need to ask, How do you feel directly? The fact that you said it is half the battle. Now let's get through it. With lots of African Americans that's how we deal with each other. We drop all the rules. Drop those rules that keep you from expressing yourself and getting through it.

Truth is the ability to present self as subject. For Lisa, being honest or truthful means presenting the same self in all social situations. However, what Lisa calls being dishonest in the younger African Americans may in fact be the ability to take the perspective of the other. Bush and Simmons (1990) define the reflexive self as "inherently changeable through social interaction . . . as the individual takes on new roles and encounters new situations, the self will continue to evolve and change" (p. 140). What Lisa describes as lying is the ability the younger African Americans have to take the perspective of the temporary referent group as the generalized other. As Charon (1992) describes:

> The individual interacts with many different groups and thus comes to have several reference groups (social worlds or societies), and he

or she shares a perspective, including a perspective used to define self, with each of them. If he or she is to continue to interact successfully with a reference group, then that perspective must, as least temporarily, become the individual's generalized other, used to see and direct the self in that group. (p. 74)

LABELS AND DISTORTIONS

As conflicts arose from individuals politically acting on their differences, so, too, did the use of labels arise. Weinstein & Deutschberger (1963) describe the act of casting others into identities that make sense for our own purposes in order to control interaction as *altercasting*. Charon (1992) defines the altercasting process: "If I can convince others who you are, I influence their definition of you and thus their action toward you, and ultimately your interaction with them" (p. 152). During the course of the OD program, participants exhibited various ways in which they engaged in influencing each other's perceptions. What was a celebration of differences the first week of the program became a menagerie of name-calling and labeling to define the actions of others in weeks five and six. Rochelle viewed the actions of those in BCD Session 3 as "cowardice." Karen perceived Lisa as "hating Whites." Tonya, Miguel, Jesus, Karen, and Kelly all see Lisa's and Karma's actions as having "too much anger." Lisa calls Karen's and Kelly's concerns "petty," while they, in turn, view her quarrel with having a European American teacher for one day out of eight weeks as "petty." Walter judges the actions of both sides of the conflict as "petty." Audre Lorde (1984) describes how the escalation in name-calling or prejudging arises:

We have all been programmed to respond to the human differences between us with fear and loathing and to handle that difference in one of three ways: ignore it, and if that is not possible, copy it if we think it is dominant, or destroy it if we think it is subordinate. But we have no patterns for relating across our human differences as equals. As a result, those differences have been misnamed and misused in the service of separation and confusion. (p. 115)

The tension, misunderstandings, and use of name-calling resulted in separation and confusion in the Opening Doors context, just as Lorde described.

From her current phase in her grounded self, Lisa's claim that she is "tired of all the multiculturalism" going on in the class stems from her perceptions of her own actions, as well as the actions of others. Only in the last four years has Lisa developed the ability to perceive herself as subject, through her study of African American history. Now, she is more consciously aware of the ways in which the Eurocentric mainstream has functioned to shape her view of self as object for over thirty years. She acts to resist self-objectification and believes others must do the same. Therefore, from Lisa's perception, *multiculturalism* is another label used by those in the mainstream to overgeneralize ethnically diverse *individuals* in order to keep them objectified. In her interview she explains how she believes the emphasis on multiculturalism, respecting the diversity of *others,* is an effort to keep *individuals* from knowing themselves as subjects:

> It's my perception about people that they're talking multicultural when they need to stop and think about who they are. I don't see the grounding. The mainstream thing doesn't mean anything. We need to know who we are first. I can't talk to you about nothing till I know who I am. And you can tell me who you are and we can go from there.

Lisa perceives the multicultural label as another effort by the mainstream to keep people of color from truly knowing and appreciating themselves as subjects. But as she makes clear in the last line, only by knowing oneself as subject is it possible to relate to others as subject as well.

OD participants described the ways, as Lorde (1984) describes, they "have no patterns for relating across our human differences as equals" and therefore "those differences have been misnamed and misused in the service of separation and confusion" (p. 115). In her first journal entry, Debra describes how the term *minority* has negative connotations for people of color.

> A graduation speaker said "minority" was a degrading word. She said that People of Color were the majority of the world, why should we be called minority in the USA? I agree with her. People of Color are

the most populous members of the world. We should be referred as
such. When I hear the word "minority" I think of a group of people
that's lesser than the "mainstream" group. It has negative connotations
to me. It's a "them" term.

The Rise of College Campus Racism video the first week of the
program elicited many discussions about the labels *separatist, militant,*
and *isolationist*. Often, these labels describe the actions of ethnically
diverse groups perceived as oppositional to the dominant out-group
perspective. However, the following excerpts of dialogue from the
ethnically diverse individuals themselves illustrate how labeling of
actions is dependent upon the personal and political perspective of the
one assigning the labels. Though somewhat lengthy, the exact dialogue
of the OD participants is recounted rather than paraphrased to suggest
the ways in which the "other" (in this case, ethnically diverse from the
European American mainstream) perceive their own actions and the
social interpretations of their personal actions.

Karma reflects on a personal experience of how teaching her
daughter historical facts that were not supported in the school
curriculum resulted in her being labeled a militant:

KARMA: They want to keep their own tradition. That's what I was
    thinking about schools and everything. I'm thinking about my
    children, and I'm thinking about teaching them. Because it's hard
    to teach them that Lincoln did not free the slaves, that Columbus
    did not, without them getting angry about their teachers teaching
    them. Because in the fourth grade is when African Americans start
    going downhill, because they start incorporating this "it is not my
    culture" thing. This is what my daughter said: "My mother told me
    that Columbus didn't do it." Then all of a sudden the teacher says,
    "You go to the principal because I'm teaching this to the students."
CELIA: This is what happens to them?
KARMA: This is what happens to them because I'm teaching them a
    certain way.
MICHELLE: The right way.
FABIAN: Yeah.
KARMA: And they're [the Eurocentric school system] saying, "No no
    no, that's not how it is. The American Indians were here first and
    let's talk about them." [And I'm teaching my daughter] "Let's talk
    about what American Indian do *you* know that was here when

Columbus arrived?" They said [to my daughter], "Look, you go
to the principal's office and we're going to call your parents, and
you're going to be in trouble because you don't teach my class, I
teach my class." You see what I'm saying? And they start beating it
and beating it into us in the classroom.

. . . And then they [African American children] start losing
interest in the class, and then the teacher starts saying, alienating
that student, because that student is talking about something they
did not put in their book. And all of a sudden your child is labeled
as a militant. That's what happened to my daughter. She got sus-
pended from school four or five different times. So how do we
positively educate our children at home for them not to go out in
society and [be] labeled as militant?

Being labeled a militant for voicing an opinion or view different
from the European American mainstream also concerned Rochelle in
group three. Her comments illustrate what Audre Lorde (1984) describes as the distortion process: the farther the experiences of the
individual are away from the mythical norm, the more those experiences will be labeled or distorted in order to keep the individual's views
subordinated. The following exchange took place:

ROCHELLE: What did you guys think about in the video when they
had the sit-ins to try to redevelop the devastated Black studies
department and the one man called them militants? How is a sit-in
militant? I was just wondering about other people's reactions
because.
DEBRA: Will you describe the definition of *militant*?
ROCHELLE: I don't know, when I think of militant, I associate that with
something, I mean, I think that society tends to view that as
something negative.
DEBRA: Right.
ROCHELLE: Like violence.
DEBRA: Violence.
ROCHELLE: Or radical, or troublemaking, or something like that.
Whereas a sit-in, to me, sounded peaceful. I mean, they didn't say
anything about any outbreaks of violence or anything like that. It
was just a way to get attention, I thought, to discuss the issues.
There was no violence there.

Rochelle explains how she believes the European American school system uses the labels as a way of justification for their own actions. She believes labels are used to maintain the Eurocentric perspective rather than face the need to change the perspective to be more inclusive of diversity.

ROCHELLE: And thinking about what happens, like, on this level [university] too. I go back to the incident where the, I think it was a president at whatever university, he was saying, "What doesn't kill you teaches you something."

DEBRA: Makes you stronger.

ROCHELLE: Yeah, makes you stronger, makes you stronger. And I thought that was ironic, you know? It seems like that's the school system's justification for, "Well, this is a learning experience for minorities or people of color." And I think about, as a student here at this university, how we [students of color], just to keep our sanity, have to view a lot of incidents in that way, you know? "Well, at least I learned something from it." Because otherwise we'd just be bombarded with this kind of thing. It's been this way all through school, you know what I mean? It's always been this way. They [European dominant school system] want us to view it as "Well, it's a learning experience for *you* [students of color]" rather than we're being denied something. I don't think that should be justification for that kind of attitude. It's always been that way, since you were in elementary school or middle school. Just learn to deal with it. At least you're learning how to get this kind of interaction with White society. And that's unfair to students of color, to use that as justification for the way they do that.

Adrianne adds historically how the distortion process has functioned to conform subordinated groups in the United States:

ADRIANNE: There were peaceful protests with Martin Luther King. And then you have the militant. Well, people saw it as militancy, the Black power. The messages of Malcolm X before he changed his, and Stokey Charmichael and Huey Newton. Recently in our school we [some African American students] had a protest and people [European Americans] saw it as negative. They saw it as negative because when you mention, what is the definition of militant, I see it as going up against or being at war with the establishment. You are challenging them.

DEBRA: Whether it's peaceful or not.

ADRIANNE: That's right. It's the challenge. You're at odds with something that's been the dominant power. It's a power struggle! A clash. You're going up against a power system and they don't want to make any changes.

DEBRA: The people who have power don't want to give it up.

ADRIANNE: When you do fight, you have to realize that you're going to be perceived as militant, like you said. They're not going to like you coming at odds making changes. And I think this is what we see here.

Individual actions that challenge the mainstream perspective are labeled as militant, no matter how peaceful the demonstration is. Rochelle explains how it happens in her present context on this university campus, and Adrianne elaborates to give a historical perspective of labeling as the establishment's strategy for confronting challenges to power. In addition to being militant, any action people of color take to associate with other people of color is perceived and labeled as separatist:

ADRIANNE: This separation issue that came up. The separation issue and how if I'm walking with you [points *to Rochelle who also is African American*] and you're walking with somebody from your race, people see us as separating. But do they see on campuses Asian students separating? [Addresses Debra] Are you viewed, when you're with your own, as being separate?

DEBRA: Hmm.

ADRIANNE: If you choose to be with your own people do you have uh.

WALTER: I don't know, I think it's kind of stereotyping.

ADRIANNE: Uh-huh. Okay.

WALTER: 'Cause like, Diane and I are both Native American. Well, I hope we're different. See, you're throwing everybody into the hat.

ADRIANNE: But it seems that here [on campus during the OD program] again, there's a pressure for minority students to get out of their groups and assimilate into the mainstream who are not willing to get out of their groups. See, the pressure's put on us. "Why are you at those tables?" Since I've been here, I've even sensed that at the cafeteria. And maybe I'm more sensitive to that because of public schools. I see the tension and the pressure and hear the questions by staff and students who say, "Well, why are all those Black kids sitting over there?"

DEBRA: Hmm, I just had a thought. What are your ideas about being separate, like when you [Adrianne] and Karma and Lisa and, you know, all you guys [African Americans in the OD program] sit together? I mean do you consider that.

ADRIANNE: No! 'cause I'm asking you, Why are you sitting together? See, here's perception. We need to check out perceptions. The perception is Black folks separate and it's not. We *all* separate. We all do. [Laughs]

ROCHELLE: This is interesting because I was just thinking that when you [Walter] said that about [how] your cultures are different and that you're both Native American

WALTER: Uh—huh.

ROCHELLE: And we [some of the OD participants in an informal group] were talking yesterday about how a lot of the Asian people, people perceive them as separating and grouping all together. But you guys have very different cultures, too. Same with us, too. We're all African Americans, but when I look at you guys [Adrianne, Karma, Lisa, Michelle, Donna], I think of it as you're not separating as Black people, but as people who came from E__ [the same undergraduate college], people who knew each other before they came here.

KAREN: Me, too.

ROCHELLE: You know what I mean? But I might look at another group and say they're all separate because they're Asian or they're Native American or you see what I'm saying?

ADRIANNE: Uh—huh.

ROCHELLE: When you're looking through your own eyes, you can see how your people are "normal" so to speak, but the others are separating because they're different. You know what I mean? They're different from you. But everybody's different. So, that's something that I talked about. That article that we read, the author, he spoke about how people look to us to be race representatives and things like that. And it seems to be difficult for society to see that. Whereas, as people of color, we have similar experiences in life, but we are still very diverse, even in our own groups. And that seems to be a difficult concept for people to grasp.

DEBRA: I saw the diversity in our autobiographies.

ADRIANNE: Uh—huh.

DEBRA: And it was incredible that everybody's story was so unique.
ADRIANNE: Uh—huh. But see, here you have visual perceptions. And I'm glad you answered that question. 'Cause see, in my school, there are definite groupings of White students, and it's okay for them to be together. No one's asking them, "Hey, why don't you get out of your group.
DEBRA: Uh—huh.
ADRIANNE: "And come over to this Black group?" It's not about race. It's about comfort level and feeling comfortable.

Rochelle's comments about separatism illustrate that a particular behavior elicited from the out-group may be perceived as negative, while the same behavior from the in-group is perceived as positive. Walter is quick to point out that any generalizations of groups is stereotyping, and instead of focusing on groups, we need to pay more attention to individuals. Adrianne tries to portray the perception of separatism as a Black and White issue. Rochelle argues that separatism is not just a White perception. She insists that perceiving behavior as well-meaning in those like us and ill-meaning in those not like us is a function of groups—ethnic or otherwise.

Charles explains that the issue is not whether to separate, but how to balance the social collective with the personal:

As educators and as people of color we must find ways to collectively work together yet still keep our individuality. We must allow ourselves to feel comfortable when we associate with those of our own culture and not let the majority culture influence our feelings and thoughts when they choose to label us as separatists, militants, and isolationists. We must also allow ourselves to freely experience and enjoy other cultures and not allow our own culture to hinder us from learning and understanding others. With a better understanding of others, much more improvement in today's race relations will be accomplished.

Personal intentions guide and direct the actions of the individual, but they represent only one particular perspective. When individuals act personally, or when they do not choose to be stifled by the social perspectives of the larger social group and act out of their unique perspective, conflict is inevitable. The twenty-one participants who bonded so quickly in the first two days of sharing that required no interaction, began to withdraw from one another when varying personal perspectives were expressed and required action. Participants noted each other's actions both within and outside the classroom setting. And as Lisa's impassioned description of being the Midnight Sister illustrates, "social identities occupy contradictory and shifting locations" (Giroux, 1992). Perceptions of truth, trust, and honesty and were gauged by the criteria of self as subject. Only those actions viewed as the individual revealing self as subject were viewed by others as honest. Discouraged participants from the first BCD session took action to make the second session personally beneficial. However, when viewed negatively by others, the same individuals inhibited themselves in the third BCD session. As some individuals acted personally (and politically) toward in-group referents and others toward out-group referents, conflicts arose. Conflict was part of the socially constructed context of Opening Doors. Conflict is a positive and a necessary condition for subject to subject relations to share personal perspectives. Charles describes this need for conflict best when he explains:

> In regards to our struggle as American people, we must realize that sometimes conflict and struggle can be very beneficial because we are finally revealing our true feelings and thoughts, giving us something to finally work with. For me, much can be learned from something I had to struggle with, and I value it much more when it has been overcome!

CHAPTER 8

Implications for Critical Teaching

*".. . an unbiased inclusive perspective, can and should
be present whether or not people of color are present"*
—hooks (1994, p. 43)

The study of the Opening Doors program provides insight into what it means to *be* and what it takes to *become* multicultural. The stories told by the twenty-one OD participants and the events that transpired in context of the OD program serve to illustrate the ways in which we as teachers can pedagogically construct the opportunity for the process of becoming multicultural in our classrooms. The process of becoming multicultural as a recursive cycle of deconstructing self as object, reconstructing self as subject, and engaging in subject to subject relations with others has several implications for educational practices. Therefore, this chapter accomplishes three goals. First, it describes the qualities of critical, multicultural teaching. Second, it discusses particular critical teaching practices that facilitate multicultural understanding. Third, I share some of ways I have applied the lessons I learned from my personal interactions with the twenty-one ethnically diverse Opening Doors participants. I share specific effects on my curriculum choices and development, as well as teacher-student interactions in my critical teaching of undergraduate teacher education courses.

QUALITIES OF MULTICULTURAL TEACHING

Historically, progressives assert that schooling and education needs to be child-centered. Understanding the individual needs of the students we intend to teach is a prerequisite for successful teaching and learning. What has not been stressed, or perhaps has even been ignored, is attention to the needs of the teacher as an individual. Teachers bring to the learning event their own intentions, interpretations, and perspectives which influence the way student needs will be perceived. Only when we know ourselves are we able to see ourselves in others. If teachers see themselves as objects, they are only able to perceive their students as objects as well. Education begins with the individual. This includes the individual teacher. Teachers must view themselves as subjects before they are able to perceive their students as subjects.

Current multicultural education practices have failed because we have misunderstood the nature of the process of becoming multicultural. Curriculum efforts have focused on student change rather than teacher change. To be successful our efforts must first be focused inward, toward our individuality as teachers. We cannot begin to understand the needs from the cultural perspectives of the students who enter our classrooms until we critically examine and account for our own worldview. We must ask the questions, Why is this so? Why do I believe this? What in my experiences has formed and shaped my views? In other words, we must begin the process of becoming multicultural by engaging in our own critical self-reflection. We must see ourselves as subjects, lest we categorize our students as objects.

To begin the process of becoming multicultural, we must begin with ourselves. We must engage in reflective activities as teachers. We must critically reflect on our own past experiences that have shaped our present selves. We must acknowledge and make explicit the influences that our present actions and aspirations have for the future. We must bring to conscious examination our historical selves which allows us to deconstruct our present selves (as the OD participants did through their autobiographical presentations), in order to gain knowledge of self as subject.

Only when we are able to consciously view ourselves as subjects can we raise our levels of social consciousness, see ourselves in our students, and break free of the positivist stronghold where we pretend what we do in classrooms is dispense objective knowledge. Only when we as teachers begin the self-transformation process (hooks, 1989) of our own perspectives will the multicultural process begin in the classroom. Becoming multicultural implies the development of an egalitarian, democratic relationship among individuals. All individuals act toward their perspective of reality, and all reality interpretations are accepted equally. When teachers adopt a multicultural perspective, they act from this perspective. They strategically formulate, plan, and implement teaching methods that reflect egalitarian ideals. Multicultural practices are those which have the following qualities:

1. Respect, include, negotiate, and dialogue with the realities from multiple perspectives, acknowledging that the personal and social realities of all students are different.
2. Encourage students and teachers to reflect inward on personal constructions to question and make meaning of the present.
3. Provide a place and a space for personal sharing and relating.
4. Pose reality as problematic and socially constructed.
5. Encourage students to face and negotiate conflict.
6. Promote a recursive cycle of external dialogue followed by internal reflection.
7. Provide opportunities for individuals (including the teacher) to find ways to familiarize themselves with perspectives and realities other than their own.
8. Encourage individuals to take responsibility to find out what they do not know or have not experienced.
9. Invite students to learn through struggle and to recognize that only through struggle can understanding be reached.

CRITICAL TEACHING PRACTICES

To describe more specifically the nine qualities of multicultural practices listed above, I suggest four types of classroom practice that contain multicultural qualities: (1) place and space, (2) dialogic teaching and the language of possibility, (3) the curriculum is ourselves, and (4) teacher as collaborative meaning maker.

The Place and Space for Multicultural Perspectives

One who teaches from a multicultural perspective structures activities that provide both the place and the space for individual perspectives in the classroom. Teacher and students alike reflect and critically examine their personal histories and constructed perspectives in order to view each other in subject to subject relations. Specific strategies that have the potential to provide the place and space for personal constructions are autobiographical assignments, dialogue journals, and multiple opportunities for small group talk and negotiation of shared perspectives. Hooks (1989) asserts several reasons why small group interaction is an important place for education for critical consciousness. First, communication between individuals is conducted in a manner that can be understood. Second, because knowledge is shared primarily through conversation, individuals need not be equally literate to participate. Third, small groups create the space where the personal experience is shared as the starting place for constructing social or collective experience.

Dialogic Teaching and the Language of Possibility

At the heart of becoming multicultural is the construction of shared perspectives. One cannot create or share perspectives with a book, music, dance, or any other objective artifact of culture. Perspectives can only be negotiated through communication with others. Shared perspectives are the rules that govern societal groups, and these rules are created through communication. As Strauss (1959) asserts:

> Group life is organized around communication. Communication. . . signifies shared meanings. . . . The members are able to participate in various coordinated activities because they share a common terminology. Groups form around points of agreement, and then new classifications arise on the basis of further shared experience. (pp. 148-149)

Points of agreement can only be reached through personal, face-to-face interaction with others. Interaction suggests the need to develop the art of negotiation. One must engage in listening, hearing, seeing, and taking the role of the other. Critical theorists suggest this personal and social transformation process is achieved through a dialectic exchange (Simon, 1987), a language of possibility (Giroux, 1985), and a pedagogy of questions (Freire, 1985). Teacher-student relations must center on negotiation where personal meanings are shared and new social perspectives are constructed. This includes asking as well as answering questions. As teachers, we must engage in authentic conversations with our students.

The Curriculum Is Ourselves

Rather than require additions to the curriculum, multicultural practices change the nature of curriculum. Since social interaction is necessary for the process of becoming multicultural to begin, the curriculum is not the books we read, the films we view, or the resource materials we explore. It is ourselves. The curriculum of multicultural teaching is talk—talk with each other through social interaction, with ourselves through critical reflection. Only through negotiating interactions with others will we share experiences and construct shared perspectives. Instead of questions about cultural artifacts, or even questions about similarities and differences, we need to pursue and ask questions of each other. We need to converse with and about the actual individuals interacting in the classroom rather than discuss the rituals and customs of some unknown group "out there." We need to know one another as subjects to construct socially shared perspectives.

Teacher as Collaborative Meaning Maker

One must be willing to share personal experiences before socially shared perspectives can be constructed. This implies that as teachers, we must also share our thoughts, feelings, and beliefs as one perspective among many in the classroom. We cannot expect students to critically reflect upon themselves and share their insecurities, fears, hopes and dreams if we are not willing to take the risk to do so ourselves. Only when we risk allowing the personal constructions of reality to be shared will new social realities be created. As hooks (1989) suggests, we must take the challenge to love.

CRITICAL TEACHING BEYOND OPENING DOORS

The summer of 1992 was a life-changing experience for me. The voices of the twenty-one Opening Doors participants permanently reside in both my head and my heart. My interactions and encounters with those individuals changed who I am and how I perceive the world. I cannot perceive the world the same way, nor can I respond to students in the same way I did before the summer of 1992.

The lessons I learned from OD participants affect me daily. When interacting with my preservice teacher education students, I often find the voices from the OD participants responding—both through my pen as I respond to weekly dialogue journals and through my voice in both formal and informal conversations. Much of what I hear myself saying came from the OD participants themselves. Gems of wisdom were said to me, and wisdom I now pass on to others.

Most (approximately 98 percent) of the preservice teachers in my classes are White and have made it to college without once encountering a person of color. When discussing multicultural issues with these students, I find their perceptions to be naive, inexperienced, and wrought with fear. They fear the unknown. Many of the perceptions they have are based on media images and stereotypes. Dealing with children of color in the classroom causes them discomfort. Two young women in particular illustrate the inexperience and naïveté of my students. At the beginning of the semester they stayed after class to discuss their fear. Both grew up in a White middle-class town, and by the age of twenty-one, had never been in contact with a person of color. Knowing that practicum placements for class were to be made in socially, ethnically, and economically diverse schools, they approached me to say that even though they were scared they felt they needed the experience and wanted to know what they could do. Accompanying their fear was their need for performance perfection. "Tell me what I need to do to be multicultural" is a request I hear often. Like all good overachievers, they wanted to "do it right." These two have not been the only ones, and each time my response is the same: Stop trying to dictate, teach, direct. Instead listen, question, and learn.

The OD experience taught me two kinds of lessons I want to share. The first I categorize as pedagogy lessons. Pedagogy lessons are those that have influenced the way I organize syllabi and structure the activities in class sessions. The second category I call content lessons. Content lessons are primarily the OD stories I internalized, and how that internalization emerges in my classroom teaching today. As Madeleine Grumet (1987) suggests, "We are, at least partially, constituted by the stories we tell to others and to ourselves about the experience" (p. 322). I could never have gained from a textbook the knowledge OD participants shared with me through their lived experiences about what it means to be a person of color in a racist society. Their lived experiences, and my own reactions to those experiences, bring a powerful perspective-changing force to my classroom.

Pedagogy Lessons

Autobiographies

The knowledge I gained from the autobiography presentations had a profound effect on the way I perceive the world and my students in the world. I begin every semester with a similar autobiography assignment for my social studies methods course. The experiences individuals share, and those they choose not to share, create a group bonding I have been unable to recreate with any other beginning assignment. Kincheloe and Steinberg (1993) assert: "The frontier where the information of the disciplines intersects with the understandings and experience that individuals carry with them to school is the point where knowledge is created (constructed). The post-formal teacher facilitates this interaction, helping students to reinterpret their own lives and uncover new talents as a result of their encounter with school knowledge" (p. 301). The deconstruction process of sharing life stories at the beginning of each semester through the autobiography assignment is a viable strategy for beginning the intersection of lived experiences and school knowledge. This activity creates an atmosphere of greater tolerance and understanding for the rest of the semester.

Dialogue Journaling

I practiced dialogue journaling prior to the OD experience, and continue to do so. Each week, students reflect on the week's readings, activities, and discussions as well as integrating what they experience in their school placements with the methods course content. The structure of dialogue journaling provides the possibility for critical self-reflection. But it takes time and energy to develop through the semester.

The beginning of each new semester pains me as I read drab, boring, depersonalized regurgitations and retellings of events that bear no resemblance to reflection or thinking but are merely summarizations. It takes several weeks of reading and responding to engage students in critical questioning. Students are too busy "playing school," trying to give the teacher what they think he or she wants. It takes a while before they catch on that I don't want that. In the beginning, my responses consist mostly of, How? Why? How do you know? How can you find out? What do *you* think about this? What about (the opposing view)? How would the opposing view respond to this?

When I return journals after the first week, I discuss the types of comments they can expect from me. I explain that the intent of my questions is to engage us in dialogue about the issues. Even with this forewarning, most are shocked to see little else but questions on their papers. Maxine Greene (1993) warns that "ideas like those associated with construction of social reality (evoking multiplicity or relativism for many who pay heed) are considered threatening to the social order as authoritatively defined" (p. 2). Students' past experiences in schooling include teachers dictating clear divisions of right and wrong answers. Therefore, most interpret my questions to engage dialogue as meaning that I, the teacher, do not agree with them, or worse, that they got it wrong.

In the next stage of journal writing, students move from distanced retelling to unsupported opinion. In true relativistic fashion, the underlying assumption in this stage is that if there is no right or wrong, whatever they say must be right. Because I am the one who has "threatened the social order" of right and wrong, I take it as my responsibility to build a "new social order" with students. The new social order is one in which suppositions and perspectives are to be supported. Here I actively engage students beyond using "I think" or "I feel" as their sole source of opinion formation. I explicitly show students how to provide a research base to back up their "feelings." Too often students want to quit at "I think it and my opinion cannot be wrong." By questioning these opinions through weekly dialogue of writing and responding, most students engage in critical reflection by midsemester.

Small Group Discussions

On any given topic, I structure class time to cycle through the following: (1) small group engagement with task; (2) small group sharing with whole group; and (3) teacher-led whole class discussion, where I provide discrepant events if needed. I have found this structure works well to provide the place and space for multiple perspectives to emerge. The key is to structure the learning experience so that as the teacher I speak last, only after all other voices have been heard. This frustrates students in the beginning because they expect the traditional ITIP model of the teacher telling and modeling what to do. When I do not provide a model for them to follow, as Madeleine Hunter (1982) suggests, students have to explore and construct meaning with their peers. They will not engage in the process of negotiation if I do not structure the activity for them to do so. Once they have engaged, I probe with questions or offer alternative interpretations. When students try to ask me questions to get at the answer my patent response is, "What do you think?" followed by, "And why do you think that?" Providing airtime for them to speak first not only allows their voices to be heard, but also affords me the opportunity to listen.

Perspective of the Other

My students are often entrenched in technocratic rationality of schooling. They firmly believe that there is a right and a wrong way to teach, that principals will tell them what to do, and that textbooks do not lie. When we analyze social studies textbooks, it becomes a challenge for me to move them to question their taken-for-granted views. Pinar (1989) contends that "only via deconstruction can reformulation of self begin, a self not frozen and overly fixed psychologically or socially, capable of perceiving and processing new information according to constantly adjusting notions of reality, the future and the past" (p. 19).

I have tried several strategies to deconstruct the taken-for-granted views of my predominantly White students in order that they may be capable of perceiving and processing new information, as Pinar suggests. We have read articles by Cherryholmes (1992), McCarthy (1992), and Popkewitz (1992) that address issues of colonial culture, power, and the omission of representation in textbooks. Students complain that the vocabulary is too tough to wade through in these readings. I have also tried reading or retelling some of the OD stories, particularly the ones about being left out of the curriculum. However, each semester when groups are asked to determine the cultural sensitivity of the textbook, all texts are viewed favorably. As far as they are concerned, all people are represented and treated equally. Unlike the OD participants, my predominantly White preservice teachers have no need to deconstruct themselves. They have not been marginalized, denied access, or made invisible by school curricula. They have had no reason to question the texts they have grown up with and view as being right.

I do not allow these assumptions to go unchallenged. Once they have declared a particular text as being culturally sensitive, I question the type of portrayal. We go back through and analyze both the pictures and the language that describe different groups. On one occasion, a group changed their minds about the sensitivity of their text. After some prompting and discussion, they realized that even though there were a number of African American children portrayed in the text, they were living in urban low-income housing, playing on blacktop surrounded by chain-link fence. The European American children were living in single-family dwellings with green grass and flowers in the yard. I have to ask specific questions about class status in images for students to move past counting numbers of instances to critically examining what the instances portray. It's hard work to enable students to perceive what they don't think exists in the first place.

Pinar (1991) argues that "by refusing to understand curriculum as a racial text, students misunderstand who they are as racialized, gendered, historical, political creatures" (p. 11). One semester, I had a class that was particularly resistant to perceiving the curriculum as racial text. The methods I employed in the past—autobiography, dialogue journals, and specific readings—only led to more rigidity, defensiveness, and anger with this particular group. The more discussion we had, the more I encountered "defensive. . . protests against what they consider to be 'white male bashing' of critical pedagogy and critical multiculturalism" (McLaren, 1995, p. 13).

Out of my own frustration at not being able to move the thinking of this class, I finally created an assignment that helped them take the perspective of the other. I assigned each student an identity (African American, Jamaican, Cuban American, Mexican American, Puerto Rican, Panamanian, Native American, Japanese, Chinese, Filipino, Vietnamese, El Salvadoran, just to name a few) and asked them to read the textbook from the point of view of this child. (If they had a fifth grade book, they were a fifth grader, etc.) They were to answer the following questions from that perspective:

1. What do you know about yourself from this book?
2. What racial or ethnic identity role models or historic heroes do you have?
3. What is your historical heritage as described or portrayed in the text?
4. What is your lifestyle? (Where do you live? What do you do? What does your family look like? What jobs might you have in the future?)
5. What is your racial or ethnic contribution to the American macro culture?
6. What evidence is there that the macroculture is receptive to your racial or ethnic identity?

The results were startling. Having to read the textbook and actually try to find "themselves" in it finally enabled some to understand the necessity of not only equal but also quality air time for perspectives. Only after being rendered non existent, or existent in a demeaning way, were my predominantly White students able to actually question this text, as well as others. The following excerpt from one of the papers illustrates the insights gained from this assignment for "Taking the Perspective of the Other":

> My name is Rosa Sojourner. I am a fifth grade student in Ms. Transmit's Social Studies class. It was another typical day of sitting dutifully while Ms. Transmit spewed forth the information she deemed important for me to learn, when it happened. The 'whiteness' of the page from my social studies page began to blind me. I soon found that I was in the land of Holt Rinehardt and Winston. I was intrigued by a sign I saw upon my entrance into this new strange land. It said I could find out all about myself by following the road that was marked African American and paying close attention to clues given along the way. Being eleven years old and somewhat unsure of myself, who I was, and how I fit into the scheme of life I jumped at this opportunity.

> I find within the land of Holt Rinehardt and Winston that the first pertinent information for me to gain about my racial heritage is not given until the fifth unit of study—two hundred pages into the four hundred page book. I see that I am black and have short curly hair. I wear no shoes, and my clothes look shabby. The grown women wear some type of bonnet on their heads. Most of the pictures I see along the way are only drawings depicting African Americans. . . . My ancestors were brought here from Africa to be sold as slaves to work on the cotton plantations, fields, or small farms. My people have no rights and I learn that I can be taken from my family at any time. . . . I know that I will grow up to work in the fields for a mistress in a big house. I feel there are many restrictions as to what I will be able to do in the future, but yet within me I have a feeling that given the opportunity I could do anything.

> I see many famous men along the way that I could look to as heroes. . . . Many men, but few women. I feel the victim of two discriminators, being female and being black. I do see many contributions that some have been noticed for from my ethnic

background, in arts, music and literature. Again, only males were mentioned.

> I am beginning to feel a little badly about myself, thinking that from most of the evidence I have seen thus far on my journey through Holt Rinehardt and Winston land is that the Macroculture out there does not seem to be receptive to my racial/ethnic identity and/or my gender role within that identity. The African American road is already over as we are really only mentioned within the one unit of text. The book goes on for several more units, but no specific mentions of African Americans are made. . . . Somehow I do not sense this equality when purveying the other roads and length that they are and the possibilities given along the way, and then experiencing my short trip.

Though it was not a requirement of the written assignment, many took on the identity and voice of a particular child reading the book. I received "letters" from "Marcia," a third-grade Cuban American; "Juanita" and her brother Esteban from El Salvador; an Iranian second grader; and a Korean third grader. The results of this assignment reinforced for me once again that "storytelling is one of the strongest traditional cultural expressions; it helps us feel whole and connected. Nothing is more critical than storytelling to defining our humanity. When telling our stories, we assert both our individuality and our connection to others, and we make others aware of our identity and history" (Pharr, 1996, p.66).

Another example depicts for me how this particular assignment provided a vehicle for critical reflection. This excerpt comes from a White male in the class who ranked his text very high for its cultural sensitivity. After the follow-up assignment he writes:

> Upon further consideration and thought I really felt that this series was very stereotypical. If we are to teach in a way that reaches all of our students then we need to incorporate many ideas and simulations. We will probably never be happy with the complete curriculum series and modification will be necessary in every series. The more I thought about it the more concerned I became with the sugar coating that this series did to show African Americans and women in our society. They only produced a bandaid to patch or hide the true

content of this series. If I had approached the series with the perspective of another ethnicity the first time I might of been more critical of the material. This text series did not reach out and look at the big picture of multiculturalism.

These two examples illustrate that pedagogically we cannot underestimate the importance and power of storytelling for building multiple perspectives. In addition, we cannot stop at employing one or two strategies for critical reflection. We must persist within the voices of resistance to seek alternatives if we are to effect radical change and multiple perspective building among preservice teachers.

Critical Confrontation

The critical questioning of the status quo and the challenging nature of my perspective do not go unnoticed by students. I stand out in the otherwise polite, Protestant, never-challenge-or-ask-why mentality of the university culture. Given the atmosphere these preservice teachers come to know and expect, encountering a course I teach is meeting the unexpected. I now expect a period of initial shock the first few weeks of the semester until students begin to understand that my interest is in the dialogue—our conversations—more than their performance on assignments. My focus and concern are not so much on *what* they do as on *how* and *why* they do. By midsemester many have learned that my expectation is for them to reciprocate my questioning. They learn to ask questions of me rather than blindly accept whatever I may say as the truth about teaching and learning. I am the one who must accept the responsibility for my expectation of questioning the teacher, and this expectation is contrary to teacher expectations that have enabled these students to succeed thus far in their academic careers. I am the one asking them to think and act differently. Therefore, I am the one who must provide scaffolding strategies that allow them to succeed within the parameters of new expectations. I am also the one who must accept the responsibility, both positive and negative, for what these new experiences bring.

Taking the risk to challenge the status quo also means accepting the responsibility for the consequences. I do not expect a conflict-free environment. As a practitioner of critical pedagogy I plan for and expect discomfort, tension, and conflict. I know that when I challenge or question taken-for-granted assumptions, there will be those who are offended. Sometimes, as McLaren (1995) suggests, "their objections to leftist political correctness amount to little more than feeling the panic discomfort of disagreement" (p. 12). Students who are socialized to obey their elders and those in positions of authority do not feel comfortable when I ask them to reexamine the underlying messages of conformity implied in these socialized teachings. When feeling discomfort or confrontation, some choose to withdraw. Others choose to retaliate.

My spring semester of 1995 illustrates the consequences of my critical questioning and challenging the status quo. I had a particularly resistant and conservative group. Like no other semester, these students were unsympathetic to the plight of children of color in classrooms. When discussing multicultural issues, I heard loud, proud, and boisterous accounts of affirmative action bashing, ESL bashing, and support of deficit views of learning. On the topic of ESL, one young White male proclaimed very righteously, "There's more of us than them. So it makes more sense to have them learn our language than us to learn all of theirs." Even when I presented statistics that showed 85 percent of teachers hired in their state were White females, these students persisted in holding on to the view that unqualified minorities were taking their jobs as teachers.

Presenting discrepant events or contradictory information to individuals who have no intention of altering their worldview is risky business—and even riskier when you are untenured faculty. However, I could not allow these views to remain unchallenged. The result was that one student filed a grievance against me. She claimed I caused her "mental and emotional anguish" and that I "personally attacked" her in class. Given the assignment to represent her understanding of fourteen multicultural terms, she turned in a New Testament coloring book that contained the characters Hannah and Michael. It was obvious through the dialogue in the coloring book that Hannah and Michael were brother and sister. She colored one character yellow and the other brown on each page to represent the fourteen multicultural terms. No written explanation was provided. When probed, she stated that she believed the meaning of the fourteen terms was self-explanatory through her coloring of the characters. She had no idea why this was unacceptable.

I viewed this conflict as similar to the OD conflict that erupted between Karma and Lisa and the rest of the group. Neither side was communicating intentions very effectively. Before we met with a mediator, this student was withdrawing from school and enrolling at another university. Papers for withdrawal and enrollment elsewhere were in the works; the decision had been made. However, after we met and each of us retold events and our intentions during these interactions, she no longer felt I was out to get her and had begun to feel that maybe she could stay after all. Through dialogue, storytelling, and mediated reflection on past events, we were able to work through the anger and resentment that often occur when personal assumptions are challenged by different perspectives.

This particular encounter ends in resolution, but not all do. Some students respond to confrontation and critical questioning by being silent during class and saving their comments for the course evaluation. One of the toughest responsibilities to accept is that in choosing to employ critical strategies in the classroom, I am also consciously choosing to receive poor student evaluations from those who do not want the status quo questioned or transformed. However, I can honestly say after completing my third-year review that the percentage of those who reject the critical reflection and examination of sociohistoric contexts I provide in my classroom is a small percentage. The overwhelming majority (85-90 percent) of my predominantly female, White students appreciate being provided the opportunity to examine teaching and learning from a critical perspective.

My commitment to critical questioning and reflection is strengthened when students return to me after class ends for the semester. Only after the course is over do many recognize the personal and meaningful conversations we had. This in turn leads to a sense of comradeship, bonding, or connection. One young woman asked me to write a recommendation and explicitly stated she thought I knew her best because of the dialogue journaling we shared. After I confronted another woman in class about the way she was devaluing specific works of children's literature through her introductory language, she intercepted me after her graduation ceremony to thank me. She said, "In your class I learned how to be a teacher, and I'll never forget that." Now, with e-mail I have ongoing conversations with students who have more questions and want to continue our conversations long after the semester is over.

Content Lessons

My intent is that the activities, illustrations, and discussions I provide in the university classroom will change the perceptions of my preservice teacher students, in much the same way the interactions with the OD participants changed mine. I want my students to be able to reinterpret or deconstruct classroom events within the sociohistoric context in which they happen in order to enhance their knowledge and understanding of the teaching-learning process.

I often use anecdotes from my experiences with the OD participants to illustrate multiple perspectives in the classroom. For instance, at least once a semester I retell Walter's lesson of patience, timing, and reflection when working with Native American students. I quote his explanation, "If you want a quick answer, then ask an easy question," to illustrate the importance of identifying and recognizing differences in cultural timing.

After a retelling one of my students was involved with a multidisciplinary team meeting concerning a Native American student in a sixth-grade classroom. The sixth grader was not completing his work. The classroom teacher explained to the mother that her son needed to be more "responsible" and establish a better "work ethic" to complete his tasks on time. After our discussion in the university classroom, my student no longer saw the sixth grader's behavior as unmotivated or lacking discipline. Instead, he viewed the child as very motivated and disciplined. Our classroom discussion caused my student to ask different questions of the sixth grader's actions. Through further investigation and direct conversation with the sixth grader, he discovered that the boy was not being lazy. He was not completing work because of his very meticulous concern for doing his work well. When asked, the child reported that he was taking extra time and effort to complete his assignments well because he didn't want the teacher to mess it up by writing all over it. The sixth grader believed that the better he did his assignments, the less the teacher would mark on them. Therefore, he was taking more time to complete the assigned tasks. My student shared with his cooperating teacher this information so that she, too, could see how the student was actually going above and beyond what was asked of him. Now instead of blaming the sixth grader for not being responsible, focus for solutions turned to changing teacher behaviors. The teacher could give him more time to complete his tasks and mark less on his papers.

When my student retold this story to the class, he was amazed and pleasantly surprised that he had an immediate encounter that related our classroom discussion to his practical experience. I thank Walter for sharing his knowledge and wisdom which I was able to pass on to future generations of teachers.

After our class discussions, students return to their practicum classrooms with perspectives that cause them to question teacher practices. A student returned to her fifth-grade classroom in which the teacher was directing an art project. The lesson was painting. After having read a Native American story, the students were to create their own Native American totems. The activity, the teacher claimed, was "multicultural." However, my student questioned the multicultural intent when three Cambodian boys in the classroom created their totems out of very Asian-type designs. The classroom teacher told them to redo their artwork because the assignment was to be Native American. Ignoring the personal perspectives of these Cambodian boys shows that the teacher's focus of the lesson was on following directions more than creating multicultural understanding.

My personal interactions with the directness and forcefulness of the OD African American women resurfaced when one of my students told the story of an African American girl in her second-grade classroom who was bossy and telling other boys what to do. My student's first reaction was to assume this bossiness was wrong and needed to be extinguished in the child. I was able to share with her some of the readings (in particular, bell hooks) I had done that helped me understand the interactions of the five African American women in the OD program. I shared how I had witnessed a similar interaction pattern in grown women, and that trying to extinguish this socialized interaction style in the second-grade girl may be fighting against a community norm. Our discussion of this pattern enabled my student to rethink her interactions with the second grader. Before sharing my experiences and readings, my student engaged in a power struggle with the second grader. She tried to coerce the child into not being bossy to others. Now, she worked to redirect the socialized cultural behavior rather than treat it as a misbehavior to be extinguished. She received much better participation from the student for doing so.

My interactions with the OD program participants enabled me to understand the subtle ways in which well-meaning European American teachers devalue the knowledge and cultural pride parents work so hard to instill in their children. In particular, the stories from Lisa and Karma came to mind when a student shared with me an experience in her practicum teaching. During a practicum experience in a second-grade classroom, one young woman was disturbed by a young African American boy who asserted ownership of his ethnic identity. One morning before school started, jazz music by a Black artist was playing on the radio in the room. The second grader recognized the music and artist and told the practicum student that she couldn't listen to that music. He reasoned that it was Black music, not White music, and it belonged to him.

My student, not recognizing this gesture of asserting ethnic pride and identity, told the child that music didn't belong to anyone and that everyone could listen just the same. She was shocked and stunned that a child "that young" could think "that way." Her premise was that everyone is equal. She didn't recognize that in this young Black man's experience things were not equal. Furthermore, from his experience, Whites take away what Blacks have. In a final semester conference, my student asked what I would have done. I suggested that I would have allowed the child to "own" his music by asking him to tell me more. I would ask; "What other music do you know by Black artists? What have you learned about them? Do you have any at home you would like to share with the class?" Instead of proclaiming he was wrong by suggesting no one owns the music, I would value his pride and owner-ship and at the same time praise him for his knowledge and interest by inviting him to share with the class what he knows.

I try to instill in preservice teachers that what they need to do most in the classroom is watch, listen, and learn. Let the students show you. The story of one of my students, working with first graders and their writing is a good illustration. The rule in this first-grade classroom was that children had to finish their journals and read them to the teacher to receive a smiley face on the paper before they could go to recess. Taking over from the teacher, my student followed the teacher's rules and drew smiley faces on the journals when they were read to her. A Korean girl in the class informed her she was drawing the smiley face wrong. The first grader took the pen and showed her how to draw the lines for the eyes horizontal instead of vertical for her paper. The child was quite explicit asserting that this was the way for hers to be drawn, and not the others.

One of the most poignant lessons that OD taught me was the dynamic fluidity of ethnicity and the effect it has on the self-esteem of individuals. I also learned that "respecting differences" or being "culturally sensitive" has little to do with curriculum materials and more to do with daily personal interactions with individuals. Charles's voice echoes in my mind the most on this subject. I have to know the individual person before mutual understanding can be reached. This is a hard lesson to relate to preservice teachers who want to do it "right." Often when asked what they will do to make their classrooms culturally sensitive, preservice teachers respond with reading multicultural literature as a strategy.

I question this patent response. Literature can certainly provide a window to experiences we might not otherwise encounter, but how teachers present or use literature can have devastating effects. I have two illustrations of this. The first is a student of mine who chose a Native American folktale to read to her students. She consciously chose the book because she knew some of her students were Native American. After the lesson, she came back to the university classroom frustrated. She claimed that multicultural literature didn't work because she had picked out a book about "their own culture" and "they didn't appreciate it." However, she never engaged in a discussion with the students about their personal perceptions of their ethnic identity. She had no idea what tribe they belonged to, or if they participated or identified with the tribe. Nor did she realize the incongruency of choosing a book that portrayed Eskimos when these students lived in an urban setting. She had not established any personal communication or trust with the students. Because there was no interpersonal understanding created between teacher and students, certainly no multicultural understanding could be achieved. This is an instance of focus on the social with disregard for the personal needs of the individual students.

The second example is a student who was assigned Arnold Adolff as a poet to present to her peers in the reading methods class. When introducing the poem she began, "I really didn't get this, I don't think it makes much sense, but I'll read it anyway." Arnold Adolff is a European American who is married to Virginia Hamilton, an African American. Arnold writes much of his poetry about his children, who are biracial. Much of the language and imagery he uses refers to skin colors. Because this woman didn't have that background knowledge (nor did she seek it out), the imagery of white skin turning red when it's cold outside escaped her.

These two anecdotes illustrate important cautions about using children's literature as a quick fix for developing multicultural understanding. We can learn from the experiences of others through the use of good literature in the classroom. Teachers need to be more conscious of the values portrayed in their choices. However, it is not the literature itself, but rather the interactions and experiences teachers provide in addition to the texts that develop or hinder understanding of multiple perspectives. The way teachers present and discuss literature with students influences the interactions and understandings developed. The implicit messages of teacher presentation can override the explicit messages of the text. Introducing a piece by saying "I don't get this" or "this is weird" or "strange" or "different" does not promote understanding, only further misunderstanding and distancing. Lastly, literature should never be viewed as taking the place of face-to-face interpersonal interactions. Reading literature still allows for a distanced watching without the need for social negotiation that only face-to-face interactions can provide.

FINAL THOUGHTS

My participation with the twenty-one individuals in the Opening Doors program in the summer of 1992 was a life-changing experience. Probably the most valuable lesson they taught me was that the choice to struggle for social transformation, to strive for achieving the goals of personal and social understanding of self and self in relation to others, is not an easy one. I often grow weary in the daily battle to "recognize the worth of all people and to instill and maintain the importance of equal respect for all" (Grant, 1977, p.65). During tough times my colleagues and I share stories of our struggle. More than once I have fantasized about how life would be easier if I could believe and practice technocratic rationality. If only I could deliver a lecture and expect students to merely write and accept the spoken word as the truth. If I could give objective tests that are easily scored and assigned a percentage. If I could go home at night with no voices of students and their stories haunting my thoughts. In times of high stress and frustration I think, wouldn't it be nice? In times of less stress and more removal for reflection, I know better.

In times of high stress I rejuvenate my spirit by revisiting the work of others to remind myself that I am not alone in my struggle "with questions of meaning and attention to the process of self production" (Kincheloe & Steinberg, 1993, p. 303). It is in this spirit of rejuvenation from the work of others that I want to end with a piece of work from

Vivian Paley (1992). This work illustrates quite well the critical process of becoming multicultural.

As I have described, multiculturalism is a socialization process. It begins with enabling small children to resolve disagreements with play-mates in the schoolyard. Paley illustrates the early beginnings of developing multicultural perspectives with children in her book *You Can't Say You Can't Play*. In her story she and her kindergartners negotiated a classroom rule for not excluding others from their play. Instead of simply implementing the rule for students to follow, Paley negotiated the meaning of the rule with her students. In their class discussions, the children shared personal accounts of times when their peers had kept them from joining. They agreed it was not fair that children treat others in ways that cause bad feelings. Paley not only gathered opinions from the children in the kindergarten class, but she also sought the opinions of the first-, second-, third-, fourth- and fifth-grade students in the school to find out if they thought the "You can't say you can't play" rule was fair. After each visit to the upper grades, she renegotiated the views of the older children with the kindergartners. By bringing in the opinions of the older children in the school, she enabled the kindergartners to negotiate and share perspectives from an even broader circle of others outside their immediate context.

At the same time students and teacher were negotiating the new rule, Paley also observed and recorded the children and their conversa-tions in a fairy tale. As children constructed their own histories within the classroom, the teacher preserved those histories in written form. As children negotiated the fairness of their actions, they also reflected on their actions when the tale was read to them. In this way, Paley enabled five-year-olds to do as the Opening Doors participants did, and as teachers who engage in critical practice do. They reflected critically on their own actions internally, then reconstructed and acted differently in the next external interaction. At the age of five they practiced the recursive cycle of external dialogue with others followed by internal dialogue with self, repeated with each weekly installment of the story and upon receiving perspectives from the older children in the school. These kindergarten students negotiated with each other in order to take the role of the other—to perceive each other subject to subject—to become multicultural. Surely we adults can learn to play well with others, too.

References

Anzaldúa, G. (1987). *Borderlands la Frontera: The new Mestiza*. San Francisco: Aunt Lute Books.

Anzaldúa, G. (1988). Tlilli, tlapalli: The path of the red and black ink. In R. Simonson & S. Walker (Eds.), *The Graywolf Annual Five: Multicultural Literacy* (pp. 29–40). Saint Paul, MN: Graywolf Press.

Anzaldúa, G. (1990a). En rapport, in opposition: Cobrando cuentas a las nuestras. In G. Anzaldúa (Ed.), *Making face, making soul: Haciendo caras* (pp. 142–148). San Francisco: Aunt Lute Foundation.

Anzaldúa, G. (1990b). La conciencia de la mestiza: Towards a new consciousness. In G. Anzaldúa (Ed.), *Making face, making soul: Haciendo caras* (pp. 377–389). San Francisco: Aunt Lute Foundation.

Au, K. H. (1981). Participant structure in a reading lesson with Hawaiian children: Analysis of a culturally appropriate instructional event. *Anthropology and Education Quarterly, 10*(20), 91–115.

Banks, J. (1981). *Multiethnic education: Theory and practice*. Boston: Allyn & Bacon.

Becker. H. S., & Geer, B. (1960). Latent culture: A note on the theory of latent social roles. *Administrative Science Quarterly, 5*, 304–313.

Benedict, R. (1934). *Patterns of culture*. Boston: Houghton Mifflin.

Bennett, C. (1990). *Comprehensive multicultural education: Theory and practice*. Boston: Allyn & Bacon.

Bereano, N. (1984). Introduction. In A. Lorde *Sister Outsider* (pp. 7–12). Freedom, CA: Crossing Press.

Blumer, H. (1953). Psychological import of the human group. In M. Sherif and M. O. Wilson (Eds.), *Group relations at crossroad* (pp. 185–202). New York: Harper & Row.

Bordieu, P. (1977). *Outline of a theory of practice*. New York: Cambridge University Press.

Britzman, D. (1995). What's this thing called love? *Taboo: The Journal of Culture and Education, 1*(Spring), 65–93.

Brown, E. B. (1988). African-American women's quilting: A framework for conceptualizing and teaching African-American women's history. In M. R. Malson, E. Mudimbe-Boyi, J. F. O'Barr, & M. Weyer (Eds.), *Black women in America: Social science perspectives* (pp. 9–180. Chicago: University of Chicago Press.

Bush, D., & Simmons, R. (1990). Socialization over the life course. In R. A. Turner (Ed.), *Social psychology: Sociological perspectives* (pp. 133–164). New York: Basic Books.

Carr, W., & Kemmis, S. (1986). *Becoming critical: Education, knowledge, and action research*. London, England: Falmer Press.

Charon, J. M. (Ed.). (1992). *Symbolic interactionism: An introduction, an interpretation, an integration* (4th ed.). Englewood Cliffs, NJ: Prentice Hall.

Cherryholmes, C. (1992). Knowledge, power, and discourse in social studies education. In K. Weiler, & C. Mitchell, (Eds.). *What schools can do. Critical pedagogy and practice* (pp. 93–115). New York: State University of New York Press.

Cliff, M. (1988). If I could write this in fire, I would write this in fire. In R. Simonson & S. Walker (Eds.), *The Graywolf Annual Five: Multicultural Literacy* (pp. 63–81). Saint Paul, MN: Graywolf Press.

Cliff, M. (1990). Object into subject: Some thoughts on the work of black women artists. In G. Anzaldúa (Ed.). *Making face, making soul: Haciendo caras* (pp. 271–290). San Francisco: Aunt Lute Foundation.

Cook-Gumperz, J. (Ed). (1986). *The social construction of literacy*. New York: Cambridge University Press.

Cross, A. (1990). *The players come again*. New York: Ballantine Books.

Delgado-Gaitan, C. (1988). The value of conformity: Learning to stay in school. *Anthropology and Education Quarterly, 19*, 354–381.

Dewey, J. (1909). *The school and society*. Chicago: University of Chicago Press.

Dillard, C. B., & Parkay, F. (1991). *Proposal for minority participation in graduate study in education program*. Washington, DC: U. S. Department of Education.

Dunn, K., & Dunn, R. (1978). *Learning style inventory*. Lawrence, KS: Price Systems.

Erickson, F. (1986). Qualitative methods in research on teaching. In M. C. Wittrock (Ed.), *The handbook on research in teaching*. New York: Macmillan.

Erickson, F., & Schultz, J. (1981). When is a context? Some isses and mehods in the analysis of social competence. In J. Greeene & C. Wallat (Eds.). *Ethnography and the language in educational settings.* (pp. 147–160). Norwood: Ablex.

Erikson, E. (1980). *Identity and the life cycle.* New York: Norton and Company. (Original work published 1959)

Frankenburg, R. (1993). *White women, race matters: The social construction of whiteness.* Minneapolis: University of Minnesota Press.

Freire, P. (1985). Toward a pedagogy of the question: Conversations with Paulo Freire. *Journal of Education, 167,* 7–21.

Gecas, V. (1982). The self concept. *Annual Review of Sociology, 8,* 1–33.

Gee, G. P. (1985). The narrativization of experience in the oral style. *Journal of Education, 167,* 9–34.

Geertz, C. (1973). *The interpretation of cultures.* New York: Basic Books.

Gilmore, P. (1985). Gimme room: School resistance, attitudes, and access to literacy. *Journal of Education, 167,* 111–128.

Giroux, H. (1985). Critical pedagogy, cultural politics, and the discourse of experience. *Journal of Education, 167,* 22–41.

Giroux, H. (1992). *Border crossings: Cultural workers and the politics of education.* New York: Routledge & Kegan Paul.

Goffman, E. (1959). *The presentation of self in everyday life.* New York: Doubleday.

Gomez-Pena, G. (1988). Documented/undocumented. In R. Simonson & S. Walker (Eds.), *The Graywolf Annual Five: Multicultural literacy* (pp. 127–134). Saint Paul, MN: Graywolf Press.

Grant, C. (1977). Education that is multicultural and P/CBTE: Discussion and recommendations for teacher education. In F. H. Klassen & D. M. Gollnick (Eds.), *Pluralism and the American teacher,* (Grant # G007501382) (pp.63–80). Washington, DC: U.S. Office of Education, American Association of Colleges for Teachers Education.

Greene, M. (1978). A question of personal reality. *Teachers College Record, 80*(1), 23–35.

Greene, M. (1993). Beyond insularity: Releasing the voices. *College ESL, 3*(1), 1–14.

Greene, M. (1994). Postmodernism and the crisis of representation. *English Education, 26,* 206–219.

Grumet, M. (1987). The politics of personal knowledge. *Curriculum Inquiry, 17,* 319–329.

Grumet, M. (1991). Existential and phenomenological foundations of autobiographical methods. In W. F. Pinar, & W. Reynolds (Eds.),

Understanding curriculum as phenomenological and deconstructed text (pp. 28–43). New York: Teachers College Press.

Hargreaves, D. H. (1967). *Social relations in a secondary school.* London, England: Routledge & Kegan Paul.

Hiebert, E. (1991). *Literacy for a diverse society: Perspectives, practices, and policies.* New York: Teachers College Press.

hooks, b. (1989). *Talking back: Thinking feminist, thinking black.* Boston, MA: South End Press.

hooks, b. (1990). *Yearning: Race, gender, and cultural politics.* Boston: South End Press

hooks, b. (1994). *Teaching to transgress: Education as the practice of freedom.* New York: Routledge & Kegan Paul.

hooks, b., & West, C. (1992). *Breaking bread: Insurgent black intellectual life.* Boston: South End Press.

Hunter, M. (1982). Mastery teaching. El Segundo, CA: TIP.

Jacobson-Widding, A. (Ed.). (1983). *Identity: Personal and socio-cultural. A symposium.* Atlantic Highlands, NJ: Humanities Press.

Kanpol, B. (1992). *Towards a theory and practice of teacher cultural politics: Continuing the postmodern debate.* Norwood, NJ: Ablex.

Kincheloe, J. L. (1993). *Toward a critical politics of teacher thinking: Mapping the postmodern.* Westport, CT: Bervin & Garvey.

Kincheloe, J., & Steinberg, S. (1993). A tentative description of post-formal thinking: The critical confrontation with cognitive theory. *Harvard Educational Review, 63,* 296–321.

Klasen, F. H., & Gollnick, D. M. (1977). *Pluralism and the American teacher.* Washington, D.C.: Grant No. G007501382, U.S. Office of Education, American Association of Colleges for Teachers Education.

Kniep, W. M. (1989). Global education as school reform. *Educational Leadership, 47,* 43–45.

Kronowitz, E. (1987). Social studies and the winds of change. *Social Studies Review, 26,* 2–26.

Lacey, C. (1970). *Hightown grammar.* Manchester, England: Manchester University Press.

Lather, P. (1986). Issues of validity in openly ideological research: Between a rock and a soft place. *Interchange, 17*(4), 63–85.

Longstreet, W. (1978). *Aspects of ethnicity: Understanding differences in pluralistic classrooms.* New York: Teachers College Press.

Lorde, A. (1984). *Sister outsider: Essays and speeches.* Freedom, CA: Crossing Press.

Lugones, M. (1990). Playfulness, "World" - travelling, and loving perception. In G. Anzaldúa (Ed.), *Making face, making soul: Haciendo caras* (pp. 390–402). San Francisco: Aunt Lute Foundation.

Markus, H. R., & Kitayama, S. (1991). Culture and the self: Implications for cognition, emotion, and motivation. *Psychological Review, 98*, 224–253.

McCarthy, C. (1992). Multicultural education: Minority identities, textbooks, and the challenge of curricular reform. In K.Weiler, & C. Mitchell (Eds.), *What schools can do: Critical pedagogy and practice*, (pp. 118–131). New York: State University of New York Press.

McDermott, R. P., & Gospodinoff, K. (1981). Nonverbal behavior: Application and cultural implications. In H. T. Trueba, G. P. Guthrie, and K. Au (Eds.), *Culture and the bilingual classroom: Studies in classroom ethnography* (pp. 212–232). Rowley, MA: Newbury House.

McLaren, P. (1995). Critical pedagogy in the age of global capitalism: Some challenges for the educational left. *Australian Journal of Education, 39*(1), 5–21.

Mead, G. H. (1934). *Mind, self, and society.* Chicago: University of Chicago Press.

Metzger, D. (1988). The challenges facing global education. *Louisiana Social Studies Journal, 15*, 13–16.

Myers, I. B., & Briggs, K. C. (1976). *Myers-Briggs type indicator.* Palo Alto, CA: Consulting Psychologists Press.

Nash, M. (1989). *The cauldron of ethnicity in the modern world.* Chicago: University of Chicago Press.

Nieto, S. (1992). *Affirming diversity: The sociopolitical context of multicultural education.* New York: Longman.

O'Brien, M. (1981). *The politics of reproduction.* New York: Routledge & Kegan Paul.

Ogbu, J. (1992). Understanding cultural diversity and learning. *Educational Researcher, 21*, 5–14.

Paley, V. (1992). *You can't say you can't play.* Cambridge, MA: Harvard University Press.

Peyton, K. (1990). Beginning at the beginning: First-grade students learn to write. In A. M. Padilla, H. H. Fairchild, & M. Valdez (Eds.), *Bilingual education: Issues and strategies*, (pp. 195–218). Newbury Park, CA: Sage.

Pharr, S. (1996, July/August). Taking the high road. *Ms*, pp. 65–69.

Phillips, S. (1976). Commentary: Access to power and maintenance of ethnic identity as goals of multi-cultural education. *Anthropology and Education Quarterly, 7*(4), 30–32.

Piaget, J. (1959). *The language and thought of the child.* New York: Humanities Press.

Pinar, W. F. (1978). Life history and curriculum theorizing. *Review Journal of Philosophy and Social Science, 3,* 92–118.

Pinar, W. F. (1981). Whole, bright, deep with understanding: Issues in autobiographical method and qualitative research. *Journal of Curriculum Studies, 13,* 173–188.

Pinar, W. F. (1989). Autobiography and the architecture of self. *Journal of Curriculum Theory, 8,* 7–36.

Pinar, W. F. (1991). Understanding of curriculum as racial text. *Scholar and Educator, 15*(1–2), 9–21.

Pinar, W. F. (1992). Dreamt into existence by others. *Theory into Practice, 31,* 228–235.

Pinar, W. F., & Reynolds, W. (Eds.). (1991). *Understanding curriculum as phenomenological and deconstructed text.* New York: Teacher's College Press.

Popkewitz, T. (1992). Culture, Pedagogy, and Power: Issues in the production of values and colonization. In K. Weiler, & C. Mitchell, (Eds.). *What schools can do. Critical pedagogy and practice* (pp. 134–147). New York: State University of New York Press.

Rosenberg, M. (1979). *Conceiving the self.* New York: Basic Books.

Saharso, S. (1989). Ethnic identity and the paradox of equality. In J. P. Van Oudenhoven & T. M. Willemsen (Eds.), *Ethnic minorities: Social psychological perspectives* (pp. 97–114). Berwyn, PA: SWETS North American.

Semons, M. (1991). Ethnicity in the urban high school: A naturalistic study of student experiences. *Urban Review, 23,* 137–157.

Shibutani, T. (1955). Reference groups as perspectives. *American Journal of Sociology, 60,* 562–569.

Simon, R. (1987). Empowerment as a pedagogy of possibility. *Language Arts, 64,* 370–382.

Strauss, A. (1959). *Mirrors and masks.* New York: Free Press.

Strauss, A., & Corbin, J. (1990). *Basics of qualitative research: Grounded theory procedures and techniques.* Newbury Park, CA: Sage.

Sue, D. W., & Sue, D. (1990). *Counseling the culturally different: Theory and practice.* New York: John Wiley.

Tajfel, H. (1981). *Human groups and social categories.* New York: Cambridge University Press.

Vygosky, L. (1954). *Thought and language.* Cambridge: MIT Press.

Vygotsky, L. (1978). *Mind in society*. Cambridge, MA: Harvard University Press.

Wallace, M. (1988). Invisibility blues. In R. S.Walker, & S. Walker (Eds.), *Multi-cultural literacy* (pp. 161–172). Saint Paul, MN: Graywolf Press.

Weinstein, E. A., & Deutschberger, P. (1963). Some dimensions of altercasting. *Sociometry, 26*, pp. 454–466.

Woods, P. (Ed.). (1980). *Pupil strategies: Explorations in the sociology of the school*. London, England: Croom Helm.

Woolf, V. (1929). *A room of one's own*. New York: Harcourt Brace.

Index

academic events, 45
action
    minimum-maximum, 35
    personal, 34, 36, 188, 193
    political, 34, 156, 157, 160, 164,
        168, 186
Akbar, Naim, 48, 109, 110
altercasting, 186
Anzaldúa, Gloria, 23, 30, 119
Au, Kathryn, 20
autobiography, 48, 49, 57, 71, 74, 75,
        85, 105, 158, 121, 200–201, 204

Banks, James, 4, 12, 16
Becker, H. S., & Geer, B., 12
Behind Closed Doors, 53, 158,
        160–170, 177–182
Benedict, Ruth, 16
Bennett, Christine, 4, 5, 16
Bereano, Nancy, 31
Blumer, Herbert, 157
Bordieu, Pierre, 12
Britzman, Debra, 22
Brown, Elsa B., 7, 21, 26, 119
Bush, D., & Simmons, R., 29, 143, 185

Carr, W., & Kemmis, S., 17
Charon, Joel M., 18, 26, 28, 31, 32, 33,
        127, 135, 143, 157, 176, 185, 186
Cherryholmes, C., 203
Cliff, Michelle, 26, 30, 119

communication
    verbal, 7
    nonverbal, 7
Comprehensive Multicultural
    Education, 5
conflict, 28, 29, 33–36, 49, 84, 159,
        167, 170, 171–180
    interpersonal, 21, 168, 182–186,
        207, 208
consciousness
    critical, 198
    critical social, 34
    in-group, 154, 196
    non european, 34
    social, 27, 38, 143, 144, 159, 160
context
    constructed, 56, 194, 215
    critical, 41–56
    learning, 11, 12
    situational, 9, 27, 29, 37, 38, 176, 183
    social, 11
    sociohistoric, 209, 210
Cook-Gumperz, J. , 20
credibility, 182
critical confrontation, 207
critical pedagogy, 207
critical questioning, 207, 209, 138
critical reflection, 21, 23, 31, 36, 121,
        127, 141, 142, 144, 147,
        161–162, 169, 180, 182, 196,
        199, 202, 209, 215

225

critical teaching, 195, 197–215
critical theory, 23
Cross, Amanda, 16
cultural aspects, 12
cultural assumptions, 31
cultural beliefs, 184
cultural capital, 23
cultural characteristics, 8
cultural difference as product
　　knowledge, 9
cultural differences, 7, 8 ,9
cultural dominance, 19,
cultural identity, 65, 88, 129
cultural pride, 70, 83, 100, 211
cultural sensitivity, 38, 203, 206, 213
cultural studies, 21
cultural tension, 88
cultural theory, 17
cultural values, 29
culture, 16, 23, 28, 70
　　as object, 17, 21, 26
　　distortion of, 103, 117
　　symbolically constructed, 17
curriculum, 26, 31, 125, 213
　　Eurocentric, 84, 118, 134
　　global approach, 6, 10
　　left out of, 77–81
　　multicultural, 198
　　process-oriented, 5, 6, 7
　　product-oriented, 5, 6, 7
　　social studies, 6, 10

Delgado-Gaitan, C., 9
Dewey, John, 11
dialogic process, 32
dialogic teaching, 198–199
Dillard, Cynthia. B., & Parkay, Forrest,
　　41, 42, 43
distortion, 189–194
double bind, 94
Dunn, Ken & Dunn, Rita, 7

education
　　democratic, 5
　　multicultural, 3, 4, 13, 26, 78, 152,
　　195–197
Erickson, Fred, & Schultz, J., 20

Erikson, Eric, 17
ethnic groups, 14, 20, 33
ethnicity 7, 10, 12, 13, 17, 18, 49, 122,
　　212
　　African American, 60, 96
　　as a perspective, 99
　　as burden of responsibility, 94, 97–99
　　as neutral, 66, 94, 99–100
　　as obstacle to overcome, 93–96
　　hatred of own, 84, 92
　　identity construction, 57, 83–100, 117
　　influences of, 87
　　influence from schooling, 93–100
　　objectified, 21, 120
　　situationally constructed, 11–12
　　social construction, 29
　　symbolically constructed, 17
　　theory, 17

Frankenburg, Ruth, 82
Freire, Paulo, 198

Gecas, Victor, 58
Gee, James Paul, 9
Geertz, Clifford, 17
Gilmore, Penny, 9
Giroux, Henry, 23, 194, 198
Goffman, Erving, 18
Gomez-Pena, G., 15
Grant, Carl, 4, 12, 214
Greene, Maxine, 23, 57, 58, 59, 201
grounded practice, 121
grouping
　　defined as, 14
　　ethnic, 55, 134, 155
Grumet, Madeleine, 23, 200

Hargreaves, D. H., 12
heritage, 84, 85, 107, 123, 126, 134
Hiebert, Elfreda, 11
historical truth, 131, 182–186
honesty
　　lack of, 161, 162, 164, 165
　　interpretations of, 182–186
hooks, bell & West, Cornell, 20, 26, 28,
　　119, 120, 144
hooks, bell, 7, 19, 20, 21, 23, 26, 30,

34, 119, 157, 160, 195, 196,
  199, 198, 211
Hunter, Madeleine, 202

identity, 16, 17, 48, 63, 131, 204, 205
  ethnic, 11, 17, 27, 28, 29, 31, 33,
    70, 82, 85, 107, 120, 122,126,
    134, 135, 142, 163, 212
  ethnic conflicts, 83, 86–93
  fixed, 23
  formation, 127, 141
  in context of schooling, 93–100
  national, 77
  personal, 17
  situationally constructed, 120
  social, 17, 48, 194
Indian giver, 98
intellectual modes, 7
interaction
  interpersonal, 9, 23, 158, 198, 213,
    214
  social, 22, 31, 32, 33, 118, 151,
    159, 160, 198, 199
  sociopolitical, 167
  styles, 14, 113
interracial dating, 60, 166
invisibility 32, 36, 154, 203
  ethnicity as an object of, 118, 134

Jacobson-Widding, A., 17
journals
  dialogue, 49
  sharing, 50
  weekly, 121, 127, 138, 161, 164,
    201–202, 204

Kanpol, Barry, 22
Kincheloe, Joe & Steinberg, Shirley,
  22, 38, 201, 214
Kincheloe, Joe, 23
Klasen, F. H., & Gollnick, D. M., 4
Kniep, W. M., 6
Kronowitz, E., 6
Kunjufu, Jawanza, 48, 109, 110

La Raza, 85
Lacey, C., 12

language of possibility, 198
Lather, Patti, 23
learning styles, 7, 10, 13–14, 20
  objectifying, 8
learning, 37
  as meaning making, 13
  as transaction, 10–11
Longstreet, William, 7
Lorde, Audre, 23, 30, 31, 34, 36, 37,
  58, 120, 142, 143, 154, 156,
  186, 187, 189
loss of language, 131–133, 135
Lugones, Maria, 15, 23, 30

marginalization, 34, 59, 61, 122, 134,
  203
Markus, H. R., & Kitayama, S., 20
McCarthy, Cameron, 203
McDermott, Ray & Gospodinoff, K.,
  20
McLaren, Peter, 204, 207
Mead, George Herbert, 18, 26, 32, 143,
  157
Metzger, D., 6
minority 15, 19, 42, 55, 98, 173, 175,
  187
  castelike, 11
  autonomous, 11
  involuntary, 11
  voluntary, 11
multicultural, 184, 187, 200, 211
  being, 23–24, 28, 154, 155, 195
  becoming, 3, 5, 12, 22, 28, 31, 195,
    199, 215
  knowledge, 37
  literature, 213
  teaching, 195–200
  understanding, 213
multiculturalism
  as perspective, 4, 10, 12, 13, 37
  as process, 5–10, 12, 13, 215
  as product, 5–10, 12, 13
Myers & Briggs, 7
mythical norm, 34, 135, 153, 189

Nash, Manning, 17, 21, 22, 29, 33, 35
Nieto, Sonia, 4

O'Brien, Mary, 23
Ogbu, John, 11, 12, 82
orientation modes, 7
other, 19, 32
  as object, 36, 120
  as subject, 142, 151
  generalized, 5, 27, 28, 33, 143, 144,
    148, 151, 153, 168, 185
  in-group, 27–28, 33, 143–156, 168,
    184, 193, 194
  out-group, 27–28, 33, 143–156,
    168, 188, 193, 194

Paley, Vivian, 215
personal histories, 100, 117–118, 158,
  197, 215
personal transformation, 198
perspectives
  anthropological, 17
  critical, 22–23, 209
  ethnic, 19
  Eurocentric, 190
  feminist, 22–23, 30
  multicultural, 3–4, 9, 13–14, 28,
    119, 197
  of other, 203
  personal, 33, 34, 36, 41, 45, 194,
    211
  postcolonial, 22–23
  postmodern, 22–23
  psychological, 23
  social, 36
  social psychological, 23, 29
  transactional, 11
Peyton, K., 20
Pharr, S., 206
Phillips, Susan, 20
Piaget, Jean, 11
Pinar & Reynolds, 100, 141
Pinar, William, 22, 57, 58, 77, 103,
  147, 203, 204
polythetic view, 21
Popkewitz, T., 203
primordial ties, 29

race, 10, 12, 16, 49, 84
racism, 48, 66, 88, 117, 120

internalized, 30, 83, 84, 92–93, 120,
  126, 144, 159
recruitment, 10
referent group, 34, 168, 186
reflective appraisal, 57, 58, 117
religion
  influences of, 73–76
research process, 50
role internalization, 28
role internalization, 32
role models
  academic, 87, 101, 109–110
  ethnic identity, 81, 101, 107–109, 150
  family, 70
  staff, 101, 110–116
role taking, 34, 36, 38, 170, 176–177,
  185, 198, 204, 205, 215
Rosenberg, M., 30

Saharso, S., 18
scenarios, 52, 158, 170–177
self construction, 26, 31
self development, 37, 38
self-affirmation, 106
self-concept, 30, 57, 135, 147
self-confidence, 107
self-discovery, 124
self-doubt, 101–103
self-esteem, 59, 65, 70, 71, 76, 81, 95,
  96, 100, 120, 123–125, 129,
  131, 134, 212
self-examination, 141
self-hate, 30, 92, 118, 120, 153
self-identity, 27, 29, 41, 45, 58, 59,
  120, 126, 141
self-judgment, 57
self-knowledge, 21, 26, 27, 34, 37, 120,
  126, 136, 141, 154
self-loathing, 30
self-perception, 135
self-pride, 123
self-reconstruction, 32
self-reflection, 27, 31, 137, 138, 161, 181
self-respect, 125
self-revelation, 36
self-transformation, 196
self-worth, 30, 95, 126

self, 18, 131, 157, 203, 214, 215
  acting, 32
  as object, 21, 22, 28, 30, 31, 32, 34,
      58, 117–118, 119–142, 144,
      147, 153, 187, 195, 196
  as subject, 22, 26, 27, 28, 31, 32,
      33, 34, 35, 36, 38, 119–121,
      125, 126, 134–142, 144, 147,
      153, 186, 187, 195, 196
  Asian, 82, 92, 144
  classroom, 183
  collective, 27, 144, 148, 149, 151
  consciousness of, 32
  construction, 30, 38, 157
  core, 29
  dorm, 183
  ethnic, 100, 117–118, 126
  fractured, 77
  grounded, 26, 27, 28, 38, 121, 124,
      125, 144, 157, 159, 187
  in relation to in-group, 27, 143–156
  in relation to others, 121, 155, 159,
      214
  in relation to out-group, 27,
      143–156
  multicultural, 26, 28, 38
  objectified, 26, 28, 117, 148, 151,
      155, 187
  personal, 22, 26, 35, 36, 37,
      117–118, 161, 168, 170
  reflexive, 18, 185
  (re)presented as subject, 143–156
  situated, 18, 22, 59
  social, 18, 22, 26, 117–118,
      157–161, 170
  symbolic, 18
Semons, M., 12
Shibutani, T., 4

Simon, Roger, 198
small group discussion, 202–203
small group presentation, 51
social comparison, 57–58
social style, 113
social transformation, 198, 214
social value patterns, 7
socialization, 37
  gender, 59, 76
  primary, 30, 117
stereotype, 7, 10, 79, 96, 117, 119, 120,
      133, 135, 193, 200
Strauss, Anselm & Corbin, Juliet, 16
Strauss, Anselm, 198
subject as object, 7
subject to subject relations, 28, 38, 39,
      155, 164, 170, 194, 195, 197,
      215
Sue, D. W., & Sue, D., 52
symbolic interaction, 22, 26, 31, 33,
      127, 135, 176

Tajfel, H., 17
The Rise of College Campus Racism,
      48, 109, 152, 158, 188
trust, 35, 136, 160, 182–186

untold stories, 101, 103–105, 118

Vygotsky, Lev, 11, 32

Wallace, Michelle, 23, 30
Weinstein, E. A., & Deutschberger, P.,
      186
West, Cornell, 23, 120
Woods, Peter, 12
Woolf, Virginia, 3, 19

You Can't Say You Can't Play, 215